CULTURE ACROSS BORDERS

Mexican Immigration

& Popular Culture

EDITED BY

David R. Maciel and María Herrera-Sobek

THE UNIVERSITY OF ARIZONA PRESS ::::: TUCSON

The University of Arizona Press
© 1998 The Arizona Board of Regents
All rights reserved

♾This book is printed on acid-free, archival-quality paper.
Manufactured in the United States of America

03   02   01   00   99   98   6   5   4   3   2   1

Library of Congress Cataloging-in-Publication Data

Culture across borders: Mexican immigration and popular culture /
edited by David R. Maciel and María Herrera-Sobek.
p. cm.
Includes index.
ISBN 0-8165-1832-7 (acid-free, archival-quality paper).—
ISBN 0-8165-1833-5 (pbk. : acid-free, archival-quality paper)
    1. Mexican Americans—Social life and customs.   2. Mexican
Americans—Cultural assimilation.   3. Popular culture—United
States—History—20th century.   4. Mexico—Emigration and
immigration—History—20th century.   5. United States—
Emigration and immigration—History—20th century.
6. Mexican Americans and mass media.   I. Maciel, David.
II. Herrera-Sobek, María.
E184.M5C85   1998   97-33899
305.868'72073—dc21   CIP

British Library Cataloguing-in-Publication Data
A catalogue record for this book is available from the British Library.

Dedicated to the memory of Ernesto Galarza and Julián Samora
—inspiring mentors, committed civil leaders,
and pioneer immigration scholars

CONTENTS

PREFACE

T his book project, like Mexican immigration itself, has been a lengthy process. The initial idea for this book derived almost a decade ago. As I researched Mexican immigration films and sought out selected studies as secondary sources, I was surprised to learn how few scholarly works existed on the cultural aspects of Mexican immigration to the United States in either country. This situation was most surprising, particularly because cultural or artistic works that have Mexican immigration as their major theme are extensive, so I chose to address this gap in some measure. Realizing that the cultural genres and motifs of Mexican immigration were varied and complex, I chose to proceed with this inquiry through the format of an edited volume. I then singled out and asked scholars who were specialists on the subject matter to collaborate with original chapters for this anthology.

While serving as Distinguished Visiting Professor in the Department of Mexican-American Studies at San Diego State University in the spring of 1989, I received financial support from the Center for the Regional Study of the Californias to organize a conference around the theme of the popular culture of Mexican immigration to the United States. The conference took place in October 1989 and was hosted by two cultural institutions of San Diego. In keeping with the spirit of the subject matter, we decided on a bilingual format for the conference — one set of presentations were in Spanish and the other in English. The scholars who attended and delivered informative presentations were Celestino Fernández, María Herrera-Sobek, José Reyna, and I. The first set of presentations was held at the Centro Cultural de la Raza in downtown San Diego. All the talks delivered there were in Spanish. The following day, the talks were repeated at the Museum of Modern Art in La Jolla, California. This time the format of the presentations and the discussion were held in English.

The encounter proved to be most valuable because it provided the editor and certain of the contributors with the opportunity to receive feedback from each other and from the audience, and I was better able to conceptualize the projected volume.

From the discussions held it seemed essential to include additional scholars who could address other critical aspects of the popular culture of Mexican immigration to the United States. Thus, contributors Juan Gómez-Quiñones, Alberto Ledesma, Genaro Padilla, and Victor Sorell came on board. It seemed that everything was now in place for the completion of a comprehensive set of original research chapters on the popular culture of Mexican immigration.

Shortly after the close of the first conference, I asked María Herrera-Sobek to serve as co-editor. She seemed an ideal choice. Professor Herrera-Sobek published one of the earliest book-length studies on immigration and culture, *The Bracero Experience: Elitelore versus Folklore*, and is a renowned scholar in the fields of cultural and folklore studies, feminist thought and literary analysis, as well as an experienced editor. Important also was that she had participated in the design of the project from the beginning.

Because the project had so changed from its original conception and much time had elapsed since the first meeting, another conference seemed in order to bring together all the participants. A second conference, *Culture across Borders: Mexican Immigration in the Popular Culture of the United States and Mexico*, took place at the University of California, Irvine, in May 1995. This conference was hosted by the co-editor of this anthology, María Herrera-Sobek, who served as overall coordinator. The purpose of the event was to encourage a dialogue between the original scholars and the newly invited ones who were participating in the anthology. The scholars who were able to participate and read their work-in-progress at the meeting were María Rosa García-Acevedo, Juan Gómez-Quiñones, María Herrera-Sobek, Alberto Ledesma, Genaro Padilla, José Reyna, and I. We were able to share our work at this gathering and offer helpful suggestions and commentary to each other.

As the semesters came and went and deadlines for the completion of the book chapters were extended, Celestino Fernández's administrative duties and responsibilities as a vice-president of the University of Arizona increased, making it impossible for him to devote the necessary time to see the project through. Another casualty of the project—also because of administrative responsibilities—was Genaro Padilla. Upon assuming his tenure as assistant chancellor of the University of California, Berkeley, he realized that his time constraints were so great that it was not possible for him to meet other commitments. Reluctantly, he also left the project. However, both generously gave constructive commentary, ideas, and encouragement to all phases of the project. Although they are not included as formal authors, their spirit and thoughts are ever present.

Other meetings took place in Albuquerque, New Mexico, and Irvine, California, between the editors who hammered out the organization and final structure of the book, edited the book chapters as they came in, and set a final resolution date for the volume.

For me, the completion of this edited volume brings both joyful satisfaction and also a note of lament, for as the saying goes, "All good things must come to an end." In the course of the preparation of this book, I learned a great deal from the insights and expertise of my collaborators on cultural and immigration studies. I also made new close friendships. It has been a distinct pleasure and an honor to have worked with such gifted scholars and *amigas y amigos muy queridos*.

DAVID R. MACIEL

ACKNOWLEDGMENTS

This book, like any project of this magnitude, required the collaboration of institutions and individuals—without their help, financial assistance, moral support, and diligence, completion of this book would not have been possible. We would, therefore, like to express our most sincere gratitude to the following specific institutions and persons.

At the institutional level, we received valuable funding from the following units of the University of California, Irvine: the Chicano/Latino Studies Program, the Latin American Studies Program, Humanities Research and Travel, Dean of Humanities Spencer Olin, "Women and the Image" Organized Research Initiative, *Chicanos in a Global Society* SCR–43 Research Funds, and the Student Academic Advancement Services. We received additional funds from the Luis Leal Endowed Chair, University of California, Santa Barbara.

At the University of New Mexico, the Center for Regional Studies provided the resources for two research assistants and for clerical support for the early formatting of the book. Its director, Tobías Durán, faithfully believed in the project from the onset and displayed personal commitment at critical stages of the process.

At San Diego State University, Paul Ganster, Founder and Director of the Center for the Regional Studies of the Californias, raised the necessary resources and enthusiastically promoted the initial conference on immigration and popular culture. The Centro Cultural de la Raza in San Diego and the Museum of Contemporary Art in La Jolla served as gracious hosts for the first conference.

In the process of completing the research on Mexican immigration films, the Director of the Filmoteca of the National University of Mexico (UNAM), Iván Trujillo, always placed at our disposal the substantial film archives, video collections, and extensive research library holdings of the Film Archives and Film Research Center of the UNAM. Many other members of Mexico's film community also generously shared research materials and personal copies of films with us.

A group of specific individuals also merit special gratitude; their dedication and professionalism greatly facilitated the course and completion of this manuscript. Andrés Valdés and Andrea Bassin proved to be excellent research assis-tants who aided the editors in important and varied tasks. María Rosa García-Acevedo was a careful supervisor of the various stages and drafts of the entire manuscript. Cara O'Flannigan creatively transformed the various word-processing formats that the contributors to this volume submitted to us into the software format used for our manuscript. In addition, at the University of California, Irvine, Stella Ginez, the administrative assistant for the Chicano/Latino Studies Program, helped with the organization of the second conference held for the project (May 4, 1995); Professor Leo Chávez, Co-director of Chicanos in a Global Society, provided SCR—43 funding; Judith Baca gave permission to use her UCI mural for our confer-ence poster; and Joe Maestas from Student Academic Advancement and the many MECHA students, such as Virginia Mosqueda, helped with the organizational mat-ters for the *Culture across Borders* conference at the University of California, Irvine. In addition, Jim Vieth from the University of California at Santa Barbara's Chicano Studies Department aided María Herrera-Sobek in tracking down copyright hold-ers for the songs cited.

A note of thanks is due to Denise Segura, Director of the Center for Chicano Studies, University of California, Santa Barbara, as well as to Ramón Miramontes and Pat Richardson from the same organization.

Our sincere thanks go to Keith Cunningham, editor of the *Southwest Folklore Journal*, for permission to reprint "Verbal Play in Mexican Immigrant Jokes."

Throughout this lengthy process, Joanne O'Hare, senior editor of the Uni-versity of Arizona Press, served as an indispensible consultant to the project. She offered many valuable suggestions and always showed strong support and patience from the time we first discussed the book as an idea in progress, close to ten years ago, to its publication.

Last, but certainly not least, as with many other of our previous cultural projects, Carlos Monsiváis, Mexico's leading authority on the country's popular culture, served as the unofficial mentor of this project from its early stages to the very present.

INTRODUCTION

Culture across Borders

o o o o
o o o o

David R. Maciel and María Herrera-Sobek

Mexican Immigration in a Binational Context

Mexican emigration to the United States is currently the most complex and difficult issue facing the two countries. Recent alarming actions directed at Mexican immigrants in the United States have forced the authorities in Mexico to respond and address the issue forcefully.[1] Concurrently, Mexican immigration has, in fact, become a salient political issue in U.S. national and state elections.[2] The controversy and debate on the issue of Mexican immigration include economic, political, social, legal, cultural, and human rights considerations. This issue is further complicated by the powerful influence of a multitude of interest groups, ranging from big business to civil rights organizations.[3] All of these pressure groups are instrumental in determining emigration policies as they relate to both countries. In the current political climate within the United States, immigration from Mexico has polarized public opinion and policy-making. On one side, the restrictionists have called for measures such as the mobilization of the National Guard to patrol the border and aid in the apprehension of undocumented workers; the hiring of a substantial number of additional border patrol agents; the upgrading of technology for the Immigration and Naturalization Service; and even the building of a wall along the U.S.–Mexican border. Responding to such concerns, the

U.S. Congress and the President enacted into law in September 1996 a bill on immigration reform that aimed at increasing sanctions against smugglers of undocumented workers, instituting various measures of control and deterrence of undocumented immigration, and regulating legal immigration more stringently.[4]

Opponents of these measures emphasize the multiple contributions of immigrants (legal and undocumented) to the economy and society of the United States. They argue that it has indeed been the labor and the efforts of immigrants such as Mexican workers that have made much of the growth and prosperity of America possible.

Immigration from Mexico to the United States, however, is not a contemporary phenomenon. It has a long historical tradition dating from the late nineteenth century and continuing to the present.[5] This immigration process involves one of the largest population movements in history. It has been estimated that around 20 percent of Mexico's total population has emigrated to the United States in less than a one-hundred-year period.[6] In fact, more immigrants have come from Mexico to the United States than from any other country.

The process of Mexican immigration to the United States derives from a combination of pull and push factors. The powerful magnets (pull factors) that draw hard-working, poorly paid workers have continuously attracted Mexican labor to the point that Mexican workers have become an institutionalized labor force in such industries as agriculture, construction, and textiles as well as in the service sector.[7]

Although a pronounced anti-immigrant xenophobic ambience currently exists in the United States and much of the political discourse is directed at curtailing immigration significantly, the reality of the trends and actual needs of the U.S. economy indicate that Mexican immigration to the United States will not cease altogether. Moreover, it might even increase in the future. Acknowledging this reality, the agricultural interests in the U.S. Southwest have already successfully lobbied the Agricultural Committee in the U.S. House of Representatives for exemptions on restrictive immigration measures, dismissing altogether the pervasive political rhetoric and anti-immigrant policies.

In addition to the pull factors, acute push factors from Mexico have resulted in immigration to the United States being a last hope and a potential safety valve for thousands of Mexican workers. Among these push factors are accelerated population growth (Mexico has ninety-one million people and its population is doubling every twenty-eight years); erratic job creation that does not come close to meeting employment needs (Mexico's labor force has increased by more than one million per year); unemployment (unemployment or underemployment is now affecting more than 50 percent of the entire labor force in Mexico); recurring economic crises (in this decade, Mexico's economic growth has not been more than 2 percent in the best of times, and has been zero or negative growth during downturns); devaluations and high inflation since the 1980s; and an increasing disparity between the affluent and all other sectors of society (close to 20 percent of Mexicans earn less than $75 a year).[8]

The crisis that began in 1994 has plunged Mexico into its most profound economic plight of the twentieth century, much surpassing the earlier 1982 crisis. Accelerated downturns of the national economy have resulted in massive layoffs that have contributed to an already alarming unemployment rate.[9] The peso devaluation not only has diminished the purchasing power of the Mexican currency but, as always, has been accompanied by rising inflation and a further erosion of the living standards of the middle and working classes. These two sectors of Mexican society account for more than 90 percent of Mexico's entire population. Furthermore, strong indicators predict that this latest crisis will not be a short-lived one. In fact, most analysts seem to concur that the recovery of Mexico will be gradual and spread out over several years.[10]

Contrary to anti-immigration political rhetoric in the United States, a large flow of Mexico's population into the United States proves valuable to the two countries for various reasons. First, for Mexico, the emigration of large numbers of its citizenry and the dividends secured from their income earnings in the United States provide significant cash flow to the country. It is estimated that the remittances sent to Mexico from wages in the United States are its second source of revenue.[11] Those resources play a vital role in the local and national economy—even in the very survival of the emigrants' families and hometowns. In addition, the yearly immigration of thousands of workers relieves economic and social pressures for demands upon the Mexican state, which is already hard pressed to meet the existing needs.[12] For the U.S. economy, Mexican immigrants have equally beneficial results. In many cases, undocumented Mexican workers are filling certain employment categories that few North American workers are willing to consider for minimum wage or less. A well-documented trend in the U.S. economy is the expansion of the service sector. This sector consistently offers unstable and low-paying jobs. A large number of Mexican immigrants have served this industry well. In addition to the service sector, undocumented workers are a critical segment of the labor force in the agricultural, domestic, construction, and textile industries. By having a large-scale labor force such as Mexican immigrants at a set wage and offering few to no benefits, North American employers are able to keep prices stable for many products and commodities.

Finally, Mexican immigrants pay local and in many cases federal taxes for which they will never claim any benefits whatsoever. Various scholars, after carrying out rigorous research projects on the economic impact of Mexican undocumented immigrants on a particular city, county, or industry, have concluded that immigrants contribute much more to the U.S. economy than they take out, and thus are major contributors both on the local and national economic level.[13] Therefore, the current status of Mexican immigration to the United States offers many incentives and clear benefits for both countries. As certain scholars and policymakers have concluded, real dangers exist and dire consequences are possible if the current situation is drastically altered.[14] The results could range from higher consumer prices in the United States for a multitude of products and services to increased social tensions and additional social unrest in Mexico.

Culturally, Mexican immigration reveals the artificiality of national political boundaries. Mexican immigrants in the United States have been major contributors to the maintenance of Mexican cultural and linguistic traditions throughout the twentieth century. The great Mexican migration to the United States at the turn of the century included numerous artists, many of whom found work as illustrators and caricaturists on Spanish-language newspapers such as *La Prensa* in San Antonio and *La Opinión* in Los Angeles. Others produced paintings and murals for stores, bars, and restaurants throughout the Southwest and the Midwest in cities such as Chicago.[15] In addition, an impressive number of Mexican immigrants continued their literary activities in the United States as journalists, creative writers, poets, and playwrights. A select few integrated themselves into the emerging film industry of Hollywood, working as actors, extras, and technicians.[16]

It is no coincidence that in the 1920s when Mexican immigration to the United States reached its peak, major newspapers in Spanish were founded in California and Texas. Also, this period marked the golden age of Spanish-language theater in the United States, which was reinforced and creatively propelled by Mexican immigrants.

Mexican immigrants, both legal and undocumented, have been instrumental in the preservation of Mexican culture, values, traditions, and the Spanish language in the United States in general, and within the Chicano community in particular. Moreover, Mexican immigrants have indeed aided in making Spanish the second most-spoken language in the United States.[17]

Additionally, Mexican immigrants have shown a marked tendency not to conform to the the classical assimilation model traditionally employed by U.S. immigration studies. Contrary to this model, a 1993 survey of children of Mexican immigrants revealed their strong propensity to reject assimilation and to display an enduring ethnic identity.[18]

Cultural Production: Theoretical Considerations

Keeping the above parameters in mind, we can construct theoretical models designed to explain literary and artistic cultural manifestations at particular points in time. A brief discussion of established cultural theories will aid in our understanding of the connection between traditional culture as such and contemporary immigrant cultural manifestations that this anthology addresses.

It is difficult to find a single, unanimously accepted, all-encompassing definition of culture. At one time, famed cultural anthropologists A. Kroeber and Clyde Kluckhohn collected various definitions of culture and found six predominating categories: descriptive, historical, normative, psychological, structural, and genetical.[19]

Carl Cafagna conceptualized culture with definitions underscoring "social heritage or learned behavior, or ideas, or standardized behavior."[20] Later in the 1960s, Edward T. Hall became more specific and highlighted ten categories of human endeavors that encompassed the concept. These were: learning, habitat, food, environmental exploitation, use of space, language, war, play, religion, and clothing.[21] Zygnunt Bauman's more abstract conceptualization offers the best insight for our purposes. He states, "The concept makes sense only if denoted straightforwardly as *the culture*; there is an ideal nature of the human being, and *the culture* means the conscious, strenuous, and prolonged effort to attain this ideal, to bring the actual life process into line with the highest potential of the human vocation."[22]

The problem with categorization, however, is that the grouping of cultural entities is not an objective activity but dependent on specific social contexts. Thus, as Bauman in his elucidating study *Culture as Praxis* points out, "domains having the fullest phenomenal resemblance may still acquire quite contradictory meanings if placed in disparate semantic frameworks."[23] With this important caveat in mind, more enlightened sociologists and anthropologists advocated for a value-bound and a value-neutral understanding of culture.[24]

Clyde Kluckhohn provided a commonly accepted definition of culture: "all of those historically created designs for living, explicit and implicit, rational, irrational and nonrational, which exist at any given time as potential guides for the behavior of man."[25]

We take this elementary definition as our kernel for the production of a theoretical model through which we can understand the forms of cultural expression as they manifest themselves in a particular geographic space and point in time.

Since theories on culture view it as essential for survival, we need to understand how cultural production manifests itself in different forms. It is our position that the production of specific cultural "products" deviating from those established ones or encapsulating a new message within accepted cultural constructs is in response to perceived threats to the survival of a group or a people. These manifestations can appear via traditional modes or newly invented ones. In this sense our conceptualization of cultural movements of culture coincide, to a certain extent, with Herbert Marcuse, the Marxist cultural thinker, who perceives "genuine culture" as applying to the "dissenting classes only: . . . the historical validity of ideas like Freedom, Equality, Justice of the Individual, was precisely in their yet unfulfilled content—in that they could not be referred to the established reality, which did not and could not validate them because they were denied by the functioning of the very institutions that were supposed to realize these ideas."[26]

Marcuse views cultural ideals as emanating from the marginal or ascending classes. According to him, such classes lose their momentum when the ruling class accepts them only to rise once again when the dispossessed rebel against the established system.

Bauman synthesizes the dialectical movement of cultural formations in society:

It seems that, in the rotation of conflicts, revolutions and institutionalization of new systems, hierarchical concepts of culture, always present, play an important though changing role. They emerge as war cries of the oppressed and dissenting; usually they end up as "bobility"-like legitimations of a new establishment. Sometimes (as in the case of the ideal of freedom, continuously reappearing in Western history, each time with an enlarged semantical referent) they resume their long-forgotten militantly critical role, but then are reformulated as a partial component of a broader principle.[27]

The variety of terms related to cultural production, such as folklore, popular culture, and mass culture, may be at times confusing, yet in our postmodern age cultural production from various sectors has been progressively converging, their boundaries, which at one time were thought to be ironclad, dissolving in the cauldron of mass culture. As Ian Chambers notes in his book *Popular Culture: The*

Metropolitan Experience (1990), "simple distinctions between high culture, between good and bad taste, between the profound and the superficial, between avant-garde and mass culture, are increasingly swamped by a wave of metropolitan connections, suggestions and sense."[28] Nevertheless, for purposes of this study we wish to clarify the cultural production terminology that we are using in the articles that follow. The term *popular culture* embraces multiple possibilities of cultural production. It is found, as Chambers enumerates, "in popular music (as opposed to classical music), the movies, popular theater (as opposed to classical theater), fashion, pop art, advertising, television, records, commercial iconography of popular experience such as Elvis Presley, beer cans, sports, comics, Coca Cola bottles, Marilyn Monroe, videos, newspapers, pulp fiction, rag magazines, newspapers, radio, magazines. Popular culture is mostly, but certainly not exclusively, derived from urban living: the city, the great metropolitan centers of the world."[29]

On the other hand, high culture may be viewed as that emanating in the most conservative museums, the concert halls, and the Shakespearean-type theaters.[30] Chambers further elucidates on "official" or "high" culture:

> Official culture, preserved in art galleries, museums, and university courses, demands cultivated tastes and formally imparted knowledge. It demands moments of attention that are separated from the run of daily life. Popular culture, meanwhile mobilizes the tactile, the incidental, the transitory, the expendable; the visceral. It does not involve an abstract aesthetic research amongst privileged objects of attention, but invokes mobile orders of sense, taste and desire. Popular culture is not appropriated through the apparatus of contemplation, but, as Walter Benjamin once put it, through "distracted perception." The public is an examiner, but an absentminded one.[31]

While popular culture is more expansive than folk culture or folklore, the latter nevertheless encompasses a great deal of cultural production. The boundaries between the two are often blurred and, in fact, in Mexico and the rest of Latin America, the term *cultura popular* is commonly used in place of "folklore."

There is no one definition for the word "folklore." When consulted, twenty-one experts on folklore did not come up with one standard definition, although the overlapping of comments did occur. One unifying thread was the consensus that folklore was transmitted through oral tradition. The following are some of the definitions proffered by renowned folklore scholars: Folklore comprises traditional creations of people, primitive (sic) and civilized. These are achieved by using sounds and words in metric form and prose, and include also folk beliefs or super-stitions, customs and performances, dances and plays. Moreover, folklore is not a science about a folk, but the traditional folk science and folk poetry.[32]

William R. Bascom's definition is quite comprehensive:

> In anthropological usage, the term folklore has come to mean myths, legends, folktales, proverbs, riddles, verse, and a variety of other forms of artistic expression whose medium is the spoken word. Thus, folk-lore can be defined as verbal art. Anthropologists recognize that an important group of individuals known as folklorists are interested in customs, beliefs, arts and crafts, dress, house types, and food recipes; but in their own studies of the aboriginal people of various parts of the world, these diverse items are treated under the accepted headings of material culture, graphic and plastic arts, technology and econom-ics, social and political organization, and religion, and all are subsumed under the general term culture. There is, however, an important part of culture which does not fall under any of these convenient headings, and which is classed separately as folklore. Folklore in all its forms, thus defined, is obviously related to literature, which is written; but folklore may never be written even in a literate society, and it may exist in societies which have no form of writing. Like literature, folk-lore is an art form related to music, the dance, and the graphic and plastic arts, but different in the medium of expression which is employed.[33]

The scholarly articles included in this anthology generally use popular cul-ture in its most comprehensive sense of meaning. That is to say, we examined contemporary novels and short stories that have not been canonized by main-stream universities (generally Chicano literature is taught under the "ethnic litera-ture" rubric), contemporary Chicano art that has not likewise achieved the bless-ings of mainstream museums, and generally B movies mass produced for the working class and the Mexican immigrant market in the borderlands.

The *corridos* examined in the Herrera-Sobek article are for the most part contemporary ballads composed specifically for movies produced in the last four decades. Most of them are not as yet in the folk tradition but belong to the contem-porary music scene.

On the other hand, the jokes cited in the Reyna and Herrera-Sobek article do belong to the folk tradition. They have been orally circulated and were collected from participants during field work.

We fully agree that the destitute and marginalized are important sources of cultural production. Nevertheless, a more expanded definition of culture would *a fortiori* encompass those elements produced by *all* members of society and not just one sector. Our study focuses on the cultural production of the undocumented and documented immigrant population and those who identify with this group, i.e., the Chicanos/as and Mexican artists, writers, and political intellectuals as well as other members of society who are sensitive to the issue. Of course there is a counter movement of cultural production structured by those who feel hostility toward the immigrant or who are passionately opposed to undocumented or even documented immigration on social, economic, and political grounds. Our study, however, concentrates on the cultural production of Chicano and Mexicano intellectuals/artists, who in general tend to be sensitive to the plight of the immigrant. Thus, the cultural production analyzed in this anthology overwhelmingly tends to defend the plight and the contribution of the immigrant. In fact, the cultural production we have seen in the Chicano/Mexicano communities arises out of a desire to defend the rights of the immigrant, whether documented or undocumented. The areas of cultural production that evidence this cultural activity include literature, art, history, folklore (folk song and humorous narratives), and film among others.

Much Chicano/Mexicano intellectual cultural production is geared toward the idealized goal of social justice for all, but more specifically, in the artistic cultural products rendered, toward the Mexican immigrant. This position is generalized and theoretically elaborated by the eminent culture critic Clifford Geertz to include a wider spectrum of society, if not all society. Geertz's view of the function of culture perceives it as a liberating force and not as a constraining one. We should view cultures, he states, "less and less in terms of the way in which they constrain human nature and more and more in the way in which, for better or for worse, they actualize it . . . Man is the only living animal who needs [cultural] designs for he is the only living animal whose evolutionary history has been such that his physical being has been significantly shaped by their existence and is therefore, irrevocably predicated upon them." [34]

Chicano/Mexicano intellectuals and artists strive through their cultural production and political commitment to afford immigrants full rights as men and women in order for them to achieve their full potential. In this sense, Chicano/Mexicano immigrant cultural manifestations are in accord with Geertz's view of

11

culture being a liberating force. We are aware that cultural products can be used negatively or positively, such as in Hitler's fascist reign. However, in our case, our cultural works go hand in hand with our political commitments, which are engaged in guaranteeing the civil rights of Mexican immigrants in the United States.

Mexican Immigration Studies: Three Perspectives

In order to better place this edited collection in the context of immigration scholarship and more fully delineate its originality and unique contributions, it is important to outline the evolution and diverse perspectives of the field of study of Mexican immigration to the United States.

Studies on immigration to the United States, while extensive, had for the most part centered upon the influx of Europeans to North America in the nineteenth century and early twentieth century.[35] This emphasis of North American scholars displayed a visible bias within an extensive historiography. There existed a serious neglect of another and equally significant immigrant wave to the United States—that of thousands of Mexicans who crossed and are still crossing the Río Grande or *la frontera* in a quest for greater economic opportunities.

As Mexican immigration became a policy issue at the turn of the century, a trend emerged for scholars on both sides of the border to contribute studies of diverse aspects of Mexican immigration to the United States. From the 1920s on, at least three perspectives of Mexican immigration studies became discernable: North American, Mexican, and Chicana/o.

North American immigration scholarship, which originated this field of study, had a peculiar evolution. Its origins coincide with the height of the process of Mexican immigration in the early decades of the twentieth century. As thousands of Mexicans migrated and settled permanently throughout the U.S. border states, the Midwest, and Far West, Anglo policy-makers and local officials became concerned about the possible negative impact of such a large population group— of whom little was known—on American institutions and society. In order to set policies and more accurately measure significance, academic studies were encouraged and even commissioned.

Thus, in the decade of the 1920s, the first formal studies of immigration north from Mexico, carried out by North American scholars, appeared. Chronologically, it would be the first "school" of Mexican immigration studies. Among these early studies, the work of Paul Taylor stands out by far. With great rigor and sensibility, he carried out an impressive research design and later published his findings on economic aspects and enclaves of Mexican immigrant labor in the United States. Besides the works of Taylor, other publications and reports addressed various issues of Mexican immigration, ranging from demographic to social aspects.[36] They all attempted to arrive at the possible consequences of the so-called "Mexican problem" on U.S. society and the labor market.[37]

As has been noted by Chicano scholars Octavio Romano, Nick Vaca, and others, much of that early U.S. scholarship was highly prejudicial and scientifically flawed.[38] For the most part, it stressed all the negative elements that were perceived about Mexican-origin culture, society and national character. Many stereotypes of Mexicans, which have become pervasive in North American academia and popular culture, had their origins in the so-called "scientific" studies of the 1920s and 1930s.

After this initial cycle of writings on the Mexican-origin immigrant population, North American scholars for the next years seemed to revert to earlier patterns of neglect regarding studies of the Mexican/Chicano community. The writings on Mexican immigrants were more on the order of journalistic and editorial pieces that appeared during the Great Depression.

In the late 1940s, Carey McWilliams, journalist, historian, and founder of *The Nation*, wrote the first general history of Mexican immigration, his classic and much-admired book, *North from Mexico*. The sensible and kindly perceptive synthesis is still one of the landmark works on Mexican immigration to the United States. Yet, for all its achievements and contributions to the field, the book was little noticed until the Chicano movement (in the late 1960s) resurrected it and gave it the recognition that it much deserved.

The next major cycle of North American scholarly writings on Mexican immigration would not be published until the late 1960s and 1970s. These studies followed an emerging concern with the rise of undocumented immigration to the United States from the Western Hemisphere, especially Mexico.[39] From that time to the present, extensive research and publications have appeared from a multitude of perspectives and disciplines with varying purposes and results.

The immigration studies of the decade of the 1970s and beyond stressed the economic significance, policy issues, legislative reforms, and demographics of immigration, and presented case studies of the impact of immigration on regions and specific cities in California and Texas.[40] The social sciences clearly dominated the scholarly inquiry on Mexican immigration. Particularly significant to the study of Mexican immigration were the fields of anthropology, economics, history, political science, and sociology.[41] Historians engaged in a strong and ambitious agenda by

13

publishing overviews and specific works on the first decades of Mexican immigration and the repatriation movements of the Great Depression, but the studies then faded from the scene.[42] Economists were much divided on their findings, some emphasizing the heavy cost of Mexican immigration for the U.S. economy while others, with similar data sets, coming up with totally different interpretations that pointed out the extensive benefits of Mexican immigrants to the U.S. economy and society.[43]

The inclusion of research on gender and women's roles in U.S. immigration studies began to make its mark in the late 1980s and 1990s.[44] Gender issues of Mexican immigration were addressed in two important anthropological and sociological studies by Marilyn Davis and Pierrette Hondagneu-Sotelo. An important article on the same topic is Silvia Pedraza's, "Women and Migration: The Social Consequences of Gender." Although these were useful first steps in a discussion of women immigrants, there is much more to be done on this theme. Currently, the misperception prevails that the majority of immigrants are male.

In terms of productivity and of the study of the most varied aspects of Mexican immigration to the United States, the Center for U.S.–Mexican Studies at the University of California, San Diego, has been at the vanguard of North American scholarship. Founder and first director, Wayne Cornelius, prioritized his and others' research on immigration. Throughout the 1980s and 1990s numerous and important studies were published by this center.

In the last few years, although there have been select valuable studies on Mexican immigration by North American scholars, they have been much outweighed by ideologically motivated writers of the restrictionist school. The overwhelming number of publications on the question of Mexican immigration can be characterized as alarmist, accentuating the negative aspects of immigration and calling for restrictionist measures. This "academic" literature models popular and journalistic reporting. Similar in nature to the xenophobic trends in the past, such literature even goes a step beyond in its harshness and racist tone. It is as if Mexican immigrants have become the single greatest threat to current American national security and well-being.[45]

Economic insecurity in a changing world mixed with latent racism and fueled by opportunistic political rhetoric spills over on academic scholarship. Various scholars are now legitimizing and substantiating the views and prejudices of opportunistic policy-makers and certain segments of the population.

The field of Mexican immigration studies had its formal beginning with the scholarship of noted anthropologist Manuel Gamio. As a response to the writings and conclusions of U.S. immigration scholars of the 1920s and beyond, Professor Gamio was commissioned by the Mexican government to carry out an extensive and original project studying social, economic, and labor issues of Mexican immigrants in the United States. After months of research and endless oral-history interviews, he wrote two important books, which were first published by the University of Chicago Press.[46]

Years later, one of the most noted demographers of Mexico, Professor Gilberto Loyo, carried out important research and synthesized the existing secondary literature in the writing of a lengthy prologue for the Spanish edition of one of Gamio's books, published by the National University of Mexico. His writing was attuned to national concern on rising immigration because of the Bracero Program. In addition, he edited an entire thematic social science journal issue on Mexican immigration to the United States. This important collection of readings was the first edited study on this subject matter in Mexican academia.[47]

The next step in Mexican immigration studies was undertaken by sociologist/historian Moisés González Navarro, who has become one of the most prolific and distinguished historians of his generation. After publishing a general overview of the social history of colonization in Mexico, he has continued to expand his comprehensive analysis of the evolution of Mexican society in subsequent multivolume studies that include valuable new research and interpretations on the historical dimensions of Mexican immigration to the United States.[48]

His student, Mercedes Carreras de Velasco, who was also a student of Luis González, the other dean of Mexican historians at the Colegio de Mexico, wrote an excellent master's thesis on the early phase of the repatriation of Mexicans in the Great Depression. Its published edition has become the standard Mexican study of this period and theme.[49]

These works, however, were isolated studies and did not reflect a central theme in Mexican scholarship. Generally speaking, Mexican scholars up until the 1970s did not address this subject with any consistency or priority. The situation began to change in the decade of the 1960s. Since that period, emerging scholars have contributed important perspectives and research findings. For the most part, these works have been carried out by anthropologists, economists, historians, political scientists, and sociologists.

Sociologist Jorge A. Bustamante, a student of Julián Samora, was the first Mexican scholar to make immigration his central academic preoccupation. Bustamante published numerous and critical articles and book chapters on the subject matter, and he fostered and prioritized the study of immigration as founder and president of the Colegio de la Frontera—Mexico's most distinguished research center for immigration and border studies.[50]

Besides the researchers at El Colegio de la Frontera, several universities in Mexico City as well as in Michoacán, Jalisco, and Zacatecas have carried out and published innovative immigration studies on the economic and regional impact of Mexican immigration waves to the United States. In the late 1970s, one of the government's principal policy institutes, the Centro de Investigación de Estudios del Trabajo (CENIET), assembled an impressive team of social scientists to conduct the single most comprehensive and rigorous research project on Mexican immigration. After years of study and data collection, various reports and published working papers were available. Overall, the research findings corrected many impressionistic assumptions, such as the numbers of Mexican undocumented workers in any set time frame, a breakdown of "sending" Mexican communities, and the work experiences of Mexican immigrants in the United States.[51]

Patricia Morales and Mónica Verea Campos, scholars and journalists, published the two existing overviews of Mexican immigration in the United States in the 1980s. Each focused her synthesis on different issues and themes. Both made valuable insights and did much to enlighten general Mexican readers on the subject matter.[52]

In the recent period, Mexican immigration studies have focused upon regional case studies. State universities and El Colegio de la Frontera continue to be central institutions engaged in the study of immigration to the United States as a priority.

Chicana/o scholarship on Mexican immigration has been original, extensive, and consistent. Almost without exception, all Chicana/o historians and social scientists have published important studies on diverse aspects of the immigrant experience. The origin of this tendency derives from the scholarship and mentorship of two noted scholars, Ernesto Galarza and Julián Samora. Ernesto Galarza wrote one of the best analyses of the Bracero Program and its labor and human dimensions, *Merchants of Labor*. He followed this publication with various studies of Mexican-origin workers in the agricultural industry in California. His books combined the rigor of academic research with the sensitivity of an observer-participant. Julián Samora was the first Chicano scholar to acknowledge the preeminence of Mexican immigration to the Chicano experience. He published the earliest overview of undocumented immigration, *Los Mojados*. In addition, he trained a whole generation of Chicano scholars who specialized in immigration studies.[53]

Galarza and Samora's valuable pioneering studies on Mexican immigration in the 1960s and early 1970s were followed by various generations of Chicana/o academics that emerged in the aftermath of the Chicano movement. Young scholars representing history and the social sciences followed suit and began to publish innovative and rigorous studies on related issues and themes of Mexican immigration. From the 1970s to the 1990s, important monographs, edited books, and journal articles by Chicana/o scholars appeared within American academia.

It is indeed remarkable that almost without exception, most Chicana/o historians or social scientists have published important research findings and perspectives on Mexican immigration to the United States. Among them are Louise Año Nuevo de Kerr, Francisco Balderrama, Pedro Castillo, Juan Ramón García, Manuel García y Griego, Mario García, Juan Gómez-Quiñones, Richard Griswold del Castillo, Camille Guerin-Gonzales, David G. Gutiérrez, David R. Maciel, Oscar J. Martínez, Douglas Monroy, Antonio Ríos-Bustamante, Ricardo Romo, Arturo Rosales, Vicky Ruíz, George Sánchez, Alex Saragosa, Denis Valdez, Emilio Zamora, and María Herrera-Sobek. The same is true for the social sciences. Gilbert Cárdenas, Jorge Castro, Leo Chávez, Julia Curry-Rodríguez, Rodolfo de la Garza, Leo Estrada, Estevan Flores, John García, José Angel Gutiérrez, Martha López-Garza, Lisa Magaña, Margarita Melville, Rebecca Morales, Christine Marie Sierra, and Rosalía Solorzano are scholars who have published substantial research pieces and have made major contributions to a better comprehension of the process and immigrant experience of Mexicans in the United States. It is most evident that the question of Mexican immigration has been a critical concern for Chicana/o scholars in the last decades, and continues to be so.[54]

Culture across Borders

Although this extensive and growing field of immigration studies has rendered important research findings on both sides of the border, one major shortcoming still exists in the scholarly literature. The cultural elements of Mexican immigration and the cultural/artistic manifestations that this immigration process has inspired have not received the academic inquiry that they merit.[55] Neither North American nor Mexican scholarship has addressed this theme, although, as the book chapters in this volume accentuate, in terms of quantity, Mexico has produced the greatest number of cultural works inspired by the immigration experience. Historical, economic, social, and gender issues have dominated immigration studies on both sides of the border.

In spite of the critical importance of the cultural dimension of Mexican immigration, until recently, and with very few exceptions, the subject had remained neglected by the scholars of both countries. For the last decade, however, Chicana/o researchers and writers have begun to include the cultural genres of Mexican immigration in their published work. This edited collection builds upon this emerging trend and attempts to go further than those existing studies. To date this is the only book-length study that analyzes and discusses in detail such a wide range of cultural manifestations: art, cinema, *corridos*, humor, and literary narratives inspired by the Mexican immigrant experience.

The contributors to this volume represent a diversity of academic disciplines and perspectives, including art history and criticism, cultural studies, film analysis, folklore, cultural history, literary criticism, and political science. A conscious attempt was made by the editors to include both established scholars as well as promising young academicians among the various contributors. Senior scholars bring years of research, published work, and reflection to their studies, and emerging researchers demonstrate innovative methodologies and novel perspectives in the themes explored. Methodologically, the chapters follow a clear trend in recent immigration studies. All of the authors emphasize the necessity of employing an interdisciplinary conceptual mode of analysis in their immigration research and published work. These scholars incorporate a wide range of source materials; analytically, they offer diverse and original interpretations in their respective book chapters.

Juan Gómez-Quiñones and David R. Maciel's article "'What Goes Around, Comes Around': Political Practice and Cultural Response in the Internationalization of Mexican Labor, 1890–1997" provides the historical framework through which we can comprehend more fully the migratory movement of Mexicans since the fateful Mexican–U.S. War of 1848 divided what is today the Southwest from its original Mexican moorings. Gómez-Quiñones and Maciel posit that an international capitalist economic system is the propelling force that drives immigrants, both men and women, to leave their homeland in search of a better life. The economic vectors are the primary fuels energizing migratory movements and directly affecting the cyclical nature of these phenomena. Thus, in times of economic prosperity, attitudes toward the immigrant are positive and surveillance units look the other way or conspiratorially wink at Mexican migration north. In times of economic depression, these forces (i.e., the police, INS, border patrol, and political demagogues) surface with a vengeance, calling for the eradication of the immigrant worker on U.S. soil.

Gómez-Quiñones and Maciel document the Mexican immigrant historical odyssey starting from the 1880s when the first hostile immigration acts surfaced in response to racist sentiment against the Chinese immigrant. They then trace the history of immigration in the early and middle of the nineteenth century, taking into account the labor movements, union organizing, and legislative acts directly proceeding from economic upturns or downturns in the U.S. economy. They explore the Bracero Program years (1942–64) and the Carter years and review what effects the newly discovered petroleum reserves had on immigration policy during the 1970s. In addition, they detail the contemporary rise of immigration rights movements and the various sectors supporting these civil rights (i.e., churches, unions—particularly the United Farm Workers of America union and Mexican American organizations).

Gómez-Quiñones and Maciel's contribution lies in making the connection between economic forces and the cultural and political ideologies that arise in response to Mexican immigration. The scapegoating of the immigrant as a major source of American decline (in spite of hard empirical data demonstrating a contrary view) is underscored in Gómez-Quiñones and Maciel's chapter. This discrepancy between empirical data and negative racist currents that seek to make the immigrant the "fall guy" creates an opposite countermovement on the part of artists who seek to "tell" the truth and give voice to the other side. This "truth" as perceived by artists is articulated by means of artistic expressions such as literary works (novels, poetry, plays, short stories) and popular culture (films, photographs, folk narratives such as the jest, and folk songs, i.e., *corridos* or ballads). Gómez-Quiñones and Maciel thus set the stage for a comprehensive hermeneutics of artistic expressions, because these expressions do not arise out of a void but are linked to a socio-historical-political context.

Alberto Ledesma in his study "Undocumented Crossings: Narratives of Mexican Immigration to the United States" approaches the representation of the Mexican immigrant from another perspective—literary texts. His fundamental concern is how Chicanos/as themselves view the Mexican immigrant experience and "fictionalize" it within their literary production. To this end, Ledesma traces the representation of the immigrant from its earliest inception, the life story of Joaquín Murieta as presented in John Rollin Ridge's *The Life and Adventures of Joaquín Murieta* (1955). Then he analyzes a Mexican perspective as presented in *Las aventuras de Don Chipote o cuando los pericos mamen* (The Adventures of Don Chipote or When the Parrots May Suckle Their Young, 1928), *Murieron a la mitad del Río* (They Died in the Middle of the River, 1948), and *Aventuras de un bracero* (The Adventures of a Bracero, 1961). He contrasts the Mexican immigrant view-

19

point with that of Chicana and Chicano narrators such as Ernesto Galarza's *Barrio Boy* (1971), Estela Portillo Trambley's *Trini* (1986), and Sandra Cisneros's *Woman Hollering Creek* (1992).

Ledesma's analytical work yields important conclusions. Chicano/a perspectives on immigration differ radically from Mexican views in that the former do not tend to romanticize or glorify Mexico or the United States but instead present the realistic struggles immigrants engage in during their quest for survival and in their search for a viable cultural identity.

Ledesma's study isolates the "distinct narrative patterns that characterize the stories of immigration written by Chicanos/as versus Mexican authors." This is an important step in recognizing the cultural and historical vectors that influence the perception of the immigrant experience.

The Mexican immigrant experience has not only found a home in literary works of art but is also evident in the plastic arts such as painting and installations. Victor Sorrell's comprehensive article "Telling Images Bracket the 'Broken-Promised Land': The Culture of Immigration and the Immigration of Culture across Borders" shows us the varied and contradictory postures resulting from United States government policy toward immigration as transcribed in history and evident in legislation and popular sentiment expressed in the hegemonic Anglo society.

The author juxtaposes the compassionate icon of open-door immigration policy as exemplified by the Statue of Liberty and an Emma Lazarus poem with the various xenophobic, anti-immigration legislative acts passed during the twentieth century by Congress. Sorrell cites numerous examples: the Chinese Exclusion Act (renewed in 1902); the Gentleman's Agreement Act; the various Quota Acts passed in the 1920s; the Alien Registration Act (1940); the Internal Security Act (1950); the Immigration and Nationality Act (McCarran-Walter Act, 1952); the Immigration Reform and Control Act of 1986; and the Immigration Act of 1990.

Sorrell examines the works of more than eighty artists whose work encompasses Mexican immigrant themes. From Yolanda M. López's "Who's the Illegal Alien, Pilgrim?" to David Avalos's "Tax Rebate," the author points out how the topic of immigration has affected the Chicano/Latino artistic world. In particular, the author analyzes the political impact that Proposition 187 had on the consciousness of Chicana/o and Latina/o artists and the resulting artistic output denouncing this infamous piece of legislation.

Furthermore, Sorrell underscores how artists cleverly articulate their concerns and express their political messages through visual imagery in spite of the ruling class's censorship.

David R. Maciel and María Rosa García-Acevedo's chapter "The Celluloid Immigrant: The Narrative Films of Mexican Immigration" centers on Mexican immigrant films as a genre and examines the significance of production, dissemination, and popularity of genre films in society. The authors first construct the theoretical framework through which analysis of immigrant films can be analyzed and apply the theories of genre previously enunciated by such film critics as Stuart M. Kaminsky in his study *American Film Genres: Approaches to a Critical Theory of Popular Film* (1974). With this theoretical model in mind, Maciel and García-Acevedo survey the immigrant film genre from its early debut in the 1920s to contemporary Mexican immigrant films of the nineties. They present an original thesis that three cinematic narratives exist that deal with the Mexican immigrant experience: Mexican cinema; the Hollywood style; and Chicano cinema. Each of the cinematic perspectives is discussed in detail through a contextual analysis of the most representative immigration narrative films.

Maciel and García-Acevedo have identified a veritable treasure of Mexican-made films with this subject matter—films such as *El hombre sin patria* (The Man without a Country, 1922), *La China Hilaria* (1938), *Pito Pérez se va de bracero* (Pito Pérez Goes Off as a Bracero, 1947), *Soy Mexicano de acá de este lado* (I Am a Mexican from this Side of the Border), *El bracero del año* (The Bracero of the Year, 1963), *Primero el dólar* (First the Dollar, 1970), *Se solicitan mojados* (Wetbacks Wanted, 1970), and *Chacales de la frontera* (Jackals of the Border, 1990). The authors divide the series of films examined into two categories: those falling within the decades 1920–70 and those filmed during the 1980–95 period. The films are analyzed for content and ideology and with respect to the representation of the Mexican immigrant. The ideological message encapsulated within the films is of particular importance—they all discourage Mexican migration to the United States.

In their examination of the Hollywood style of immigration films, Maciel and García-Acevedo trace the evolution and ideological constructs of North American immigration films beginning in the early silent-movie period and continuing to the present. The authors conclude that the principal thesis or message of the films is the need to control our southern border and better regulate or deter illegal immigration from Mexico.

21

The third narrative film approach concerns the rich contributions of such Chicano immigration films as *El Norte, Born in East L.A.*, and *My Family/Mi Familia*. In the view of Maciel and García-Acevedo, the Chicano immigrant film is the one cinematic genre that offers complexity, humanism, and a deep sensibility toward the Mexican immigrant experience.

Maciel and García-Acevedo offer the first detailed historical analysis of narrative films with the immigrant worker theme. The archival work undertaken, the comparative model employed, and their analysis of the ideological constructs underpinning these films makes this chapter an outstanding contribution to both film studies and Chicano/Mexican studies.

María Herrera-Sobek's article "The *Corrido* as Hypertext: Undocumented Mexican Immigrant Films and the Mexican/Chicano Ballad" examines the importance of *corridos* (ballads) and *canciones* (songs) in structuring the story line in Mexican immigrant films. The corrido tradition has served immigrants well as an artistic literary form through which they can articulate their desires, hopes, dreams, plans, grievances, sadness, happiness, love, disillusionment, and so forth.

Most likely the first corrido enunciating the immigrant experience is "El Corrido de Joaquín Murieta," which may date from the 1850s when the adventures of the celebrated Chicano rebel transpired. Joaquín identifies himself as an immigrant from Hermosillo, Sonora. Thereafter, corridos from the 1860s depict Mexican immigrant cowboy adventures, then the railroad building era, the Mexican revolution, the Great Depression era, the bracero era of the 1940–1960s, and contemporary corridos from the 1970–90 period—all portray the Mexican immigrant experience in its full complexity. It is not surprising that these ballads introduce the topic of immigration in a film, develop the narrative, or serve as a coda within the film's structure. Films such as *Pasaporte a la muerte* (Passport to Death), *Arizona, Maldita miseria* (Damned Misery), and others utilize the corrido to highlight specific episodes. Thus the corrido is an important element within the total structure of the film. It is an element that can stop the story line to reflect on the immigrant experience, aid the flow of the narrative by foreshadowing events in the story line, or underscore important ideological messages inscribed within the film's text.

The study most significantly contributes to the understanding of the function of intertextuality and the crossing of boundaries between genres in the construction of a film's story line and "message." It points to the importance of popular culture and oral tradition in capturing the audience's attention. It also demonstrates the skillful integration of older traditional modes of expression (the ballad) with contemporary, technologically advanced ones—film.

José Reyna and María Herrera-Sobek's chapter, "Jokelore, Cultural Differences, and Linguistic Dexterity: The Construction of the Mexican Immigrant in Chicano Humor," provides further evidence of the pervasiveness of the immigrant experience in popular culture. Reyna and Herrera-Sobek's study examines folk narratives belonging to the jest or joke category vis-à-vis the representation of the Mexican immigrant. Reyna and Herrera-Sobek point out the importance of immigration as a topic within the Chicano joke tradition.

Collectively, as the summaries of these chapters attest, this book is a first step in addressing the cultural dimensions of Mexican immigration to the United States. These chapters clearly demonstrate how the issue and process of Mexican immigration have indeed inspired creative and powerful cultural manifestations — art, corridos, fiction, films, humor, and plays on both sides of the border.

Notes

1. *La Jornada*, 7 May 1996, pp. 1, 2.

2. The current anthology by Bruno Leone, *Immigration: Opposing Viewpoints* (San Diego: Greenhaven Press, 1994) traces the divergent political positions and views on Mexican immigration.

3. See Julian L. Simon et al., "Why Control the Borders?" *National Review* (February 1993) for various articles that touch on this issue.

4. Mónica Verea, "The U.S. Immigration Debate and Its Consequences for Mexico," *Voices of Mexico* (October-December 1995), pp. 18–21.

5. See David R. Maciel, "The Unwritten Alliance: Mexican Policy on Immigration to the United States," *The World and I* (July 1986), pp. 676–699 for an overview and periodization of Mexican immigration.

6. Moisés González Navarro, *Población y sociedad en México (1900–1970)* (Mexico: UNAM, 1974), details this process with rigor in this work. His most recent study, *Los extranjeros en México y los mexicanos en el extranjero 1821–1970* (Mexico: El Colegio de México, 1994), updates the early publications.

7. The edited volume by Wayne Cornelius, *The Changing Role of Mexican Labor in the U.S. Economy* (La Jolla, Calif.: Center For U.S.–Mexican Studies University of California, 1989) covers this theme in great detail.

8. Jorge Castañeda discusses and analyzes the Mexican contemporary crisis in great detail in *The Mexican Shock: Its Meaning for the U.S.* (New York: New Press, 1995).

9. "México en su peor momento," *Baja California* (7 May 1996), pp. 2–4.

10. Sidney Weintraub, "Mexico's Painful Detour on the Way to the Promised Land," *The San Diego Union-Tribune*, 12 May 1996, p. 5.

11. The study by Juan Díaz-Canedo, *La migración indocumentada a Estados Unidos: Un nuevo enfoque* (México: Fondo de Cultura Económica, 1980), is to date the most complete analysis of the remittances of Mexican immigrants in the United States to Mexico and their overall economic significance.

12. Interview with Carlos Monsiváis, Mexico City, 12 June 1995.

13. Michael Piore's *Birds of Passage: Migrant Labor and Industrial Societies* (Cambridge: Cambridge University Press, 1979) argues this point well.

14. Interview with Manuel García y Griego, Irvine, California, 14 June 1995.

15. David R. Maciel, "Aztlán and Mexico: Mexico in Aztlán: The Dialectics of Chicano/ Mexicano Art," in Richard Griswold del Castillo et al., *Chicano Art: Resistance and Affirmation* (Los Angeles: U.C.L.A. Wright Gallery, University of California Los Angeles, 1991), pp. 110–111.

16. George Hadley-García's pictorial history, *Hispanic Hollywood: The Latinos in Motion Pictures* (New York: Carol Publishing Group, 1990) narrates this story well.

17. A. Aguirre, "Language Use in Bilingual Mexican American Households," *Social Science Quarterly* 65:2 (June 1984), pp. 567–571.

18. See the excellent book chapter by Leo Chávez and Rebecca G. Martínez, "Mexican Immigration in the 1980s and Beyond: Implications for Chicanas/os" in David R. Maciel and Isidro D. Ortiz, eds., *Chicanas/Chicanos at the Crossroads* (Tucson, University of Arizona Press, 1996), pp. 52–81.

19. A. Kroeber and C. Kluckhohn, *Culture: A Critical Review of Concepts and Definitions.* Papers of the Peabody Museum (New York: Vintage, 1952).

20. Carl Cafagna, "A Formal Analysis of Definitions of 'Culture,'" in *Essays in the Science of Culture*, ed. Gertrude E. Dole and Robert L. Carneiro (New York: 1960).

21. Edward T. Hall, *The Silent Language* (Greenwich, Conn.: Fawcett Publications, 1959).

22. Zygmunt Bauman, *Culture as Praxis* (London: Routledge and Kegan Paul, 1973), p. 3.

23. Ibid., p. 9.

24. Ibid., p. 3.

25. Kroeber and Kluckhohn, p. 97.

26. Bauman, p. 15.

27. Ibid.

28. Iain Chambers, *Popular Culture: The Metropolitan Experience* (London: Methven, 1986).

29. Ibid.

30. Ibid.

31. Ibid.

32. Maria Leach et al., *Funk and Wagnalls Dictionary of Folklore, Mythology and Legend* (New York: Funk and Wagnalls Co., 1950).

33. Ibid.

34. Clifford Geertz, "The Transition to Humanity," *Horizon in Anthropology* (London: 1965), p. 47.

35. Reed Veda's excellent interpretative synthesis, *Postwar Immigrant America* (New York: 1994), covers this point in fine detail.

36. Paul Taylor, *Mexican Labor in the United States* (Berkeley: University of California Press, 1928).

37. See the publications by Victor S. Clark, *Mexican Labor in the United States* (Washington, D.C.: 1908); and Emory S. Bogardus, *The Mexican in the United States* (Los Angeles: University of Southern California Press, 1934).

38. Octavio Romano, "The Anthropology and Sociology of Mexican-Americans: The Distortion of Mexican-American History," *El Grito* 2:1 (Fall 1968), and Nick C. Vaca, "The Mexican-American in the Social Sciences, 1912–1970, Part I," *El Grito* 3:3 (Spring 1970), and Part II *El Grito* 4:1 (Fall 1970).

39. Wayne Cornelius, *Illegal Mexican Migration to the United States: Research Findings, Policy Implications, and Research Priorities* (Cambridge: 1977) summarizes many of the studies of this period and traces the direction of research in progress.

40. For an example of such studies, see Harry E. Cross and James A. Sandos, *Across the Border: Rural Development in Mexico and Recent Migration to the United States* (Berkeley: Institute of Government Studies, University of California, 1981).

41. The review article by Jorge Durand and Douglas E. Massey, "Mexican Migration to the United States: A Critical Review," *Latin American Research Review* 27:2 (1992), provides a useful analysis of social science immigration research.

42. Arthur F. Corwin, ed., *Immigrants and Immigrants: Perspectives on Mexican Labor Migration to the United States* (Westport: Greenwood Press, 1978) is a representative historical study that covers a wide historical period and themes.

43. See Julian L. Simon, *The Economic Consequences of Immigration* (New York: Oxford University Press, Mass.: 1989).

44. See Marilyn P. Davis, *Mexican Voices/American Dreams* (New York: Henry Holt, 1990); Pierrette Hondagneu-Sotelo, *Gendered Transitions: Mexican Experiences of Immigration* (Berkeley: University of California Press, 1994); and Silvia Pedraza, "Women and Migration: The Social Consequences of Gender," *Annual Review of Sociology* 17 (1991), pp. 303–325.

45. The books by Vernon M. Briggs, *Mass Immigration and the National Interest* (New York: Armonck, 1992); Daniel James, *Illegal Immigration: An Unfolding Crisis* (Lanham, Md.: University Press of America, 1991); and John Vinson, *Immigration out of Control: The Interests against America* (Monterey: 1992) are representative of this recent trend of U.S. immigration scholarship.

46. Manuel Gamio, *Mexican Immigration to the United States* (New York: Arno Press, 1969); and Gamio, *The Mexican Immigrant* (New York: Arno Press, 1969).

47. Gilberto Loyo, *El inmigrante mexicano* (Mexico: 1969).

48. See Moisés González Navarro, *Cinco crisis mexicanas* (México: El Colegio de México, 1985) and *La pobreza en México* (México: El Colegio de México, 1985).

49. Mercedes Carreras de Velasco, *Los mexicanos que devolvió la crisis* (Mexico: Secretaría de Relaciones Exteriores, 1974).

50. Among Bustamante's extensive publications are *Espaldas mojadas, materia para la expansión del capital norteamericano* (México: El Colegio de México, 1977); and Jorge Bustamante and Wayne A. Cornelius, eds., *Flujos migratorios hacia Estados Unidos* (Mexico: Comisión sobre el Futuro de las Relaciones México–Estados Unidos, 1989).

51. CENIET, "Informe final sobre los emigrantes mexicanos en Estados Unidos" (México: Secretaría del Trabajo y Previsión Social, 1979).

52. See Patricia Morales, *Indocumentados mexicanos: causas y razones de la migración* (México: Grijalbo, 1989); and Mónica Verea, *Entre México y Estados Unidos: Los indocumentados* (México: 1942). More recent studies published in Mexico include David M. Heer, *Los mexicanos indocumentados en los Estados Unidos* (Mexico: Fondo de Cultura Económica, 1993); and Roger Díaz de Cossío, Graciela Orozco, and Esther González, *Los mexicanos en Estados Unidos* (Mexico: SITESA Sistema Técnicos de Edición, S.A. de C.V., 1997).

53. Ernesto Galarza, *Farmworkers and Agri-Business in California, 1947–1960* (Notre Dame: University of Notre Dame Press, 1977); Galarza, *Merchants of Labor: The Mexican Bracero Program* (Charlotte, Calif.: McNally and Loftin, 1964); and Julián Samora, *Los Mojados: The Wetback Story* (Notre Dame: University of Notre Dame Press, 1971).

54. The very recent studies by David G. Gutiérrez, *Walls and Mirrors: Mexican Americans, Mexican Immigrants and the Politics of Ethnicity* (Berkeley: University of California Press, 1995) and *Between Two Worlds: Mexican Immigrants in the United States* (Washington, D.C.: 1996), clearly reflect the continued importance of Mexican immigration to Chicana/o scholarship.

55. See the recent two-volume anthology on Chicano history and culture, David R. Maciel, ed., *El México olvidado: la historia del pueblo chicano* (El Paso and Ciudad Juárez: University of Texas, El Paso/Universidad Autónoma de Ciudad Juárez, 1996), for further discussion of this theme.

1

"WHAT GOES AROUND, COMES AROUND"

Political Practice and Cultural Response in the Internationalization of Mexican Labor, 1890–1997

o o o o
o o o o

Juan Gómez-Quiñones and David R. Maciel

Mexican immigrants are cultural makers and political actors. How the cultural and political are interactive may be examined through a review over time of immigrants as subjects and objects. Mexican immigrant workers, both women and men, in the United States and Mexico are part of an international capitalist economic system, and their mobility is part of a larger pattern of international history.[1] Foremost, the human act and group phenomenon of emigration are so complex as to overpower available analogical concepts and paradigms. Further, to look at immigration is to look at the receiving society. This attempted cultural prolegomenon to a tentatively comprehensive map of Mexican immigration in the United States covers various themes. Interpretive analysis based on the literature will be used in this chapter incorporating the paradigmatic, the personal, the international, the historical, the economic, the social, the cultural, the perceptual, and the political.

Prolegomena — the Personal and the International

Capital has long been international, and capitalist actions here galvanized the workforce wherever they have extended.[2] The nineteenth-century workforce included not only manufacturing workers of Manchester but also slaves of the U.S. cotton-producing South, transoceanic sailors, and mine workers of Arizona and Sonora. Population movements are recurrent phenomena in world history. Within different groups and areas they have varying significance socially, economically, culturally, and politically. The personal and the structural account for the phenomena of the internationalization of labor; its economics and politics have been the case with Mexican workers in the United States.

Immigrants and native workers interrelate and interact economically and socially. Nearly all workers in the United States have been affected by immigration, primarily because the majority are the descendants of earlier immigrants.[3] Immigrants replenish the work force and are particularly vulnerable to exploitation, whether their immigration has resulted from force, recruitment, or choice.

From a perspective emphasizing personal will and context immigration becomes a mode of workforce action for individuals and groups when workers cross borders and continents to obtain more favorable conditions. In fact it has been a form of worker proaction.[4] When workers have chosen or been forced to cross borders, it often has been due to economic exploitation and political domination in their home areas, often combined with specific local circumstances and individual family context. The choice and will to emigrate may be personal, but the move into existing work arrangements and practices continually shapes the larger workforce into one that is diverse, stratified, and divided.

History and continuing transmigration patterns are a processual influence.[5] Mexican immigration is much more than the transmittal of patriarchal social practices or the sorry anecdotes of the sojourner in strange lands. Neither these nor other aspects of its complex process can be likened to taffy in a push-pull machine. To characterize immigrations strictly in terms of market/product, or employees and employers, would unreasonably obscure state actions. The internationalization of Mexican labor involves clear actions by two states and the weight of their interrelated history. The immigrant phenomenon brings together two labor markets and two discrete national labor movements, yet the immigrant's personal decision brings a step into another national history, another class formation. A review of immigrant volitions, work situations, politics, and cultures reveals the deep complexity of modern times, a unique time in world history.

Socially, once settled in the new area, immigrants may maintain their customary forms of organizing and elaborate or adopt different ones in the new situation. Moreover, immigrant workers interact with local workers and communicate their labor-political heritage and practices to a wider sector of their working peers. In areas such as the U.S. Southwest where migration from Mexico is often recurrent, the immigrant's experience with advocacy and organizing in Mexico is carried into the United States and vice versa. Immigrants transmit, create, and recreate culture. They build ethical communities as well as spatial ones and organize a range of social groups. Immigration also results in new cultural adaptations in the immigrants' places of origin. For instance, women who are left behind—or migrate—adjust their family, labor, and civic roles, and these adjustments in turn may become part of the next generation's cultural formation. Some immigrant workers may hope that labor shortages in the U.S. will improve their individual situation, that benign state actions will materialize, or that educational programs will provide answers and lessen their plight. Wherever immigrants are exploited, some seek to organize, and occasionally some acquire leverage in collective protection.

Culturally, immigrant workers respond in various ways, including cultural constructions. Immigrants are carriers of ideals, experiences, and myths, so the exploitation and oppression of a specific immigrant workforce by capitalist forces can stimulate culturally premised efforts to achieve collective security for workers, both in a given workplace and in general worker movements. But these are not the only possible responses. Immigrants may form non-union groups, pooling part of their wages for mutual assistance. They may form cultural groups devoted in part to legal defense or civic representation for advocacy and lobbying. These workers may organize education efforts to improve their literacy for job or civic enhancement. Immigrants may engage in cultural politics of various kinds and ways. They have not one priority or identity but multiple ones. This becomes evident by the issues discussed in the following chapters.

Contrary to stereotypes or essentialist views on Mexican immigrants, their perceptual expressions have varied and changed throughout Mexican immigrant history. Immigrants perceive themselves and are perceived. Their own perceptions are a powerful force in their lives, linked to the whys, wherefores, and consequences of immigration. The receiving society sees immigrants in various ways. Mexicans born in the United States have a range of views and can hold quite contrary views at the same time. New immigrants have views on motives, ethics, regional origin, and classes of immigrants. Mexican immigrants often see other immigrants treated differently, treated better.

Politically, efforts to establish collective security have resulted in a broad range of conflicts and have taken various forms during the past hundred years. The discriminatory oppression by economic elites in the United States of native-born Mexicans and Mexican immigrants has fueled two historically continuing mass movements: civil rights empowerment and trade unionism.[6] Immigrants agitate periodically for political and economic power in the workplace. The successes and failures of immigrant workers in gaining greater shares of the profits they produce indicate the strengths and limits of organized labor efforts as well as the constraints of individual situations.

History and Population

The social duality of Mexican immigrant/Mexican native-born arose during the mid-nineteenth century, with its legacies of an annexationist war and an economy that entailed slavery. During these decades the early immigrant cohorts arrived.[7] In California, Arizona, and Texas Mexicans were attacked for their immigrant status and work participation, and these attacks ostensibly directed at foreigners spilled over to include native-born U.S. Mexicans. Although Mexican immigration antedates 1910 by some sixty years and three generations, political groups such as the "Know Nothings" targeted Mexican and other immigrants in the Southwest.

The post-1848 arrivals fitted a social die, which in turn had foundational consequences for later arrivals. There were an estimated 125,000 native-born Mexicans in the Southwest in 1848; by 1900 there were more than 200,000—and more than half of the Mexican people in the United States were either immigrants or the children of immigrants. This fact underscores the importance of continuing immigration in the late nineteenth century to the growth and maintenance of a population of Mexican origin in the United States.

Settlement patterns in the United States shifted some over the years. About 90 percent of the immigrants between 1850 and 1910 chose the Southwest. Over the years, immigrants to the Midwest increased, particularly to Illinois, as well as to the Northwest and points east of the Mississippi. Yet, certain areas were more impacted by immigrants, and immigrant life and culture were more elaborate in these regions. Plural differentiations and leadership appeared in all areas. Status, income, education, cultural sophistication, and leadership positions specific to different places and times characterized the immigrant sector of Mexican communities in the United States.

By the 1880s Mexicans populated the workforces of mining, railroads, live-stock, and agriculture with representation in a variety of "urban" industries in the Southwest. Craftspersons and small-trades persons also migrated there. Racism prevailed: Mexicans were under certain circumstances useful, but they were also a subspecies of the human population. Mexicans fitted certain jobs and certain con-ditions. In effect, discrimination produced job unity. Equally significant were pat-terns of demography, gender, class, religion, and employment, i.e., where the im-migrants came from, where they located, and what work they performed. Some patterns continued into the twentieth century as new ones appeared.

Structures, Motivations, and Economics

The individual's decision to emigrate occurs in an economic structure cre-ated by other individuals with vastly more power. Specific aims and decisions ac-count for this context over time. Though not sufficient in the Mexican case to explain the worldwide interaction of migration and capital, it provides a broad framework that is helpful.[8]

The most advanced forms of capitalism develop cyclically at the expense of the less advanced. Appropriation of the labor force and resources of less developed areas is significant to the incremental accumulation of capital. Given this process, there is no need for any orchestrated initiative concerning labor emigration. All that is needed is the unfolding economic and political force of capital. Workers recruit themselves, pay for themselves, and strengthen the power of capital over themselves. Consequently emigration is not only circumstantially related to eco-nomic development but is a direct structural characteristic of the evolving capitalist mode of production.

The effort by owners of capital to maintain and increase the profits on their investments is a constant stimulant to the process of economic, technological, so-cial, and integrative expansion. In industry and agriculture, the productivity and lower cost of the immigrant worker create conditions favorable to investors, allow-ing the appropriation of surplus value and maximizing the profits realized from the products of labor and investment. The norm sought is more work, lower costs, and increased profits.

In times of high demand for labor, the idle or underemployed labor popula-tion, formed in part by immigrant workers, can be drawn upon to meet increased production or service needs. During cyclical periods of production decrease, im-migrants can readily be eliminated from the labor force because they lack legal protection and are the least unionized. Immigrant workers are also exploited ideo-logically by political agents representing one agenda or another. During periods of economic crisis, antagonism rises between labor and owners of capital. Through deliberate manipulation, or circumstantially, immigrant workers are held up as lightning rods for public discontent thus diverting antagonism from those actually responsible for the crises, those who have an interest—politically—in furthering the scapegoating scenario.

Mexican emigration motivation has been complex and so have its changing contexts. Throughout the twentieth century, the following variables have generally been identified, among others, as significantly influencing Mexicans to migrate to the United States: agricultural productivity and agricultural commodity prices in Mexico, agricultural productivity and the rate of capital investment in the United States, and farm wages in both countries.[9] At the core of Mexican immigration has been the question of individual or family subsistence or financial improvement beyond subsistence in a context of underdevelopment. The causes underlying Mexican immigration to the United States arguably can be traced to disparities in the formation and integration of the national economies of the two nations.[10] During the colonial period, these disparities were reflected in the economic infrastruc-ture, ownership of production, and class structure. Although the southern entity was stronger initially, it was surpassed by the northern one, which modernized more effectively. Mexico faced an enormous task of social integration and suffered repeatedly the economic consequences of destructive civil wars. Possibilities were limited for the development of a viable national manufacturing sector. Clearly Mex-ico was not an undeveloped country, but the nature of production and speed of development were inadequate to meet the needs and possibilities of the country and insufficient to keep up with change worldwide.

These weaknesses slowed national economic integration, making it difficult for Mexico to regulate foreign economic investment and avoid international politi-cal coercion and military threats. The ruling elites could neither consolidate nor pursue effective consistent policies of national development. When the integration of regional economies accelerated, the control of major resources was in the hands of North American and European interests. Mexican ownership was limited to a bourgeois *comprador* sector whose interests were subordinate to foreigners in in-vestment, management, technology, and distribution. Yet, though uneven, Mexican development and job creation continued; however, population displacement also occurred, affecting both laborers and members of the lower middle class.

Beginning in the nineteenth century and through the twentieth century, the relationship between Mexico and the United States became one of interdependency, advantageous to the United States and less advantageous to Mexico.[11] Indeed the United States has impacted the economic development of Mexico in a variety of ways, including the direct appropriation of resources and influence over its government's policies. In recent times this has been accomplished through labor immigration, direct investment, loans and interest on loans, and political understanding between the two governments. In this context, immigration—the movement of a labor force—represents a fundamental link between national labor, production, and sales markets, and their relative interdependence.

Migration was stimulated by economic conditions in both the changing rural and urban areas of the Mexican north and north-central regions and by the rapidly growing demand for labor during the development of the southwestern United States.[12] The construction in the 1880s and 1890s of North American-owned railroads linked to the United States facilitated the movement of Mexican labor on an increasing scale for this and other purposes, a movement ultimately underwritten by the workers themselves. Mexican workers and their families migrating to former Mexican territories in California, New Mexico, Texas, Arizona, and Colorado joined the resident Mexican inhabitants and nonwhite workers at the bottom of the labor force. There they and their descendants continued to face extreme exploitation and intense nationality and racial chauvinism, which reflected historical patterns of social conflict within the United States. Concurrently Mexican workers, as a consequence of class exploitation and racism, struggled to organize for the defense of their economic and ethnic interests and their cultural life.

Economic change and state regulation constructed and reconstructed immigrant communities and also successive generations of native-born U.S. Mexicans. Specifically, Mexican migration generally consisted of the migration of labor—historically and economically a continuous phenomenon.[13] In the 1920s immigrants divided according to legal and nonlegal entry, the result of expanding and changing government regulation. Other divisive factors stemmed from the distinctiveness of Mexican immigrants from different regions, the shared experience of crossing particular borders, and the existence, or lack, of large Mexican populations in destination communities. There is a noticeably critical attitude about the immigrant experience by immigrants themselves that is apparent in the *corridos* of the day, commentaries in newspapers, literary writings, and in the dialogues and humor of plays and *carpas*. Nationality and class are often salient motifs in these expressions.

33

Social Relations and Social Space

Immigration is affected by a constellation of complex regional elements from the Mexico–United States border.[14] This is an area of convergence, conflict, exchange, dependence, interdependent national economies, state authorities, interactive nationalities, and cultural characteristics. While U.S. claims were established through military conquest and coercion, an effective administrative frontier was not realized until the third decade of the twentieth century and not surveilled extensively until the fifth decade. In effect the U.S.–Mexico border has been open longer than closed; obviously the overwhelming majority of Mexicans in Mexico did not emigrate.

Mexican immigration has several distinctive characteristics.[15] Despite the hostility they encounter, Mexican immigrants are believed by many to have — and believe themselves to have — a particularly positive immigrant ethic. Since the settlement of the Southwest by *mestizos*, particularly since the nineteenth century, migration northward from Mexico has been a continuous process with marked familial aspects involving both women and men. Migration across the Mexican border has been multivaried: permanent, periodic, circular, temporary; it has been both legal and undocumented. Mexican immigrants to the United States are diverse as to class and subcultures. The migration occurs over a lengthy border area with scant major natural obstacles; the border cross can be but a step, and moreover the crosser steps often into Mexican resident communities.

When control is desired by groups in the U.S., the border becomes a conflictual space. More than other groups, Mexican immigrants have been used as scapegoats for the periodic cycles of economic depression and the failure of capital enterprise and the U.S. government to remedy them. And more than many other groups, Mexicans have persisted in their proactive affirmations.

Mexican immigrants have been socially and regionally diverse with differing political attitudes, yet they tend to share specific attitudes.[16] The commonly stated reasons for immigration are lack of employment and low wages. Workers are dissatisfied with their status at home and seek to change it by moving. Immigrants are often individuals with initiative who "see" into the future and are willing to take risks. They are presumably willing to question authority or tradition. Allegedly, many immigrants display a strong desire for an eventual permanent return to Mexico. Many repeatedly visit their home areas in Mexico. The gist may be that some stay in the United States but many more return to Mexico — those who journey with the goal of acquiring capital for very specific purposes.

Mexican immigrants also share other characteristics. In comparison with other immigrants and with the general U.S. Mexican-origin population, immigrants from Mexico are younger. Mexican immigrants often have relatives who immigrated earlier to the United States and with whom they retain family ties. Among legal immigrants, the breakdown by sexes is nearly equal; among the undocumented, men outnumber women. Many women originally migrate as dependents of men, but they do not remain dependents in many cases. Independent women also migrate alone or in groups. The lower educational and skills levels of many immigrants have predisposed them to be disadvantaged vis-à-vis European immigrants, native-born whites, blacks, and U.S.–born Mexicans. However, there is a diversity in the skills and educational levels of Mexican immigrants; they usually have come from the lower-income half of their home communities, but not from the bottom. Moreover, there have always been immigrants with professional or semiprofessional training and a few with modest capital.

The concentration of Mexican immigrants in the U.S. workforce varies, but there are clusters in certain occupations.[17] Determining the numbers and occupational and sectoral distribution of immigrant workers in the U.S. economy has been problematic due to the difficulty in obtaining unbiased statistical information. Although immigrants have located in most sectors of the economy, occupying a wide range of occupations and nearly all occupational categories, the majority have concentrated principally in the areas of agriculture, industry, and services. Specific occupations with a high concentration of Mexican workers have included assembly and light manufacturing in the plastics, electronics, garment, and furniture industries, as well as general labor and construction. Mexican immigrants have also worked in hotels, restaurants, and private homes. Many jobs for immigrants have generally required little technical skill or knowledge of English. Although the number of Mexican agricultural workers (both immigrant and U.S.–born) has declined because of mechanization, they still constitute the largest sector of that workforce. Mexican immigrant workers are particularly concentrated in jobs considered unattractive, demeaning, dangerous, dirty, temporary, or comparatively poorly paid — i.e., "Mexican work."

Since the late nineteenth century, Mexican immigrant workers have taken part in labor organizing to some degree or another, struggling side by side with Mexican American workers as well as others. Moreover, from the 1900s through the twentieth century, immigrants joined and sometimes led labor efforts in mining, agriculture, and industry as well as in some trades. Yet, they often faced the same discrimination in unions that they received from employers and from other workers.

Politics and a Regulatory Order

Legislation in the United States pertaining to immigration, both Mexican and other, has tended to reflect the overall need of the U.S. economy for foreign labor.[18] Understandably, the principal general function of immigration laws has been to regulate the supply of labor, but there are important constant exceptions. The enforcement of these laws has also reflected the prevailing attitudes and economic situation of the United States as a whole — and the Southwest in particular — and the power of specific political figures. The Department of Labor, the Department of Agriculture, the State Department, and police agencies have worked in conjunction with organized interest groups to invoke policies and practices that have affected migration patterns and Mexican labor on both sides of the border. Contrary to a common misperception, these laws have not been universally applied nor have they been applied irrespective of class, ideology, or color.

Prior to 1882 no major federal restrictions or quota laws regulating immigration existed, although the Act Concerning Aliens of 1798 authorized deportation of immigrants. Two basic liberal concepts determined an ostensible open-door policy: the United States was to be an asylum and place of opportunity for all, and migrants of any nationality would be absorbed into the giant labor force of United States society. In short, the need was for mass labor without restriction.

The basic aspects of labor regulation and explicit racism were visible in legal and political practices by 1882.[19] Congress in 1882 passed the Chinese Exclusion Act, which underscored the racist sentiments of North American labor and the tendency to scapegoat nonwhites. Following that, in 1883 the first general U.S. immigration law was enacted. It established a head tax and provided for the exclusion of certain categories of people. In 1885 Congress passed the first Alien Contract Labor Law; its primary goal was to prevent employers from importing "foreign labor" that would replace Anglo workers.

The economic organizations and relations of production from 1848 through the early decades of the twentieth century reflected a need for labor in the United States and a transformative dislocation of labor in Mexico.[20] In the second decade of the twentieth century, the phenomenon of Mexican immigration was in a transitional phase from nineteenth-century to twentieth-century motivations and patterns. Several events stimulated emigration from Mexico between 1910 and 1920, such as the growth and expansion in the U.S. Southwest, the increased labor demands caused by World War I, and postwar economic expansion in the United States.[21] In addition, the social and political upheavals in Mexico from 1910 through 1920 had a significant role in shaping the modern Mexican state and society and also had cultural and demographic consequences for the population. More immediately, these events greatly affected the process of immigration. According to the 1920 U.S. census, 486,416 individuals born in Mexico resided in the United States. At most, Mexican immigrants made up some 4 percent of the total number of immigrants (6,541,039) entering the United States between 1911 and 1921.

For Mexico and the United States the 1920s marked new phases in social and economic development that affected immigrants. Shortly after World War I, European and Asian immigration into the United States decreased as a result of the restrictions established by the Exclusion Law of 1921 and the Quota Act of 1924.[22] The legislation established a quota system that numerically restricted immigration on the basis of a national-origin formula that allocated numbers of visas to specific nationalities. Mexican labor, however, was not overtly limited by the quota system.

Benefiting from a large pool of exploitable labor to expand the rising economic infrastructure of the Southwest, industrialists and politicians continued to encourage the movement of Mexicans there.[23] U.S. entrepreneurs argued that Mexicans were a source of inexpensive abundant labor, and thus Mexican immigration was an economic asset to U.S. economic growth.[24] The Department of Agriculture asserted that Mexican labor was important for reclamation projects. And the State Department contended rhetorically that the application of the quota system to the American republics such as Mexico could hinder the foreign policy efforts of Pan-Americanism—that is, the policy of U.S. hegemony over Latin America. These perspectives expanded the range of views on the Mexican.

A debate on the exclusion of Mexican immigration from quotas flared between 1926 and 1930. At this time other voices rose to complain that immigration from Mexico had increased both absolutely and relative to total immigration. A large-scale anti-Mexican campaign developed. Three major arguments for restricting further Mexican immigration emerged: Mexican labor displaced Anglo native workers and kept wages low; the economic benefit derived from a cheap labor force was a short-term gain and a long-term cost; and the Mexican nationality posed a social threat to the "white race" because Mexicans were *mestizos*, i.e., miscegenated, thus inferior. These views were, in turn, supported by allegedly "objective scientific studies," which rationalized the racist beliefs common to many whites.

State regulation of borders and border crossers increased. In 1924 the Border Patrol was authorized and thereafter expanded, both in personnel and in budget

37

appropriations for minor surveillance on the Canadian border and for major deportation work along the Mexican border.[25] This marked a dramatic change in the
situation for many Mexican workers; their status changed from being merely immigrant workers whose entry without an official visa was incidental to that of
potential fugitives from the law. Moreover, the public concept and condition of
"illegal worker" was introduced into labor relations, modifying the pattern of interaction between Mexican workers and their communities — some were now "legal"
and others "illegal." In contrast, employers escaped liability and became adept at
heightening the fears of undocumented immigrants to increase their profit margins.

Arrivals and Departures

The question of numbers is important to the issue of immigration from
various perspectives, but particularly in regard to the concentration and condition
of arrivals.[26] Considering need, proximity, and facility, Mexican immigration has
been modest in relation to total U.S. immigration and also has been characterized
by significant immigrant returns. Emigration from Mexico during the twenties and
thirties was unusually intensive and then declined. Only in the second half of the
1920s and again in the period from 1955 to 1964 did Mexican immigrants account
for up to 15 percent of all immigrants coming to the United States. However,
Mexico was the largest single source of immigrants for temporary farmwork. Yet to
judge from statistics on expulsions, Mexico was also the greatest source of undocumented entrants and of immigrants singled out for deportation.

Mexican immigration reached high tide between 1927 and 1929 and began
to ebb in 1930. The four years from 1930 through 1933 saw a reversal in immigration due to the acute economic depression in the United States and in spite of
continuing depressed conditions in Mexico. The decrease also resulted from programs of deportation. During the 1930s only 27,900 Mexicans entered on permanent visas. By then Mexican immigration again accounted for only 4 percent
of arrivals.

Yet, Depression years also had labor and civic organizing by immigrant and
native-born Mexicans as well as a surge in Spanish-speaking cultural activity.[27] As
wages dropped to subsistence levels or below, Mexican and other migrant workers
sought organization. Labor conflicts, some along ethnic lines, others multiethnic,
flared against employers.

To defuse the frustration in the U.S. labor sector and public opinion in
general, government policy was implemented to repatriate Mexican workers.[28]

Some Mexicans returned to Mexico of their own accord, but both repatriation and voluntary returns were the results of a systematic campaign against Mexicans by federal, state, and local authorities and private agencies. Both Mexican and U.S. Mexican-origin citizens left, including large numbers of U.S.–born children of Mexican parents. Perhaps approximately 500,000 people left the country. After the Depression eased and world war needs loomed, the importation of Mexican labor again became desirable. Within little more than a decade, the U.S. government and U.S. employers attracted, repelled, and recalled Mexican labor in a massive anguished circularity.

New national and international factors impacted immigration both in the United States and in Mexico during the 1940s. Immigration resumed, stimulated in large part by war and postwar needs and by the 1942 Emergency Farm Labor Program, the Bracero Program, which was a significant reformulation of the historical labor exchange.[29] This program, initially Public Law 45, eventually Public Law 78, created a new infrastructure through formalized bilateral agreements for agricultural labor. Later it was extended for other work, in effect a revised resumption of large-scale importation of Mexican workers but now for temporary jobs. At the behest of U.S. employers between 1942 and 1964, 4.5 million Mexican workers participated.

Concurrent with the formalized program, legal immigration continued, although slowly. Immigration through permanent visas continued in the forties, reaching a modest total of 54,500 for the decade. Although Mexican immigration was allowed and labor was needed, pejorative attitudes toward people of Mexican origin did not change. Discriminatory prohibitions against Mexicans using public facilities persisted. Ethnic conflict occurred in parts of the Southwest, especially in Los Angeles during the forties. Labor strife, once feared in many areas, again occurred during and after World War II, targeting immigrant and native-born Mexicans.

Coinciding with reviews of immigration laws by the U.S. Congress during the fifties and sixties, the Bracero agreement was amended and extended several times. On July 13, 1951, Public Law 78 was signed, authorizing the further employment of Mexican workers. To facilitate matters for employers, the U.S. government ceased to be a responsible party to contractual arrangements. These became much weaker, earning the program opprobrium. Beginning in 1955, Congress extended the Bracero Program six more times until December 31, 1964.

Undocumented immigration from Mexico also increased from the 1940s on. On the one hand, Mexican workers could save time and expense by avoiding official channels, and on the other hand, employers could avoid the red tape of the Bracero Program. They could even pay lower wages. When the economic recession of the mid-fifties occurred, public sentiment turned against Mexican immigration.[30] In 1954 government measures to curtail or control undocumented Mexican immigration accelerated. These set the stage for what came to be known as "Operation Wetback," a campaign that sought to deport all undocumented workers, perhaps involving one million detentions. This effort established a new benchmark in relations with immigrants; increased police surveillance and militarization became a part of labor regulation.

The sixties was a major decade for immigration, as had been the twenties. As the economy of Mexico became more dependent on the United States, a greater number of Mexican workers entered the U.S. labor force in general. For Mexican employment, the importance of agriculture stabilized, while other sectors of the economy, such as manufacturing and services, grew. Consequently, some Mexican workers moved from seasonal to more permanent occupations.

In the mid-sixties the Bracero Program ended amid a chorus of diverse arguments often used to object to formal immigration, charges that would have been as valid (or invalid) in 1942 as in 1962. Among these were arguments involving trade unions, deplorable conditions, ethnic pride, "no Mexicans, period," and free labor markets. As modest as regulation of labor had been initially, some employers preferred unregulated labor. Mexican American organizations criticized the Bracero Program because it led to abuses of workers, and many U.S.–Mexican individuals believed the program stigmatized them. Some questioned further immigration in large numbers.

Importantly, as the Bracero Program ended, a liberal majority in the U.S. Congress passed a revised general immigration and nationality law, Hart-Celler, in 1965.[31] Two results followed: limits for legal Mexican immigrants were kept relatively modest, and hence, Mexican legal immigrants were outnumbered each year by undocumented workers. Moreover, extended and nuclear families involved both. Documented Mexican immigrants faced discrimination in employment and in a range of services and situations. Access to social services, adult education, and job improvement training was limited. The government ignored immigrant needs in these areas generally, and private services were scant. The results of this situation contributed to the disadvantaged statistical profile of Mexican immigrants.

From the sixties to the eighties, the Mexican community in the United States grew in complexity—numerically and in political significance—while immigrants became an increasingly important part of U.S. society and economics. The U.S.–

born immigrants, now as in the past, were the majority. Presumably mostly short-term undocumented Mexican workers may have fluctuated between 0.5 to 1.5 million people in these years. In 1980 there were approximately 50,000 legal daily commuters, but an astounding 8 million cases of deportation were recorded from 1924 to 1980.[32] Though "cases" do not equal individuals, the enormous number of undocumented immigrants who were received and deported is significant. In sum, a mass of people had participated in this immigrant experience. Those who remained in the United States built or influenced multifaceted communities that represented a mosaic of subregional cultures drawn from all parts of Mexico.

Responses and Activism

Varied and broad-based political, social, and economic activities in the United States marked the 1960s and 1970s as years of cultural and historical transformation for the Mexican community. This burst of activity, called *El Movimiento* (the movement), encompassed civil rights activity, the arts, the land rights issue, agricultural unionization, women's rights, urban labor and educational issues, the establishment of political organizations, the resurgence of a community-based political left, and increased political ties with Mexico. The roots of the movement sprang from the objective economic and social conditions of Mexicans and thus from the failure of U.S. agencies to deal with Mexicans as U.S. citizens or immigrants.

Movement organizations affected immigrant laborers in specific ways. For example, the Crusade for Justice, an organization based in Colorado, emphasized employment access and equities. Women's organizations such as the Chicana Welfare Rights Organization and the Comisión Femenil Mexicana advanced the social and political rights of immigrant women. Student groups were a major support force in all boycott efforts, campaigns in defense of undocumented workers, and even in several regional labor conflicts. La Raza Unida Party raised some labor and immigration questions. Agricultural labor organizations emphasized workers' rights.

As the Vietnam War decelerated and the economy faltered during the early seventies, anti-immigrant rhetoric increased again concurrent with high inflation, unemployment, and the threat of economic depression. Though the nondocumented received official notice, the hysteria itself was about "immigrants." The specter of an unprecedented number of "illegal" immigrants from Mexico was raised by politicians, the INS, and conservative political groups hoping to evoke anti-Mexican sentiments in the general public. In effect, legal and nonlegal immi-

41

grants were blamed for the country's economic ills. Emotional propaganda was directed at the Anglo middle class and blue-collar worker, and conservative public pressure led officials to attempt new legislative controls. And a new argument against immigration—the need for national security—was introduced and used to justify police-agency surveillance of immigrant rights groups.

The State's Visible Hand

Legislators in the 1970s presented a virtual cascade of U.S. legislation to reform provisions of the McCarran-Walter Act of 1952 and the Immigration Act of 1965. Measures appeared at both state and national levels, but all were designed to impact Mexican immigrants and workers.[33] As a whole, these measures created a blueprint for state action vis-à-vis Mexican immigration. In 1972 Congressman Peter Rodino introduced a seminal bill to amend existing immigration legislation. The bill sought to make employment of undocumented workers a crime and provided penalties for employers who knowingly hired illegal workers. Although the bill passed the House of Representatives, it failed in the Senate. The Rodino measure succeeded in becoming a symbol of anti-immigrant sentiment and a lightning rod for immigrant rights activists. Mexican American organizations lobbied federal and state officials on behalf of immigrants more than ever before, and immigration loomed as one of their major issues.

Some years later in October 1976, the Ninety-third Congress passed Public Law 94–571, amendments to the Immigration and Nationality Acts, known popularly as the Eilberg Bill (Western Hemisphere Act), which marked the priorities for the late twentieth century. The law had several major provisions, including a limit of 20,000 permanent resident visas for all countries in the Western Hemisphere. This made legal permanent immigration from Mexico far more difficult.

Then in 1977, President Jimmy Carter presented an executive plan to the U.S. Congress, ostensibly to enforce U.S. borders.[34] The Carter Plan sought to synthesize past experience, including measures designed to please business interests and assuage public resentment. For employers, the plan offered labor without employment benefits or rights for temporary workers. For the public hostile to immigrants, the plan promised more effective methods of control and deportation of undocumented immigrants. Presumably for Mexican Americans and the Mexican government, the plan included provisions for amnesty and temporary work. The Carter proposal was presented to Congress in 1978, but did not pass during the session. Then employment figures began rising, and pressure on the undocumented-worker issue slackened. When in 1979 and 1980 employment declined, multifaceted pressure against further immigration resurfaced, once again singling out Mexicans.

Unilateral immigration policy became a potentially bilateral issue in U.S.–Mexico relations during a brief period when Mexico discovered vast oil reserves. In attempts to secure concessions in energy, the Carter administration sought both to pressure and appease Mexico's administration. Speculation arose that the Mexican executive would explore a protected guest-worker proposal for the ongoing labor exchange. Meetings took place between Presidents Jimmy Carter and José López Portillo, but although immigration was discussed, no policy was publicly announced by either government.

Both governments, however, indicated a willingness to study migration concurrently. In its final report, President Carter's Select Commission on Immigration and Refugee Policy [35] favored sanctions against employers, some form of worker identification, limited amnesty, modest increases in immigration ceilings, and increased expenditures for surveillance. These measures became part of the 1982 Simpson-Mazzoli immigration bill, which did not pass. This bill was drafted while an extensive project to study immigration was underway by Mexico's Department of Labor. This agency was also to report its findings and offer policy recommendations. The creation of these commissions indicated political vacillation concerning the issue of Mexican undocumented immigration, or the lack of will to mediate between the economic and the political, which accounts for the immigrant population's circularity.

The choices available in the 1980s remained problematic. In reviewing immigration policy options, there was no single government policy alternative that was satisfactory to all parties. The trend was toward tighter regulation and enforcement of immigration, greater police power in the area of immigration, and greater selectivity of immigrant workers for specific needs. Mexican American opinion varied; internal minorities favored extremes ranging from no immigration to open immigration, but the majority clustered around a centrist position — some continuing immigration according to law with no discrimination.

Preceded by intricate and convoluted lobbying, the Immigration Reform and Control Act (IRCA/Simpson-Rodino) went into effect in November 1986.[36] Ostensibly the law emphasized border surveillance and implied the hope of increasing the migratory labor pool. Tellingly, there were two provisions for allowing additional agricultural laborers in the immediate future, Special Agricultural Worker (SAW) and Replenishment Agricultural Worker (RAW). Moreover, employers were required to verify status of employees or face sanctions. Provided undocumented immigrants met certain specific requirements, "amnesty," or a regularization of status, was made possible for more than two million Mexican undocumented workers. By January 1989 a total of some three million applicants from all nationalities had come forward, far below alarmist expectations.[37]

Undocumented immigration, however, continued. The price individuals had to pay to be transported across the border jumped and so did the price for fraudulent documents. Arrests increased also. Many Mexican workers who were still undocumented clearly faced a worsening situation of persecution and exploitation. Public opinion in the late eighties and early nineties became harsher against undocumented workers, and surveillance of the border, work sites, highways, and neighborhoods increased. Perhaps more than in previous times, the social nexuses between documented and undocumented tightly intertwined. Undocumented school children were at risk. Immigrant organizing, social and civic, heightened, though it differed among areas. Citizenship petitions dramatically increased.

The IRCA threshold signaled hardening times.[38] In its proposed Immigration Enforcement Act of 1995 the Clinton administration emphasized border surveillance, deportations, and admission curtailment while leaving immigrant policies to local governments.

After considerable drafts and negotiations by both the Senate and House of Representatives, and responding to election politics, a comprehensive immigration bill was passed on September 28, 1996, and signed into law by President Bill Clinton three days later. Specifically, the law encompassed the following points: it doubled the Border Patrol force to 10,000 over a five-year period; constructed a triple fence along the San Diego–Tijuana border; made it easier to deport undocumented workers by speeding up the paperwork and appeal process; barred undocumented workers from Social Security benefits and public housing; set up pilot projects to check job applicants' immigration status; toughened sanctions for smuggling; made it more difficult for low-income U.S. citizens or legal immigrants to bring their relatives to the United States as legal immigrants; curtailed welfare benefits for legal immigrants; and made it harder for immigrants to prove discrimination by employers.[39]

44   Contentions and Cultures

The presence of Mexicans within the United States has been a focus of contention among a variety of interest groups nationally as well as regionally.[40]

Opposition to Mexican immigration has come from community sectors and has involved both objective and subjective factors. Some studies of U.S. inhabitants have indicated that a majority opposes Mexican immigration, and some would even support forcible removal of some of the Mexican population.

There is a tradition of anti-Mexicanism that has infiltrated the general society. This tradition has been buttressed by strong emotional and objective forces, which have galvanized the social wrath and economic frustration of exploited, over-taxed Anglo blue-collar and white-collar wage earners as well as other immigrant groups and their progenies. These groups have few progressive political leaders. Some have been concerned with alleged overpopulation. Others have expressed concern for an allegedly threatened ecological balance, social harmony, and persistence of the "American" way of life. The labor unions and AFL-CIO leaders have often opposed Mexican immigration. Traditional racist or quasi-militarist groups (e.g., Ku Klux Klan, Veterans of Foreign Wars) have been active against Mexican immigration and immigrants for more than one hundred years. Additionally, policy planners and policy makers increasingly have voiced concerns about the internal and external security of economic and political organizations in the United States.

Repressive strategies of the seventies and eighties have been renewed by the INS and government police agencies, supported by conservative politicians and some scholars. Proponents have presented a barrage of accusations and justifications founded on what they acknowledge to be educated guesses, i.e., questionable statistics. Among the issues raised have been the following allegations:

1. Mexican immigration is increasing exponentially, and the arrival of many millions of undocumented Mexican aliens presents a threat.
2. Undocumented workers take jobs away from U.S. citizens; they are in direct competition with poor whites and members of minority groups for jobs.
3. Undocumented workers are a burden on public, social, educational, and medical services, i.e., on the U.S. wage earner and taxpayer.
4. Undocumented workers are responsible for increasing rates of crime; they are a threat to a peaceful society and public morality.
5. Undocumented workers undermine existing wage rates and unionization efforts.
6. Undocumented workers and their families are a threat to the

demographic and ecological balance vital to sustaining natural resources because they add to the pressure on resources in heavily
populated areas.

7. Undocumented workers jeopardize U.S. political and military security because they are not loyal to the U.S. government.

Contrary to these perceptions, there is no historical or contemporary evidence that the immigrant Mexican population has created a "problem" in relation to any of these charges. These charges consist of inflammatory rhetorical
statements made in response to fears and phobias recurrent in U.S. history and
voiced periodically by demagogues of one kind or another. Indeed the "problem"
is that of a population that is vulnerable economically and has minimal human and
civil rights.

From the mid-eighties on, a more sophisticated articulation of anti-immigrant arguments has circulated. Immigrants supposedly have undermined the pros-
pects of a welfare state that could provide more and better social services to the
native-born population. Immigrants have impeded, if not made impossible, progress
toward extension of welfare services to in-need constituencies. The targets of this
argument have been liberals and progressives whose goal has been to raise the
standard of living of many in the United States through government-initiated or
-assisted social programs.

Responses

For Mexican-origin communities within the United States, the political situation regarding immigration has been a difficult one.[41] Much of the U.S. public
views Mexicans, citizens or not, as "alien." Given these attitudes, there is limited public sympathy evoked by gross violations of Mexican people's civil and human rights.

At times of economic development, specific U.S. economic interests have
supported Mexican immigration: farmers, labor-intensive railroad and mining com-
panies, construction firms, labor-intensive manufacturing industries, service opera-
tions, and smaller employers of all kinds. Generally, whether large or small, some
businesses periodically have favored Mexican immigrants because they are economic, efficient producers and profit generators.

During all the deportation crises, when repression has intensified, so has
resistance and its expression.[42] Since the turn of the century, when the individual

and mass deportations began to occur, some organizations and individuals have sought to defend undocumented Mexicans. The eighties signaled a new era for transborder worker organizing across parts of the United States. These parties have included legal-defense groups, advocacy groups, service centers, church committees, civil rights organizations, a few persons from the African and Asian communities, and certain progressive sectors of the trade-union movement.

Moreover, in answer to repressive tactics against immigrants, other alternatives have emerged from generalized community-wide debates.[43] Activity in defense of undocumented workers has consisted of conferences and mass demonstrations, advocacy before the federal government, and the forming of organizations and coalitions. The Mexican American Legal Defense and Education Fund (MALDEF) has been particularly important. Key battles have involved public opinion, judicial issues, legislation, and legal defense. Lawyers and allied researchers have won a number of important cases pertaining to the defense of undocumented workers. Strong support from elected and national leaderships of Chicano/Latino organizations has also been important.

Understanding that important interests are at stake, some foundations and U.S. government advisors have put forth proposals underscoring the injustices suffered by undocumented workers and recommending developmental solutions. Reflecting the desire to increase the economic relationship between the two countries, these proposals have suggested regulated guest-worker programs. Yet because these programs do not confer full rights for workers, they could actually increase the economic dependency of Mexican workers on their employers and detract from the potential organized strength of workers.

Up to the 1980s, a functional coalition had formed comprised of U.S.-Mexican-origin organizations, business interests, academic groups, churches, interested parties in Mexico, and civil rights activists. They were bound ideologically on the issue of the primacy of human rights, which all individuals possess and all states ought to protect. Immigrants—documented or not—arguably enjoy constitutional protection, particularly that guaranteeing civil rights.

Pro-immigrant supporters have converged and diverged. Potentially the most important—and most problematic—support for Mexican immigrants has been that of the trade unions. Churches have provided solace to immigrants and in some cases a base for immigrant life, but have not been ready advocates. However, churches have increased their pro-immigrant rights advocacy, particularly the Catholic Church, which has counted many outstanding advocates. The most direct, though the most vulnerable, support for immigrant rights has come from immigrants themselves. And the most intense ideological politics regarding immigrations continue to be within immigrant groups.

Labor Insurgence Again

Hermandad Mexicana, founded in 1951, has been active in serving and involving Mexican immigrant workers; it has been a cross between a mutualistic organization, a notary and counseling center, and a labor-support committee.[44] It reportedly has had members or sympathizers in auto-part manufacturing, aerospace-part manufacturing, industrial electronics, furniture making, industrial molding, medical supplies, plastics, and hotel and hospital services. Apart from publicized protest activity against INS practices, there is ample record of direct action by La Hermandad in labor conflicts or unionization. It has insistently promoted worker rights through litigation, advocacy, and mass mobilization, unilaterally and through coalitions, for more than two decades, as other immigrant-defense efforts have risen and passed. Yet Hermandad's major impact dates from the 1980s.

During the seventies an important source of community organizational support for immigrant workers was the Centro de Acción Social Autónoma–Hermandad General de Trabajadores (CASA-HGT), now defunct, with chapters in California, Texas, and Illinois.[45] One of its branches, Comité Obrero en Defensa de Indocumentados/das en Lucha (CODIL), was involved in labor conflicts in the greater Los Angeles area. In addition, CASA sought to maximize workers' organization and participation in unions, and the organization contributed to a greater awareness of the need to organize and defend undocumented workers.

All agricultural organizing projects have had strong immigrant participation. Organizing efforts across the Southwest and Midwest have depended on the initiative and courage of vulnerable immigrant workers, and farm labor organizing has proved difficult.

Undocumented workers have long maintained covert networks of support.[46] They have on occasion resisted raids and deportations at the workplace, supported by legal residents in California, Illinois, and Texas. Acts of worker self-defense have taken place that many who see these workers as helpless or passive would not have believed possible. In April 1976, led by Nicolás García, CODIL began a campaign during events at Ortho Mattress to stop INS raids at factories and to provide undocumented workers with union representation. It also sought to form defense committees at workplaces. CODIL worked to promote the passage of resolutions on the rights of undocumented workers with several unions, including the ILGWU, the UAW, the UE, the Carpenters, the Teamsters, and others.

Despite the hegemony of anti-immigrant voices within the AFL-CIO, several Mexican-origin activists continued during the seventies to pressure unions and to form several independent worker-organizing committees and agricultural unions.[47] And not least of all, they attempted to create an umbrella union, the International Brotherhood of General Workers, Local 301. Examples of this worker-protest tendency were particularly evident in California, Illinois, Arizona, and Texas. They occurred in light manufacturing, some industrial plants, garment factories, canneries, and among agricultural workers. Given the limited number of organizers and resources, the successes were notable. Court cases were won, contracts were signed, and often workers responded positively.

Some of CASA's organizers continued these efforts through the eighties, linking them with efforts in Arizona, Texas, the Midwest, the border area, and the interior of Mexico. These often involved former Raza Unida activists or Mexican unionists. The fledgling organizations all emphasized specific projects and stressed ending abuses of migratory workers on both sides of the border, along with campaigning for pro-union education. The sum total of their achievements was impressive. The clearest and most comprehensive popular statement on undocumented Mexican workers was the "Carta de Derechos para los Trabajadores Indocumentados," issued at the international conference in Mexico City in April 1980, "Primera Conferencia Internacional por los Derechos Plenos de los Trabajadores Indocumentados," which was attended by representatives of more than eighty organizations. A number of key concepts emerged, such as a transborder bill of rights, an immigrant legal-defense fund, aggressive unionization, a development fund for home communities, and mechanisms to safeguard immigrant financial transactions. In August 1982, the Primer Congreso Nacional de Trabajadores Migratorios was held, attended by several hundred representatives at Ahuacatlán de Guadalupe, Querétaro, México. Among the major results were the Sindicato Nacional de Trabajadores Migratorios de México, the Sociedad Cooperative Multiactiva "Sin Fronteras," and the Sociedad Cooperativa Impormex.

Though Mexican transborder workers have often been undocumented, their participation in organizing can be seen in several sectors of the economy and in many unions.[48] Union policies toward undocumented workers have been of three types: (1) exclusion by formal means, (2) token membership without substantively attending to their needs, and (3) direct organization and effective defense activity.

In deciding which course to take, leadership and public awareness have been important, as has been the proportion of undocumented workers in the industry. Craft unions have tended to limit undocumented workers as well as other Mexicans. More often, industrial unions have tended to include undocumented members but have not always defended their rights. A few unions have both organized and actively defended these workers.

Some sectors of the labor movement have acknowledged undocumented membership.[49] Several specifically have taken the initiative to include such workers. The Farm Labor Organizing Committee (FLOC); the United Farm Workers of America (UFWA); the Arizona Farm Workers (AFW); the Texas Farm Workers (TFW); the International Longshoremen and Warehouse Workers' Union (LWWU); the International Ladies' Garment Workers' Union (ILGWU); the Retail Clerks International Unions; the United Electrical, Radio, and Machine Operators of America; the United Auto Workers (UAW); and the Teamsters all began to support the unionization of undocumented workers during the seventies. By the eighties, these union locals had a significant number of undocumented members. Moreover, as several immigrant services centers formed, they encouraged unionization. Among them are One-Stop Immigration and Education Center in California, the Maricopa Project in Arizona, and local project offices in Texas and the Midwest.

Many conservative labor leaders have called for more restrictions on the immigration of workers from other countries. Such a position is grounded in the premise that undocumented workers take jobs away from U.S. citizens. In the eighties, however, senior regional AFL-CIO officials took a commendable step with a project to assist immigrant workers to secure their civil and labor rights. Eventually a result of this interest was the California Immigrant Workers Association (CIWA).[50] Apart from ongoing educational efforts, two notable organizing drives supported by CIWA occurred with construction drywallers (carpenters) and manufacturing workers at American Racing (machinists).

Conclusion

To examine Mexican immigrants and immigration reveals seemingly disparate positions, denial and faith. One ready conclusion in critically reviewing the history of Mexican immigration to better understand the cultural, social, and political phenomena is its uniqueness as part of a modern world situation but with specific state locus. At the core of this uniqueness is the experience of the individual. In each of the themes referred to in the overview at the beginning of this chapter, the historical process and contemporary situation of the Mexican immigrant are dynamically complex. To date none of the scholarly literature offers a complex historical processual view of Mexican immigration. Perceptions of and by Mexican immigrants are contradictory and potent. Mexican immigrants are economic and political actors and pariahs in a multitude of ways. Socially they constitute major segments of two distinct U.S. regions, the Southwest and the Midwest. Culturally the evolution of immigrants and immigrant communities continues across regions. However convoluted debate of public policy may be, the voices that take up the debate speak not only on immigrants but on the country as a whole, whether in optimistic or pessimistic tones.

Up to a point, situating Mexican immigrants in broad frameworks is advantageous. The world economy provides a large context that prevails over regional histories, in degree if not in kind. Yet, individual agency and creativity is blurred. Such a thesis marginalizes individual immigrant experiences.

A critical review of Mexican immigration leads to questions about U.S. historical development, its cultural traces, representations, and continuities. Notions of U.S. history seemingly are the filtered results of the ideological biases of liberal writers on this subject. The consensus view that historians have propagated is of an idyllic society of craftspeople, artisans, farmers, merchants, and manufacturers —a society permeated by Euroamericans and governed by republican ethics, virtues, and practices. Yet, the treatment of colored immigrants and populations has disturbed the elegance of this consensus vision; persecution and exploitation have presumably been aberrations. Over time, contradictory images have challenged consensus views. However, proponents and antagonists within the discourse have had little time or patience with specifics of groups, regions, variations in cultural manifestations, and sequences of change. Ironically, the proffered undersides to these visions are telling.

Presumably the contours of Mexican immigrant patterns should be enlightened by writers with progressive ideological-organizational biases. However, most writers who combine some interest in ethnicity and worker politics subcontextualize in their writing the "one big radical movement" shibboleth. In their eyes the ultimate end is a perfect radical movement, with perfect social integration, political consciousness and faultless radical leadership. In sum, confrontational immigrant activity among people of color, particularly Mexicans, is well-meaning but confused. To the small extent it occurs, it is subversive and insubstantive. The progressive is in a critical mode but one similar to that of the financial elites.

When considering Mexican immigration and its relation to the economic and cultural development of the United States, four as yet theoretically unrelated realities loom that impact Mexican immigrants and U.S. development: (1) To compare slavery and "free" labor, even under the most disadvantageous conditions, would be of little worth. Yet African slavery and the racist context it created is as important an element in the formation of the United States as mercantile capitalism, Protestant Christianity, and European gendering. And it is as contextual to Mexican immigrant labor as the historical systemic relations between Mexico and the United States. (2) As advanced as U.S. capital development may be, it is founded on a mass labor pool that is devalued and delimited in relation to other sectors of the society including some white women. The devaluing of Mexican labor is an extreme manifestation of this practice. (3) In the space of one hundred years, while Mexicans were immigrating or available, the United States went relatively rapidly from regional economies based on mercantilism, trades, farming, and slave labor to industrial and postindustrial economies, stamping regions differently. With these changes, regional concentrations and calibrations of change were integral to U.S. social development. Mexican immigration economically and socially has been much affected by changes since 1900, as this has occurred in the main regions of the West and Midwest, particularly in the states of California, Texas, and Illinois. The social, economic, and political participation of immigrants varies in these three areas historically, and their contentions have particular importance. (4) The benign view holds that the United States has welcomed immigrants, but the record evidences selection and exploitation of immigrants through public-policy discourse focused on control without provision of services to provide for immigrant needs. Without such services, their vulnerability is arguably insured. Mexicans are used while made outcasts. Indeed there are *immigrants*—and *immigrants*.

The reception of Mexican immigrants says much about progressive political and cultural potentialities in the United States. There is evidence that some Mexican immigrants have arrived with the expectation that they would collaborate in radical labor and political organizing. Arguably a preference or proclivity for ethnic exclusivity on their part has been superseded by the chauvinist exclusiveness of others in radical organizing. Exclusiveness has reduced the radical radius both politically and culturally. An explanation to the limits of radicalism in the United States is to be found, not among the plutocracy and its police agents, but among the Euroamerican radicals themselves. As part of their cultural life, Mexican immigrants have participated civically through their own initiative and enriched the cultural ambience of U.S. society; however, they have not been eagerly sought out or enthusiastically welcomed by progressive labor and political groups. Emigrant Mexicans to the United States represent a unique example of an international trend whose specifics are not fully appreciated in comparative studies. Both the lives of immigrants and the issues of Mexican immigrants and the rights of the undocumented have taken place in a changing historical context amid successive economic and political crises. These specifics have involved a shifting mosaic of ideology, tactics, and leadership and the inter-relationship of domestic and foreign-relations issues for both the United States and Mexico.

There are two pervasive conditions. Antagonistically, from the early decades to the 1990s, an ideological propaganda campaign fomented popular feelings against the Mexican immigrant worker. Hiring immigrants, regardless of the legal status of the workers, was a tradition for many big or small businesses and for much of agriculture. Employers benefited but did not overtly support immigrant rights. Employers had little to say in the media in regard to immigrant workers, yet they supported political groups or spokespersons who made exaggerated accusations against Mexican immigrants — even as North American regional integration proceeded. Economic realities and political actions contrasted, and cultural animosity remained privileged.

Immigrants have historically addressed their disempowerment through social constructions and self-agency. Through the decades immigrants have built complex communities based on cultural and political traditions that subsume workers independent of their legal status. These are communities constructed and reconstructed under assault. A de facto accessible border, a workforce in part outside the law, continuing deportations, and widespread cultural denigration seemingly would produce a weakened, intimidated, disenfranchised, suppressed sector of the workforce. Yet, some immigrant workers have resisted such discriminations and organized for their labor and civil rights through the eighties and nineties. Hence, in many areas defense and organization activities as well as cultural manifestations are available to both documented and undocumented workers.

Mexican immigrants have been grist for the mills of some troubled academics as well as for exploiters. Troubled but comfortable, the attitude of scholars — even among those seemingly empathetic — is one of superiority over their subjects. The discussions during the twentieth century have ranged over whether Mexican immigrants are barely salvageable, a net liability, or "loyal." To some scholars immigrants represent a "dilemma" that is a choice between negatives, while others simper over whether the immigrant process, as employee-employer relation, is but a contestation of "dreams" rooted in a misunderstanding that therapy and publications will resolve. It is instructive to note the posture of power and the dehumanization that are evident in designations such as "alien," "illegal," and so forth. How existentially absurd for humans from England or Russia to call humans from Sonora or Coahuila "alien." The cultural voices of immigrants and their cultural constructs reaffirm what is too often denied—their freedom and responsibility.

To contest the overt and covert anti-immigrant thrust the defense of the advancing immigrants for decades was orthodox and limited. It comprised self-help groups, unionization efforts, and some supportive assistance, in total involving a minority of activists. In the early seventies a few Mexican activists centered primarily in southern California, Texas, and the Midwest changed the rules of the "alien" game. They were supported by an equally small number of humanitarians and older progressive activist veterans of the thirties and forties. Through sheer will and indefatigable work, they built a movement of support that included both legal and undocumented immigrant workers, recent political emigrés from Mexico, a few academicians, artists, and some main leaders of the resident Mexican who eventually obtained Mexican labor support in some U.S. unions. These were followed by students, later by political, civic, and legal services organizations and, indirectly, by some in Mexico's political circles.

Conscious cultural expression marked this movement and was pervasive in its development. Eventually, this operational coalition—for it had no emphatic structural or ideological unity—won some public support and more thoughtful consideration of the issue of immigrant rights. In particular, considerable effort had been expended on the rights of the undocumented worker to equality on the job and to education for children, as well as on the radical idea that immigrants contributed to society, and thus were entitled to equality. Some achievements occurred. In turn the anti-immigrant force responded, gaining political and public support and putting some human rights liberals and progressives on the defensive. Immigrants have again been demonized and objectified.

As has been demonstrated repeatedly, the immigrant workers' issues cover many agendas: foreign relations bargaining, human and civil rights, and ethnic solidarity. There is also the simple agenda of pursuing opportunity for whatever game is at hand. It has been and is a workers' issue; the rights of workers are best secured by workers themselves. These rights can be secured by organization in civic associations and unions, regularization of status for those in the United States, and through *just* immigration provisions for immigrant workers in the future. These rights are continually tested as are the tolerance and appreciation for cultural enrichment, as is faith in the future, as are human rights.

Exploitation of workers and disregard of fundamental rights of entire sectors are not unique to the United States. What is unique to the United States is a historically evolved expression combining nativism, chauvinism, and racism repeated for political purposes. Traditionally this has been linked to economic, social, and political domination by a small complex of special interests over a majority of producers in the United States and the world. This feature of U.S. society has been expressed most notably in the treatment of Mexican immigrant workers and around the issue of Mexican immigration. Yet, the Mexican immigrant worker is a predominant choice for certain labor needs despite repeatedly being the subject of deportation and denigration. To be sure, these are opposed by political actions and constitutional debates; this too happens in the United States. The cultural and political construction and reconstruction of the U.S.-Mexican community and immigrant sector continues; cultural material gives us human testimony of these historical actions.

Notes

1. See Estevan Flores, "La circulación internacional del trabajo y de la lucha de clases"; Juan Gómez-Quiñones, "La política de exportación de capital e importación de mano de obra," *Historia y sociedad* 20 (1978); and Harry Cleaver, *Reading Capital Politically* (Austin: University of Texas Press, 1979). For literature in reference to aspects of Mexican immigration, see J. Durand and D. S. Massey, "Mexican Migration to the United States: A Critical Review," *Latin American Research Review* 27 (1992). For overviews of Mexican immigration, see Lawrence A. Cardoso, *Mexican Emigration to the United States 1897–1931* (Tucson: University of Arizona Press, 1980); Mark Reisler, *By the Sweat of Their Brow: Mexican Immigrant Labor in the United States, 1900–1940* (Westport, Conn., Greenwood Press, 1976); and Jorge Durand, *Más allá de la línea* (Mexico D.F.: Consejo Nacional para la Cultura y las Artes, 1994). For exploitation of immigrants, see James D. Cockcroft, *Outlaws in the Promised Land* (New York: Grove Press, 1986); for manipulative views of the Mexican immigrant see Mauricio Mazon, "Illegal Alien Surrogates: A Psychohistorical Interpretation of Group Stereotyping," *Aztlán* 6 (Spring 1975). For a sensitive study with special attention to women, see Pierrette Hondagneu-Sotelo, *Gendered Transitions, Mexican Experiences of Immigration* (Berkeley: University of California Press, 1994).

2. A point agreed on by a diversity of analysts from right to left; see S. Larson and B. Nissen, eds., *Theories of the Labor Movement* (Detroit: Wayne State University Press, 1987); and V. I. Lenin "On Trade Unions" (Moscow: Institut Marksima-Leninizma, 1970).

3. The literature on immigration and immigrant workers in the United States and Western Europe continues to proliferate. References, particularly informed references, to

Mexican workers are now common beginning with Oscar Handlin's ostensibly classic *The Uprooted* (Boston: Little Brown, 1951); the absence also is obvious in the work of notable labor historians of the past decades, such as David Brody's *Workers in Industrial America* (New York: Oxford University Press, 1980). Nevertheless, these works are important to the appreciation of the interaction between immigration and labor.

4. Useful for data and interpretation on immigrant actions and migration currents and contexts impacting on the United States and some other parts of the world are Michael Piore's influential *Birds of Passage* (Cambridge: Cambridge University Press, 1979); Mary M. Kritz et al., eds., *Global Trends in Migration: Theory and Research on International Population Movements* (New York: Center of Migration Studies, 1983); Saskia Sassen, *The Mobility of Labor and Capital* (Cambridge: Cambridge University Press, 1988); and John Laslett, "Challenging American Exceptionalism: Overlapping Diasporas as a Model for Studying American Working Class Formation, 1810–1924," *Newberry Library Papers in Family and Community History* 87 (April 1987). For European patterns of return migration, see J. D. Gould, "European Inter-Continental Emigration—The Road Home: Return Migration from the U.S.A." *Journal of European Economic History* 9 (1980); and Dirk Hoerder, "Immigration and the Working Class: The Remigration Factor," *International Labor and Working Class History* 21 (1982). On the relation between state policies and traditions of public opinion, see Michael C. Lemay, *From Open Door to Dutch Door: An Analysis of United States Immigration Policy since 1820* (New York: Praeger, 1987); and John Higham, *Strangers in the Land: Patterns of American Nativism, 1860–1925*, 2nd ed. (New Brunswick, N.J.: Rutgers University Press, 1988).

5. Arguable overviews of ethnicity and the process of immigrants' assimilation in the United States are Alan M. Kraut, *The Huddled Masses: The Immigrant in American Society, 1880–1921* (Arlington Heights, Ill.: Harlan Davidson, 1982); John Bodnar, *The Transplanted: A History of Immigrants in Urban America* (Bloomington, Ind.: Indiana University Press, 1985); and Thomas Archdeacon, *Becoming American: An Ethnic History* (New York: Free Press, 1983). On women, work, and immigration, see Natalie Sakoloff, *Between Money and Love: The Dialectics of Women's Home and Market Work* (New York: Praeger, 1980); and Hasia R. Diner, *Erin's Daughters in America: Irish Immigrant Women* (Baltimore: Johns Hopkins University Press, 1983). On dual and segmented labor markets, see P. Doeringer and Michael Piore, *Internal Labour Markets and Manpower Analysis* (Lexington, Mass.: Heath, 1971); P. Doeringer and M. Piore, "Unemployment and the Dual Labour Market," *Public Interest* (Winter 1975); David M. Gordon, *Theories of Poverty and Underemployment: Orthodox, Radical, and Dual Labour Market Perspectives* (Lexington, Mass.: Lexington Books, 1972); Richard Edwards, Michael Reich, and David M. Gordon, *Labour Market Segmentation* (Lexington, Mass.: Lexington Books, 1975); and D. M. Gordon, R. Edwards, and M. Reich, *Segmented Work, Divided Workers: The Historical Transformation of Labor in the United States* (Cambridge: Cambridge University Press, 1982). Dual and segmented labor theories are a major debate within labor economics: see Glen G. Cain, "The Challenge of Segmented

Labor Market Theories to Orthodox Theory: A Survey," *Journal of Economic Literature* 14 (December 1976); Barry R. Chiswick, "The Economic Progress of Immigrants: Some Apparently Universal Patterns," in William Fellner, ed., *Contemporary Economic Problems* (Washington, D.C.: American Enterprise Institute, 1979); and R. Loveridge and A. L. Mok, *Theories of Labour Market Segmentation: a Critique* (The Hague: M. Nijhoff, 1979).

6. The debate over the economic causes and effects of immigration is continuous. See in particular George Borjas, *Friends or Strangers: The Impact of Immigrants of the U.S. Economy* (New York: Basic Books, 1990); and W. R. Böhning, *Studies in International Labour Migration* (New York: St. Martin's Press, 1984). For some insights on the class intra-relations between native-born workers and immigrants, see Stephen Castles and Godula Kosack, *Immigrant Workers and the Class Structure in Western Europe*, 2nd ed. (Oxford: Oxford University Press, 1985); and Jonathan Power, *Migrant Workers in Western Europe and the United States* (Oxford: Pergamon Press, 1979). Concerning some relations of native-born and immigrants in organized labor, see Charles Sabel, *Work and Politics: The Division of Labor in Industry* (Cambridge: Cambridge University Press, 1982); Gerald Rosenblum, *Immigrant Workers: The Impact on American Labor Racialism* (New York: Basic Books, 1973); Charles Leinenweber, "Socialism and Ethnicity," in John Laslett and Seymour Martin Lipset, eds., *Failure of a Dream? Essays in History of American Socialism*, 1st ed. (Garden City, N.Y.: Anchor Press, 1984); A. T. Lane, *Solidarity or Survival? American Labor and European Immigrants, 1830–1924* (New York: Greenwood Press, 1987); and A. Gwendolyn Mink, *Old Labor and New Immigrants in American Political Development: Union, Party, and State, 1875–1920* (Ithaca: Cornell University Press, 1986). For a series of articles on worker culture with some attention to immigrants see the special issue, *Journal of Contemporary History* 13 (April 1978). On the relation between religion, culture, and activism including immigrants, see "Religion and the Working Class," *International Labor and Working Class History* 34 (Fall 1988). For immigrant community building in the United States, see Josef Barton, *Peasants and Strangers: Italians, Rumanians and Slovaks in an American City, 1890–1950* (Cambridge, Mass.: Harvard University Press, 1975); and Ronald Takaki, *Strangers from a Different Shore: A History of Asian Americans* (Boston: Little Brown, 1989). For Europe, see Gary Cross, *Immigrant Workers in Industrial France* (Philadelphia: Temple University Press, 1983); and Hans Christian Buechler and Judith Marie Buechler, eds., *Migrants in Europe: the Role of Family, Labor, and Politics* (New York: Greenwood Press, 1987).

7. For analysis of population growth and recorded census figures, see Oscar Martínez, "On the Size of the Chicano Population: New Estimates, 1850–1900," *Aztlán* 6 (Spring 1975); Roberto Villarreal, "Model for Estimating the Spanish Surname Population of Texas, 1860–1920" (unpublished manuscript, 1973); Allyn Campbell Loosley, "Foreign Born Population of California, 1848–1920" (master's thesis, University of California, Berkeley, 1928); Georges Sabagh, "A Critical Analysis of California Population Statistics with Special Emphasis on Census Data, 1850–1870 (master's thesis, University of California, Berkeley, 1943); and Terry O. Jordan et al., "Population Origins of Texas, 1850," *Geographical Review*

59 (1969). For attitudes toward Mexicans, see Richard A. Peterson, "Anti-Mexican Nativism in California, 1848–1853: A Study in Social Conflict," *Southern California Quarterly* 62 (Winter 1980), and Arnold De Leon, *They Called Them Greasers: Anglo Attitudes toward Mexicans in Texas, 1821–1900* (Austin: University of Texas Press, 1983).

8. For interpretive analysis of the interaction of worker population movements and qualitative and quantitative advances in the economy and production, see James O'Connor, "The Global Migration of Labor and Capital," in Antonio Ríos-Bustamante, ed., *Mexican Immigrant Workers* (Los Angeles: UCLA, CSRC, 1981); Manuel Castells, "Immigrant Workers in Advanced Capitalism," *Politics and Society* 5 (1971); Stephen Castles and Godula Kosack, *Immigrant Workers and Class in Western Europe* (London: Oxford University Press, 1973); and Thomas Brindley, *Migration and Economic Growth* (Cambridge: Cambridge University Press, 1954).

9. See the works of Roger Bartra, *Estructura agraria y clases sociales en México* (México: Editorial Era, 1974); Armando Bartra, *La explotación del trabajo campesino por el capital* (México: ENAH, 1979); Claude Meillassoux, *Mujeres, graneros y capitales* (México: Siglo Veintiuno, 1977); and Luisa Pare, *El proletariado agrícola* (México: Siglo Veintiuno, 1977). A short informative local study is Adrián de León Arias, *Política económica, estructura agraria y migración* (Guadalajara: Universidad de Guadalajara, 1983); and the basic Jorge A. Bustamante, "The Historical Context of Undocumented Mexican Immigration to the United States," in Antonio Ríos-Bustamante, ed., *Mexican Immigrant Workers in the U.S.* (Los Angeles: Chicano Studies Research Center, University of California Los Angeles, 1981). There are several dozen articles and several books on the causes of emigration from Mexico. See Jorge Bustamante et al., *México–Estados Unidos, bibliografía general sobre estudios fronterizos* (México: El Colegio de México, 1980), pp. 59–97. For one assessment of causes, see Wayne A. Cornelius, "Causes of Mexican Migration to the United States: A Summary View," *Perspectives in American History* 7 (1973); and Cornelius, *Mexican Migration to the United States: The View from Rural Sending Communities* (Cambridge, Mass: MIT/CIS, 1976). For a major study on change and mobility in Mexico, see Moisés González Navarro, *Población y sociedad en México 1900–1970*, 2 vols. (México: UNAM 1974).

10. Informed discussions are Harry E. Cross and James A. Sandos, *Across the Border: Rural Development in Mexico and Recent Migration to the United States* (Berkeley: University of California Institute of Government Studies, 1981); and Jorge Durand, *Más allá de la línea* (Mexico: Consejo Nacional para la Cultura y las Artes, 1994). On Mexico's development, see Fernando Rosenzweig Hernández, "La economía novo-hispana al comenzar el siglo XIX," *Ciencias políticas y sociales* 9 (1963). For some comments on historical contrasting development, though labor transfer is not referred to explicitly, see Josefina Vásquez and Lorenzo Meyer, *México frente a Estados Unidos* (México: El Colegio de México, 1982); and John H. Coatsworth "Obstacles to Economic Growth in Nineteenth Century Mexico," *American Historical Review* 83 (February 1978).

11. See the essays in *Mexican–U.S. Relations, Conflict and Convergence*, ed. Carlos Vásquez and Manuel Garcia y Griego (Los Angeles: UCLA/CSRC, 1983); and Richard Fagen, "The Realities of U.S. Mexican Relations," in Ríos-Bustamante, ed., *Mexican Immigrant Workers in the U.S.* (Los Angeles: Chicano Studies Research Center, University of California Los Angeles, 1981).

12. See Lawrence Cardoso, *Mexican Emigration to the United States, 1897–1931* (Tucson: University of Arizona Press, 1980); Mark Reisler, *By the Sweat of Their Brow: Mexican Immigrant Labor in the United States, 1900–1940* (Westport, Conn.: Greenwood Press, 1976); and D. Massey et al., *Return to Aztlán: The Social Process of International Migration from Western Mexico* (Berkeley: University of California Press, 1987). For literary materials, see Arturo Madrid-Barela, "Alambristas, Mojados, Norteños: Aliens in Aztlán," *Aztlán* 6 (Spring 1975). On community building experiences, see Roberto A. Alvarez, *Familia, Migration and Adaptation in Baja and Alta California 1800–1975* (Berkeley: University of California Press, 1987); Judith Fincher Laird, "Argentine Kansas: The Evolution of a Mexican American Community, 1905–1940" (Ph.D. diss., University of Kansas, 1975); and Francisco Rosales and Daniel T. Simon, "Mexican Immigration Experience in the Urban Midwest" in *Indiana Magazine of History* 57 (1981).

13. See Gilberto Loyo, "Notas preliminares sobre la migración de mexicanos a los Estados Unidos de 1900 a 1967," in Manuel Gamio, *El inmigrante mexicano* (México: UNAM, 1969). See also Jorge Bustamante, "The Historical Context of Undocumented Mexican Immigration to the United States," *Aztlán* 3 (Fall 1972); and Bustamante, "Commodity Migrants: Structural Analysis of Mexican Immigration to the United States," in Stanley Ross, ed., *Views across the Border* (Albuquerque: University of New Mexico Press, 1978).

14. See essays discussing immigration and the border in E. Mendoza Berrueto, ed., *Impactos regionales de las relaciones México–Estados Unidos* (México: ECM, 1984); and Johns R. Weeks et al., *Demographic Dynamics of the U.S.–Mexico Border* (El Paso: Texas Western Press, 1992). For a summary history, see Romeo Flores Caballero, *La frontera entre México y Estados Unidos* (Monterrey: UANL, 1976); and R. A. Fernández, *The Mexican Border Region* (Notre Dame: Notre Dame University Press, 1989). For essays on various aspects of border interaction, see Roque González Salazar, ed., *La frontera norte* (México: El Colegio de México, 1981); and Stanley Ross, ed., *Views across the Border* (Albuquerque: University of New Mexico Press, 1978). For monographic studies, see Niles Hansen, *The Border Economy: Regional Development in the Southwest* (Austin: University of Texas Press, 1981); Lawrence Herzog, *Where North Meets South* (Austin: University of Texas Press, 1990); and John House, *Frontier on the Rio Grande* (Oxford: Clarendon Press, 1982). For studies on the border, see *International Guide to Research on Mexico* (Tijuana and La Jolla: El Colegio de la Frontera Norte/Center for U.S.–Mexican Studies, University of California at San Diego, 1986); and E. Stoddard et al., *Borderlands Sourcebook: A Guide to the Literature* (Norman: University of Oklahoma Press, 1983).

15. See Manuel Gamio, *The Mexican Immigrant: His Life Story* (Chicago: University of Chicago Press, 1931); Gilberto Loyo, "Notas Preliminares"; Leo Grebler et al., *The Mexican American People* (New York: Free Press, 1970) chapters 3–5; and Arthur Corwin, ed., *Immigrants—and Immigrants: Perspectives on Mexican Labor Migration to the United States* (Westport, Conn.: Greenwood Press, 1978). For recent immigrants, information is available in Consejo Nacional de Población, *Encuesta en la frontera norte a trabajadores indocumentados* (Mexico: CONAPO, 1986); and Douglas Massey and K. Schnabel, "Background and Characteristics of Undocumented Hispanic Migrants to the United States: A Review of the Literature," *Migration Today* XI (1983).

16. See Manuel Gamio, *Mexican Immigration to the United States* (Chicago: University of Chicago Press, 1930); Enrique Santibañez, *Ensayo acerca de la inmigración mexicana en los Estados Unidos* (San Antonio, Tex.: Clegg Co., 1930); and Stella Leal Carrillo, "Importancia económica y social de la población mexicana en Estados Unidos de Norteamerica" (thesis, Universidad Nacional Autónoma de Mexico, 1963).

17. Manuel Gamio, *Quantitative Estimate Sources and Distribution of Mexican Immigration into the United States* (México: Talleres Gráficos y Diario Oficial, 1930). See also Mark Reisler, *By the Sweat of Their Brow* (Westport, Conn.: Greenwood Press, 1976), pp. 3–17; José Hernández Álvarez, "A Demographic Profile of Mexican Immigration to the United States, 1910–1950," *Journal of InterAmerican Studies* 8 (1966); and the impressive discussion in Jesús Antonio Machuca Ramírez, *Internacionalización de la fuerza de trabajo y acumulación de capital* (Mexico: INAH, 1990), pp. 119–241.

18. Gilbert Cárdenas, "United States Immigration Policy Toward Mexico: A Historical Perspective," *Chicano Law Review* 2 (Summer 1975); Marion T. Bennet, *American Immigration Policies: A History* (Washington, D.C.: Public Affairs Press, 1963); and Robert L. Bach, "Mexican Immigration and the American State," *International Migration Review* 12 (Winter 1978).

19. Kitty Calavita, *U.S. Immigration Law and the Control of Labor, 1820–1924* (Orlando, Fla.: Academic Press, 1984); and Roger Daniel, *Politics of Prejudice* (New York: Atheneum, 1968).

20. This is discernable in Victor S. Clark, "Mexican Labor in the United States," *Bulletin of the Department of Labor* 78 (1908); and Gerald Nash, *The American West in the Twentieth Century* (Albuquerque: University of New Mexico Press, 1977).

21. For figures on Mexican immigration, see Annual Reports of the U.S. Immigration and Naturalization Service and its predecessor agencies. There is considerable print material expressing views on Mexican immigration. For example, see R. F. Foerster, *The Racial Problems Involved in Immigration from Latin America and the West Indies to the United States* (Washington, D.C.: Government Printing Office, 1925); and R. I. Gares, "Mexican Immigration," in U.S. House of Representatives, *Western Hemisphere Immigration* (Washington, D.C.: Government Printing Office, 1930).

22. Robert A. Devine, *American Immigration Policy, 1924–1952* (New Haven: Yale University Press, 1957); Sidney Kansas, *United States Immigration, Exclusion and Deportation* (Albany: M. Bendler, 1948); and S. Kansas, *Immigration and Nationality Act, Annotated* (Buffalo: W. S. Hein, 1953).

23. See Manuel L. García y Griego, "The Bracero Experiment: U.S. and Mexican Policy Responses to Mexican Labor Migration, 1942–1955" (Ph.D. diss., University of California, Los Angeles, 1988), pp. 1–64; and Ernesto Galarza, *Merchants of Labor, The Mexican Bracero History* (Santa Barbara: McNally and Loftin, 1964).

24. U.S. Congress, Senate Committee on Immigration, *Hearings on Restrictions of Western Hemisphere Immigration* (70th Congress, 1st session, 1928). Many of the views had been expressed fifteen years earlier in a hearing by the Dillingham Commission, *Report of the Immigration Commission*, vol 1. (42 vols., Washington, D.C.: Government Printing Office, 1911), pp. 689–691 and vol. 25, passim; note the dictionary of races and people.

25. For memories and observations of changes in border vigilance, read Clifford Alan Perkins, *Border Patrol: With the U.S. Immigration Service on the Mexican Boundary, 1910–1954* (El Paso: Texas Western Press, 1978). For a summary of monitoring activities and proposals, see Juan R. Garcia, *Operation Wetback: The Mass Deportation of Mexican Undocumented Workers in 1954* (Westport, Conn., Greenwood Press, 1980).

26. The firsthand observations of Enrique Santibañez, Manuel Gamio, Paul S. Taylor, and Ernesto Galarza are valuable. And see Leo Grebler et al., *The Mexican American People*, chaps. 3–5; J. Craig Jenkins, "The Demand for Immigrant Workers: Labor Scarcity or Social Control," *International Migration Review* 12 (1978); and K. Calavita, *Inside the State: The Bracero Program, Immigration and the INS* (New York: Routledge, 1992).

27. Ernesto Galarza, "Life in the United States for Mexican People: Out of the Experience of a Mexican," in National Conference of Social Work, *Proceedings* (1929). On community cohesion, see Rodolfo Acuña, *Occupied America: A History of Chicanos* (New York: Harper & Row, 1988), "Mexican American Communities in the Making: The Depression Years," pp. 198–250; and Paul S. Taylor, *Mexican Labor in the United States, Migration Statistics, IV* (Berkeley: University of California Publications on Economics, v. 12, no. 3, 1934), pp. 25–50. See also comments of Ernesto Galarza, *Merchants of Labor: The Mexican Bracero Program* (Santa Barbara: McNally and Loftin, 1964), pp. 28–29. For relations between Mexico's administration and the U.S. communities, see Carlos H. Zazueta, "Mexican Political Actors in the United States and Mexico," in C. Vasquez and M. Garcia y Griego, eds. (Los Angeles: UCLA/CSRC, 1983); and Francisco E. Balderrama, *In Defense of La Raza* (Tucson: The University of Arizona Press, 1982).

28. For one report on repatriation, see "Nuevos grupos de repatriados de California," *La Prensa*, 14 August 1931. See also F. Balderrama and R. Rodriguez, *Decade of Betrayal: Mexicans Repatriated in the 1930s* (forthcoming); Mercedes Carreras de Velasco, *Los mexicanos que nos devolvió la crisis, 1929–1932* (México: Secretaría de Relaciones Exteriores,

1974); and Abraham Hoffman, *Unwanted Mexican-Americans* (Tucson: University of Arizona Press, 1974). There are several published articles on repatriations, the depression, and labor conflict.

29. The major books by Ernesto Galarza provide direct analysis of the specific workings and consequences of the labor exchange. See also Manuel L. Garcia y Griego, *The Importation of Mexican Contract Laborers to the United States* (San Diego: Program in United States–Mexican Studies, University of California, 1981); Leo Grebler, *Mexican Immigration to the United States: The Record and Its Implications* (Los Angeles: Graduate School of Business Administration, UCLA, 1965); and Richard B. Craig, *The Bracero Program* (Austin: University of Texas Press, 1971). For a view from Mexico during these times, see José Lázaro Salinas, *La emigración de braceros: visión objetiva de un problema mexicano* (México: Cuauhtemoc, 1955).

30. Julián Samora, *Los Mojados: The Wetback Story* (Notre Dame, Ind.: University of Notre Dame Press, 1971). As to how Mexican workers fared inspection, see *Our Badge of Infamy: A Petition to the U.N. on the Treatment of the Mexican Immigrant* (New York: Committee for the Protection of the Foreign Born, 1959). For a Mexico view of United States conditions for Mexicans, see Máximo Peón, *Como viven los mexicanos en Estados Unidos* (México: Costa Amic Editores, 1966).

31. The 1965 Immigration and Nationality Act, 89th Congress, 1st Session. See also *Report of the Select Commission on Western Hemisphere Immigration* (Washington, D.C.: Government Printing Office, January 1968).

32. Gilbert Cárdenas, "Mexican Labor: A View to Conceptualizing the Effects of Migration, Immigration and the Chicano Population in the United States," in Charles Teller et al., *Cuantos Somos: A Demographic Study of the Mexican American Population* (Austin: Center for Mexican American Studies, University of Texas, Austin, 1977); and Julián Samora, *Los Mojados: The Wetback Story.*

33. For analysis of Mexican documented and undocumented immigration issues related to changes in law, see Gilbert Cárdenas, "United States Immigration Policy toward Mexico, a Historical Perspective," *Chicano Law Review* 2 (1975); for general policy discussion, see Charles B. Keeley, *U.S. Immigration: A Policy Analysis* (New York: The Population Council, 1979); and U.S. House of Representatives, Committee on the Judiciary, *Illegal Aliens: Analysis and Background* (Washington, D.C.: Government Printing Office, 1977).

34. See materials in Antonio Ríos-Bustamante, ed., *Immigration and Public Policy: Human Rights for Undocumented Workers and Their Families* (Los Angeles: Chicano Studies Research Center, University of California Los Angeles, 1977; CSU Dominguez Hills, Labor Studies Program); and One Stop Immigration and Education Center, "The Invisibles," Conference Report (Los Angeles: May 1977).

35. U.S. Select Commission on Immigration and Refugee Policy, *U.S. Immigration Policy and the National Interest* (Washington, D.C.: Government Printing Office, 1981), and U.S.

Congress, *Select Readings on U.S. Immigration Law and Policy* (Washington, D.C.: Congressional Record Service, 1980).

36. "Immigration Reform and Control Act of 1986," House of Representatives, 99th Congress, 2d session, Report 99-1000 (14 October 1986); and Mexican American Legal Defense and Educational Fund, "Summary of the Immigration Reform and Control Act of 1986" (Los Angeles: MALDEF, 27 October 1986). For the policy debate at the time, see Nathan Glazer, ed., *Clamor at the Gates: The New American Immigration* (San Francisco: Institute for Contemporary Studies, 1985). For public views of undocumented workers at this time, see Edward E. Telles and Frank D. Bean, "Undocumented Migration to the United States: Perceptions and Evidence," *Population and Development Review* (December 1987). For proposals considered, see W. A. Cornelius, "The Reagan Administration Proposals for a New U.S. Immigration Policy: An Assessment of Potential Effects," *International Migration Review* 15 (1981). For a partial critique of the politics of the act, see Antonio Rodriguez et al., "The Struggle against the Immigration Control Act," *Chicano Law Review* 8 (1985). For an informed review of congressional and organizational politics leading to IRCA, see Christine Marie Sierra, "In Search of National Power: Chicanos Working the System on Immigration Reform" (unpublished paper, University of New Mexico Political Science Department, 1993). For an analysis on the confluence and contradiction of immigrants and Mexican Americans, see David G. Gutierrez, *Walls and Mirrors, Mexican Americans, Mexican Immigrants and the Politics of Ethnicity* (Berkeley: University of California Press, 1995). For a historical perspective, see Aristide R. Zolberg, "Reforming the Back Door," in V. Yans-McLaughlin, ed., *Immigration Reconsidered* (New York: Oxford University Press, 1990).

37. For the economic status of Mexican immigrants, see Francisco L. Rivera-Batz, "The Declining Socioeconomic Status of the Mexican Immigrant Population in the U.S., 1980–1990" (Teachers College, Columbia University, Institute for Urban and Minority Education, 94-4); see also the provocative interpretations of Douglas S. Massey et al., *Return to Aztlán: The Social Process of International Migration from Western Mexico* (Berkeley: University of California Press, 1987). For information on those covered by the 1986 law, see CASAS (Comprehensive Adult Student Assessment System), *A Survey of Newly Legalized Persons in California*, prepared for the California Health and Welfare Agency (San Diego: CASAS, 1989); see also "IRCA: Tabulations Prepared from the Legalized Population Survey" (U.S. Department of Labor, 1992). For a critique of IRCA see José A. Bracamonte, "How INS Can Make Amnesty Successful," *L. A. Examiner*, 7 December 1986. Mark Gibney, *Strangers or Friends: Principles for a New Alien Admissions Policy* (Westport, Conn.: Greenwood Press, 1986), provides scenarios on the notions of "community" and "citizenship" possible among 1980s immigrants.

63

38. See American Immigration Lawyers Association, "Advocacy Update" (Washington, D.C., 10 March 1995); John Willshire Carrera, "Immigrant Students: The Right of

Access to Public Schools," *Immigration Newsletter* 20 (1991); Lucas Guttentag and Antonio Maciel, "Employers Sanctions and Proposals for a National Identity Card," *Immigration Newsletter* 21 (1993); Cathi Tactaquin, "International Perspective on Migration," *Poverty and Race* 4 (1995), and Doris Meisner, "Testimony," INS, 14 March 1995. For an activist response, see José Jacques Medina, "Not Born in the U.S.A.," *International Union Rights* 1 (1993).

39. See María Puente, "GOP Retreats in a Compromise Immigration Bill"; and Mark Potok, "Immigration's Other Side: Interdependence," *USA Today,* 30 September 1996, pp. 19A–20A.

40. Juan Gómez-Quiñones, *Chicano Politics, Reality and Promise, 1940–1990* (Albuquerque: University of New Mexico Press, 1990), chapter 4; and Juan Gómez-Quiñones, *Mexican American Labor, 1790–1990* (Albuquerque: University of New Mexico Press, 1994), passim. Numerical information on Mexican native-born and Mexican immigrants is available from census reports. Particularly useful are the 1940, 1950, and 1970 reports and the reports of the former Immigration Commission and current INS. On the issues raised by legal and undocumented immigrants from agency perspectives, consult U.S. Congress, *Illegal Aliens: Issue Brief Number 1B 74137* (Washington, D.C.: Congressional Record Service, 1978), and U.S. Select Committee and Immigration and Refugee Policy, *U.S. Immigration Policy and the National Interest: The Final Report and Recommendations* (Washington, D.C.: Government Printing Office, 1981). For summaries of the main concerns motivating limiting or ending immigration, see Otis L. Graham, *Illegal Immigration and the New Reform Movement* (Washington, D.C.: Federation for American Immigration Reform, 1980). For analysis of media coverage, consult Celestino Fernández, "Newspaper Coverage of Undocumented Mexican Immigration During the 1970s: A Qualitative Analysis of Pictures and Headings" in *History, Culture and Society: Chicano Studies in the 1980s* (Ypsilanti, Mich.: Bilingual Press, 1983). For political responses related to immigrants, see the documents and essays in the publications edited by Antonio Rios-Bustamante, and for contrast to these, see Peter Skerry, *Mexican Americans: The Ambivalent Minority* (New York: Free Press, 1993). For immigration public opinion, see Gallup Opinion Index Reports, *Immigration* November 1983 and January–February 1985.

41. See Estevan T. Flores, "Post-Bracero Undocumented Mexican Immigration to the United States and Political Recomposition" (Ph.D. diss., University of Texas, Austin, 1982); and the publications of Antonio Rios-Bustamante on immigration.

42. For views at the time as well as documents and analyses, see Ríos-Bustamante, ed., *Immigration and Public Policy*; and Ríos-Bustamante, *Mexican Immigrant Workers in the U.S.* In the latter, see the essay by Margarita Melville.

43. For views opposing immigrant rights, see the article by Rodolfo O. de la Garza, "Mexican Americans, Mexican Immigrants and Immigration Reform" in Glazer, ed., *Clamor at the Gates* (San Francisco, Calif.: ICS Press, 1985), and others listed therein; see also

Lawrence Miller et al., "Attitudes toward Undocumented Workers: The Mexican American Perspective," *Social Science Quarterly* 65 (June 1984).

44. "Hermandad Mexicana," *Voz Fronteriza* (February 1978); and Jesús Mena, "Testimonio de Bert Corona. . . ." in *201, Homenaje a la Ciudad de Los Angeles* (Los Angeles, 1982).

45. See issues of *Sin Fronteras* and "Reporte de la Secretaría de Asuntos y Sindicales (CASA-HGT, unpublished report, circa 1979); Arturo Santamaría Gómez, *La izquierda norteamericana y los trabajadores indocumentados* (Mexico: Ediciones de Cultura Popular, 1988); and David Gutiérrez, "CASA in the Chicano Movement: Ideology and Organization in the Chicano Community" (Stanford: Center for Chicano Research (SCCR), Stanford University, 1984).

46. Luis R. Negrete, "La lucha de la comunidad mexicana," in Ríos-Bustamante, ed., *Mexican Immigrant Workers*; Gómez-Quiñones, *Mexican American Labor*, pp. 224-227; and Camilo García Parra, "The Social-Cultural Consequences of Trust" (Ph.D. diss., University of California, Los Angeles, 1985).

47. Interview with Juan José Gutiérrez (December 1988), notes in author's possession; see also "Editorial," *Voz Fronteriza* (May/June 1983).

48. Personal collection of papers from National Coalition for Fair Immigration Laws and Practices (1976-1978); California Conference on Immigration and Public Policy (1977); International Committee on Immigration and Public Policy (1977-1978); see also José Jacques Medina, "Organization and Resistance: CODIL," *Sin Fronteras* (June 1977); "La Conferencia Internacional," *Voz Fronteriza* (May 1980); and "Conference: 'From Theory to Practice,'" *Voz Fronteriza* (May/June 1983).

49. José Jacques Medina, "INS Out of the Factory-Worker Resistance," *Sin Fronteras* (September 1976); and Fidel Gómez, "Workers Experience Resisting the Migra," *Sin Fronteras* (April 1978). See also Santamaría Gómez, *La izquierda norteamericana y los trabajadores indocumentados* (Mexico: Ediciones de Cultura Popular, 1988). In contrast to these, see John W. Crewdson, "The New Migrant Militancy," *The New York Times*, 16 April 1978. On undocumented workers in organized labor, see "Who Organizes the Undocumented," *Voz Fronteriza* (November/December 1978); American Friends Service Committee, *Undocumented Workers in the U.S. Labor Market* (Pasadena, Calif.: AFSC, 1980); and Rebecca Morales, "Transitional Labor: Undocumented Workers in the Los Angeles Automobile Industry," *International Migration Review* 17 (1983).

50. CIWA materials in author's possession.

2

UNDOCUMENTED CROSSINGS

Narratives of Mexican Immigration to the United States

○ ○ ○ ○
○ ○ ○ ○

Alberto Ledesma

Mexican undocumented immigration has recently become a significant issue in the political arena, especially in California. The growing population of Mexican immigrants with their perceived "need" for social services, education, and cultural space has created a backlash against all immigrants—documented and undocumented—a backlash that has manifested itself in such varied forms as the Federal Immigration Reform and Control Act of 1986, California's English-only movement of the late 1980s, and 1994's Proposition 187.[1]

Yet this is not the first time that Mexican immigrants have become the subject of increased concern in the United States. Although Mexican immigrants have too often gone unnoticed by American society, they are usually rediscovered during adverse economic times and blamed as the major cause of the problem. Even though they are momentarily singled out, their point of view is generally not solicited. Fortunately, however, historical Mexican immigrant experiences have been recorded in narrative. Fictional accounts of immigrant experiences have been present in many of the short stories, dramas, and novels produced in Mexico and the American Southwest since the United States defeated Mexico in 1848. Often the stories related by these narratives have not been fictional at all, but rather factual accounts of what it has meant to live marginally as a Mexican immigrant in what has been the most powerful nation-state on earth. Given the politics of the time and the significant corpus of Chicano works that we now have, one question we may ask is how Chicana and Chicano narrative works have chronicled the historical undocumented immigrant experience? How have stories written by Chicanas and Chicanos, mostly the children of generations of Mexican immigrants, reflected the experience of Mexican immigrants living in the United States, particularly those Mexican immigrants who by accident of circumstance have had to traverse the border without the benefit of "papers"?

The Origins

Scholars of the literature have long recognized the importance, thematic and otherwise, of Mexican immigration in the formation and articulation of Chicana/o narratives. Indeed, in *Literatura chicana: texto y contexto*, one of the first major anthologies of Chicana/o literature, the process of Mexican-American migration within the United States and Mexican immigration into the United States is posited as "a root experience of socioeconomic nature which has been a fact of life imposed on the Chicano and his ancestors across the centuries." [2] More recently, Edward Simmen in a revised anthology of short stories that he originally edited in 1971 as *The Chicano: From Caricature to Self-Portrait*, has observed that "because the border is virtually impossible to monitor, each day increasing numbers of Mexican nationals are crossing it," and this, he contends, is "bringing a fresh voice and vision to [Chicano] literature." [3] But what have the characteristics of these fresh voices been?

A brief review of the way that Chicana/o narratives have been interpreted by literary scholars demonstrates that even though critics have recognized Mexican immigration as an important formational element of Chicana/o narratives, a more complete assessment of how the literature represents its immigrant legacy is necessary. Especially when it comes to identifying early Chicana/o literary representations, the immigrant question beckons. As Juan Bruce-Novoa has pondered, "at what point can an immigrant Mexican writer be considered Chicano?" [4]

Some literary critics present stories written by and about Mexican immigrants as documents of Chicana/o experience. Consider, for example, Nicolás Kanellos's research on turn-of-the-century narratives published in Spanish-language newspapers. His rediscovery of *Las aventuras de don Chipote o cuando los pericos mamen* (The Adventures of Don Chipote or When Parakeets May Suckle Their Young), which was originally published in 1928 (reprinted in 1984), should certainly be considered a major accomplishment. This narrative, written by the Mexican immigrant journalist Daniel Venegas, tells the humorous story of a Mexican peasant who emigrates to the United States to find economic prosperity. The story, written in Spanish and originally serialized in the Mexican immigrant newspaper *El Heraldo de México*, narrates the experiences of Mexican immigrants who come to the United States only to return to Mexico disappointed by the exploitation that they were confronted with. Kanellos, however, refers to this Mexican immigrant tale as *"la primera novela chicana"* (the first Chicano novel).[5]

Kanellos's assertion is intriguing because the narrative that he calls the "first Chicano novel" is thoroughly immigrant in character. In Kanellos's words, works such as *Don Chipote* "can be considered forerunners of the Chicano novel of the 1960s in their identification with the working-class Mexicans of the Southwest, their popular use of dialects, and their political stance as regards to the government and society of the United States."[6] So far as I know, his contention has not been challenged.

What is significant, however, is that *Don Chipote*'s story predominantly relates an undocumented immigrant experience. After Don Chipote de Jesús María Domínguez, the protagonist of the novel, travels to the border in 1924, he finds that the doors are not open to him. He then is forced to find a job that may earn him enough money to cross the border illegally.[7] Don Chipote's crossing of the border constitutes an important and defining episode of the novel, and his immigrant status dictates the chain of events that occur afterward. Because he does not satisfy the immigration law requirements, he is forced to take any job that is available and to seek aid from other immigrants who better know American society.

The underlying assumption of Venegas, both as the author and implied narrator, is that most of the immigrants who cross the border after the Mexican Revolution are, like Don Chipote, governed by their undocumented condition. Venegas's purpose here is to discourage immigrants like Don Chipote from coming across the border. In one of his many editorials Venegas states, *"La mayoría sólo viene a los Estados Unidos a dejar todas sus energías, a ser maltratados por los capataces y humillados por los ciudadanos del país."*[8] (The majority of Mexican immigrants come to the United States only to leave all their physical energy, to be mistreated by foremen and humiliated by the citizens of the country.)

Don Chipote finds that although the United States offers better wages, there are hidden costs that immigrants like himself must pay. For example, he can find only menial jobs, laying railroad tracks or washing dishes. His condition as an undocumented worker makes him easier to manage by bosses who overwork and underpay him. He cannot lobby for better working conditions or strike for labor rights, because doing so would get him deported. Indeed, the protagonist learns that he is even looked down upon by "his own people" for not being able to speak English. In a scene that occurs after he befriends another undocumented immigrant, Policarpo, Don Chipote learns that there are some Mexican immigrants who consider that speaking Spanish is a sign of inferiority. Venegas's apparent indignation is not based on the fact that there are Mexican-Americans who refuse to help Mexican immigrants; rather, he is offended by the fact that some Mexican-Americans, as if ashamed, "refuse to speak their own language." The subtle reality that Venegas implies in Don Chipote's chance meeting with this person "who by his aspect looked Mexican," is that Don Chipote's inability to speak English also determines his socioeconomic class status.[9]

The tragi-comic climax of this novel illustrates to what degree Don Chipote's dreams and aspirations are predetermined and circumscribed by his immigrant reality. Just as he has begun to enjoy his new cultural surroundings, Don Chipote is arrested by the police and deported by an immigration judge.

Although it seems that the moral of Don Chipote's story applies to all Mexican immigrants, the novel's didactic conclusion can be interpreted only as a comment on the plight of the undocumented. Interestingly, a scene described in the epilogue is identical to one described when the novel opens. As in the first chapter, the epilogue places Don Chipote in an idyllic pastoral setting in Mexico. Unable to appreciate the beauty of his surroundings, Don Chipote works feverishly because he has so many children to feed. Yet, unlike in the novel's beginning, in the epilogue Don Chipote does not dream about becoming rich. Instead, as illusory images begin to envelop his imagination, Don Chipote stops himself, enlightened by his recent experience. Venegas writes, "*y pensando en ésto, llegó a la conclusión de que los mexicanos se harían ricos en los Estados Unidos: Cuando Los Pericos Mamen*"[10] (and thinking of this, he arrived at the conclusion that Mexicans will become rich in the United States: When Parakeets May Suckle Their Young).

This conclusion must be placed in its proper perspective. We presume that Don Chipote's comment addresses all Mexican immigrants, regardless of race, class, or other elements of variance. It does not. Don Chipote's comment refers to other immigrants like himself—Mexican men, undocumented immigrants—who allow themselves to endure great hardships as sojourners in the United States, deluded by the prospect of earning a fortune.[11]

Kanellos's statement that *Don Chipote* is "the first Chicano novel," or at least a precursor to Chicano novels of the sixties, must be acknowledged as a significant claim. What this claim assumes is that the historical undocumented immigrant experience is a "precursor to," if not a constituent of, collective Chicana and Chicano experience. Even though Kanellos frames his claim by specifically stating that what *Don Chipote* and Chicano novels have in common, is "their identification with the working-class Mexicans of the Southwest, their popular use of dialects, and their political stance as regards to the government and society of the United States,"[12] his assertion that *Don Chipote* is "the first Chicano novel" concretely implicates the subject of the novel—undocumented immigrant experience—as a thematic element of the experiences that produce Chicanos.[13] Kanellos's finding argues that the connections between *Don Chipote* and Chicano novels are profound. Both at the level of what the novel says—its themes—and at the level of how it says it—its style—the connection is made. To what extent the subject of undocumented immigration affects how *Don Chipote* is written remains to be examined. However, there can be no question but that undocumented immigration deeply influences *Don Chipote's* thematic content.

Unlike with Kanellos, for other literary scholars the scope of what Chicana/o narratives are is problematized by questions of how extensively immigrant points of view dominate the story. Héctor Calderón asks, "Are Mexican writers and expatriates traveling through or living in Texas and California to be included among Chicano writers?"[14] In the case of Ramón Saldívar's exhaustive and highly influential work, *Chicano Narrative: The Dialectics of Difference* (1990),[15] Mexican immigration is read as an important historical background and context to the genesis of Chicanas/os. What is provocative, however, is the kind of immigration Saldívar is referring to. His contention that "for Chicano narrative, history is the subtext that we must recover because history itself is the subject of its discourse"[16] would suggest that the history of generations of immigrants that most Chicanos are a product of is or should be represented by Chicano narratives. Although Saldívar's contention is significant, the fact remains that most Chicano literary criticism has overlooked the experience of Mexican undocumented immigrants recorded by Chicano narratives.

However, some few works such as Barbara Harlow's "Sites of Struggle: Immigration, Deportation, Prison, and Exile,"[17] María Herrera-Sobek's *Northward Bound*, and Genaro Padilla's "The Mexican Immigrant as *: The (de)Formation of Mexican Immigrant Life Story"[18] have begun to explore Chicana/o literary products from the point of view of the immigrant subject, distinguishing, in the process, that there is a difference between Mexican immigrant and Chicano literary articulations. Genaro Padilla, for example, has argued in "The Mexican Immigrant" that

Mexican immigrant ethnographic works have undergone such manipulations that "the Mexican immigrant [has been] given voice in a text only to have the name that identifies the autobiographical utterance textually concealed, canceled by a fabricated name."[19] Indeed, Padilla notes how the ethnographic convention of re-placing the "informant's" proper name with an invented generic name has meant that "the Mexican immigrant, therefore, has too often remained an anonymous entity, a cipher to be assigned meaning in a sociological play of statements."[20]

The prime example that Padilla cites to illustrate his observation is John J. Poggie's *Between Two Cultures: The Life of an American-Mexican* (1973).[21] He notes that although the text that Poggie offers is presented as an immigrant's autobiog-raphy, the standard convention of using a pseudonym to protect the privacy of the subject informant makes the autobiography more akin to fiction. The question of who authors the text remains ever-present.

In spite of this, Padilla contends, there are moments when the informant manages to assert something unique to his own experience, when he manages to reveal a particular part of his life that the social scientist fails to appropriate as a characteristic of the group he is studying. This "autobiographical moment," as Padilla calls it, is evidence that the social scientist is not in total control of what is being said. As Padilla states, "the asterisk will always loom before us as the symbol of the social scientist's ownership of the text, but within the asterisk's concealment of the face and name is a voice we hear calling its own presence."[22]

Padilla's discussion focuses on the way that sociologists appropriate indi-vidual immigrant autobiographical statements in order to make generalized obser-vations about all Mexican immigrants; he is not, however, addressing how Chi-cana/o narratives represent immigrants directly. If Padilla were to consider the way that Chicana/o narratives have reflected Mexican immigrant experience, he might conclude that Mexican immigrant voices have been well represented by the litera-ture. Novels such as José Antonio Villarreal's *Pocho* (1959),[23] Ernesto Galarza's *Barrio Boy* (1971),[24] Estela Portillo Trambley's *Trini* (1986),[25] and Arturo Islas's *Rain God* (1984)[26] have Mexican immigration as an important thematic element. Short stories on immigrant themes have also been prolific: for example, Sandra Cisneros's *Woman Hollering Creek*,[27] María Helena Viramontes's *Cariboo Cafe*,[28] and major works such as Gloria Anzaldúa's collection of essays and poems, *Borderlands/ La Frontera: The New Mestiza* (1987)[29] have affirmed not only that Chicana/o lit-erature involves immigrant experience, but that immigration is a fundamental part of who Chicanas/os are.

Indeed, critics such as Alfred Arteaga and José David Saldívar have recognized the power of immigrant symbols such as the border as expressions of Chi-cana/o marginality.[30] For example, Arteaga has stated in *An Other Tongue* that "the border as a discursive and existential fact does something to the interpretation of Chicano writing."[31] Yet if the symbol of the border "does something" to the way that Chicana/o writing is interpreted, how does the epistemological condition of being undocumented affect the way that Chicana/o narratives represent Mexican immigrant experience in the United States? Certainly, if we accept the premise that Chicanos and Mexican immigrants are not the same, and if we accept Genaro Padilla's argument that the "Mexican immigrant has too often remained an anony-mous entity,"[32] should we not expect some degree of misrepresentation by Chi-cana/o authors who themselves have to "assign meaning" to the Mexican immi-grant experience? After all, Chicana and Chicano authors who write about Mexican immigration tend to produce narratives that are not about immigrant experiences they personally lived; more often they must imagine experiences that their parents went through, and thus render stories translated from what others have experienced.

Mexican and Chicano Depictions of the Undocumented

In order to gauge how Mexican undocumented immigrant experiences are represented by Chicana and Chicano narratives, it is necessary to compare these narratives of Mexican immigration to the creative works that Mexican authors have written on the subject.[33] This kind of comparison yields three beneficial results: first, it shows what structural similarities and differences—major themes, meta-phors, and symbols—characterize the way that Mexican immigration narratives are rendered by Mexican and Chicana/o authors; second, it demonstrates how the "nationality," if not the "nationalism," of the authors influences the style, struc-ture, and/or tone of how undocumented immigration stories are told; and third, it bears out the terms by which undocumented immigrant identity has been defined and constructed by Chicana/o versus *mexicano* narratives. What becomes apparent after surveying narratives of Mexican immigration to the United States written by both Mexican and Chicana/o authors is that there exist two major paradigms by which stories of undocumented Mexican immigration to the United States are related, paradigms determined by a nationalist subjectivity.[34]

The emigration of Mexican workers to the United States has been a subject of various important Mexican narratives of the twentieth century. Indeed, works like Agustín Yañez's *Al filo del agua* (1947)[35] and Carlos Fuentes's *La región más transparente* (1958)[36] have provided a focus not just on the plight of Mexican immigrant braceros, but also on the social role that immigration has played in defining the characteristics of the Mexican nation that emerged after the decade-long revolution it experienced at the beginning of this century. These narratives are often referred to as *bracero* narratives — stories of documented and undocumented Mexican immigrant workers who travel to the United States, but only temporarily, in search of jobs that may earn them quick fortunes.

Mexican bracero narratives have been so prolific that one may argue that they constitute an independent genre. Over the years, such works as Luis Spota's *Murieron a mitad del río* (1948),[37] José de Jesús Becerra González's *El dólar viene del norte* (1954),[38] Héctor Raúl Almanza's *Huelga blanca* (1950),[39] Jesús Topete's *Aventuras de un bracero* (1948),[40] Magdalena Mondragón's *Tenemos sed* (1956),[41] and Herminio Corral Barrera's *Los fabricantes de braceros* (1980)[42] have portrayed the lives of Mexican men and women who have crossed the border looking for work. Sometimes the themes alluded to by bracero narratives have to do with the plight of the undocumented. Often, as Herrera-Sobek has discovered in *The Bracero Experience: Elitelore versus Folklore* (1979), the most important themes "deal with prejudice, ill-treatment, and poor wages, and in general present the bracero experience as a wretched and unbearable one."[43]

The Mexican perspectives on both documented and undocumented immigration form a highly nationalistic narrative discourse. This nationalist subjectivity is principally characterized by repeated references to Mexican patriotism and national loyalty, which romanticize Mexico while simultaneously vilifying the United States. The discourse is also marked by the negative portrayals of *pochos*—Mexican immigrants or the children of immigrants who show evidence of having acculturated to American society. In addition to this nationalist subjectivity, Mexican immigration narratives are also typified by an emphasis on group class consciousness and on the trials and tribulations of *los pobres*—poor Mexicans who struggle to survive amid capitalist rapacity.

One of the novels that best represents the nationalist and class perspectives common to most Mexican narratives of immigration and that merits detailed attention is Spota's *Murieron a mitad del río*. Like many bracero narratives, Spota's novel seeks to expose the harsh treatment that Mexican immigrants are subjected to as they work long hours for menial wages. The novel, like Venegas's *Don Chipote*, also seeks to warn potential braceros away from venturing northward. Yet unlike Venegas's narrative, Spota's novel bases its observations on explicit undocumented immigrant experience. He writes, "*He querido reseñar la historia de unos cuantos mexi-*

canos que se embarcaron en la aventura de cruzar la frontera, en busca de dólares." [44] (I have attempted to sketch the experience of a few Mexican workers who embarked on an adventure of crossing the border, in search of dollars.) The novel, as well as the extent of the adventure, lasts as long as the protagonist, José Paván, and his friends, Lupe Flores, Luis Alvarez and "Cocula," struggle to survive as "illegal" immigrants in the United States. This struggle provokes changes in the way that the four adventurers perceive themselves, changes that occur because of the way that they are treated as Mexican immigrants and because of the conditions they face as exploited laborers.

As with *Don Chipote*, the scene of the protagonists' border crossing in *Murieron a mitad del río* is crucial. However, in Spota's novel the border crossing is where the story begins, not a midpoint experience between life in Mexico and life in the United States. Spota gives very little detail about why Paván and his friends resort to crossing the border illegally or about what leads up to their adventure. Rather, the novel starts off *in medias res* with Paván and his friends caught in the darkness, in a sand bank in the middle of the Río Grande. The lights that search for them in the darkness represent much more than lights; they are metonymic referents to the Border Patrol, reminders that the crossing and permanence of Paván and his friends into the United States depends on their ability to remain invisible, out of sight. Thus their submersion in the river also symbolizes their submersion into a new social role. Suddenly they must learn how to live in the shadows, not knowing the language that is spoken to them, uninformed about any rights that they may have, and unable to protest their plight. Luckily, they are able to evade detection the first time they cross the river. The experience is so traumatic, however, that the timid Cocula gets left behind to fend for himself. Once the remaining three are on Texas *terra firma*, they realize that they must constantly hide.

From the beginning, the novel focuses on twenty-year-old José Paván's point of view. Yet unlike Venegas's Don Chipote, Paván is a nontraditional undocumented immigrant, having abandoned his life as a student in order to pursue his dream of enjoying the wonders of American metropolitan life. Like Don Chipote, however, Paván is a representative immigrant, a figure whose experience in the United States is premised on the actual experiences of many Mexican braceros before him.[45]

As a result of the difficult experience that Spota's undocumented immigrants undergo in crossing the river, Paván is compelled to reassess the practicality of crossing the border. Now in the United States, he and his friends feel a unique self-awareness, a nervous uncertainty about how to behave and what to do.[46]

The uneasiness that Paván and his comrades feel is created by their new condition as undocumented immigrants.[47] Evidently, the questions that Paván asks himself are motivated by situations that he did not ponder in Mexico; he did not anticipate having to evade a ubiquitous Border Patrol or that he could starve without a job. The language that Spota uses to communicate what Paván is thinking has a prophetic quality that alludes beyond his individual experience; the fact that Spota uses the second-person future perfect tense "you will" during Paván's meditations is significant. Leo R. Chavez has written in his book *Shadowed Lives: Undocumented Immigrants in American Society* (1992) that "undocumented immigrants are constantly aware that at any moment they could be apprehended and deported from the country."[48] Evidently, this awareness—fear of what may come—dominates Paván's thoughts.

The by-product of Paván's existential ponderings about being undocumented is the enhancement of his appreciation for Mexico, Mexicans and Mexican culture. This perspective, however, is not automatically assumed when Paván crosses the border. His opinion of the United States sours gradually as one negative experience after another transpires while he is away from Mexico. Spota writes, *"En Texas, ser mexicano no es una nacionalidad sino un oficio. El peor, y más despreciable de todos."*[49] (In Texas being Mexican is not a nationality but a job—the worst and most despicable of all.)

As the story proceeds, it becomes clear that even though Paván and his friends have found good-paying jobs, their undocumented situation makes them vulnerable to exploitation. Interestingly, it is an American of Mexican descent who first takes advantage of them, the foreman Domingo Mascorro. Mascorro exercises strict control of his subordinates, cruelly forcing them to work as hard as they can digging potatoes.

It is one of the other workers, an overzealous and more cynical fellow undocumented immigrant by the name of Benito Fortis who gives voice to what Paván and his friends are beginning to feel about Mascorro. Fortis states, *"¿Viste a Mascorro? Igual que el gringo: hipócrita. Esos son los peores."*[50] (Did you see Mascorro? Just like the gringo: hypocrite. Those are the worst.) Yet even though Paván dislikes Mascorro, he is not willing to make categorical value judgments as Fortis does. Instead, Paván rationalizes that it is Fortis's bumpkin unsophistication that engenders his frustration.[51] The presumptuous view that Paván has of Fortis reveals his biases. Paván feels that because he is educated and because his skin is "white," he is a different kind of undocumented immigrant than Fortis. And indeed he is treated differently from his friends by Leslie Walker, the boss's wife, who has an affair with him. However, Paván cannot escape being an undocumented immigrant. Mascorro, envious of all the favors that Paván has been getting from Leslie Walker, decides to call the Border Patrol.

After running away from certain deportation, Paván and his friends face greater misfortunes. No longer do Paván and his friends appear as sympathetic figures; the lengths that they are willing to go to in order to secure dollars seem extreme, tragic. But even desperate plans fail them.

Finally, as Paván and Luis travel northward, they run into Cocula—the friend who had been left behind the first time they crossed the river. Cocula had managed to cross the border with relative ease by assuming a false identity, purchasing the Social Security card that once belonged to a legal immigrant. [52] Paván learns that there is a way to remain in the United States without facing what he has faced as an undocumented immigrant. Thousands of legal immigrants sell their papers when returning home, Cocula tells him. However, Paván has no opportunity to use the new information before the Border Patrol arrests him.

As Paván is being repatriated home, certainly his meditations are full of remorse. Most importantly, what Paván learns is that being undocumented dehumanizes the individual, makes it so that one has no choice but to resort to desperate means in order to survive. It is this final understanding that seems to be the moral of Spota's narrative; Paván finally understands that the promise of wealth that the United States represents to undocumented immigrants is nothing more than an empty promise.

Spota's story, however, does not sufficiently explore the factors that motivate Mexican workers such as Paván and his friends to willingly undertake such drastic endeavors. Rather, Mexico, the homeland, is romanticized by the story. Indeed, in *Murieron a mitad del río*, Mexican immigrants are portrayed as having given up too easily on Mexico.

Spota is not the only writer to suggest this of Mexican immigrants. Another author to make such a statement is Jesús Topete, who has gone even further. His autobiography, *Aventuras de un bracero*, which focuses on his experience as a legally contracted Mexican immigrant seasonal worker (a *bracero*) offers a perspective of Mexican immigration that is similar to Spota's. What can be said about Topete's work, however, is that if Mexican undocumented immigration is portrayed as a form of slavery in Spota's novel, in Topete's autobiography life as a contracted bracero is presented as indentured servitude. Topete recounts all the major joys and sorrows that he experienced during his life as a bracero: the excitement and expectation of leaving Mexico, bound for the United States; the pleasant camaraderie that he formed with men from all over Mexico, who like him journeyed to an unknown land; the strenuousness of working long hours at a labor camp planting seed, washing dishes, and harvesting an infinity of potatoes; the bittersweet longing and nostalgia that he felt for his homeland, which was partly a result of his inability to fully explore his new world; and the ecstasy of the return to the motherland after a long and difficult absence. In other words, Topete chronicles the events that transpired from the time that he managed to contract himself to his return back home. He offers a book that, in the words of the editor, Gutierre Tibón, helps the reader love Mexico even more.[53]

Interestingly, Topete's story is set during the same historical period as Spota's, some time just before the end of World War II. However, whereas Spota's story takes place in Texas, Topete's story takes place in California's San Joaquín Valley and centers mostly on "legal" and temporary immigration. From the beginning of his narration, moreover, Topete tries to detach himself from what he observes, describing the events that transpired during his bracero adventure in a journalistic matter-of-fact way, much like a classic travel narrative.

While Jesús Topete's adventure to the United States is brief, there are clearly aspects of his experience that he cherishes. In this sense, Topete's experience north of the border seems quite distinct from Spota's narration, as it is relatively pleasant. Although Topete seems bothered by some aspects of his trip—he and his fellow braceros are abused and treated like cattle—he nonetheless enjoys the friendships that he forms with the other workers.[54] In short, he is willing to put up with the abuse that the Bracero Program represents as long as he can rely on the support and brotherhood of his compatriots who are also participants.

When confronted with Mexican American women, however, Topete passionately asserts his disgust with what they represent, in the process manifesting a chauvinism that reveals not just sexism and racism, but also a mild nationalist belligerence. As part of a large group of men who has traveled to the United States to work, a group of men housed in camps more akin to prisons, Topete's disgust for Chicana workers seems surprising. His presumption that the Chicanas he describes are not what American women are supposed to be like is premised on the idealized assumption that American women are statuesque and blond. It could be argued that because the women are also brought in to work along with the men and because they are of Mexican heritage, Topete's disgust is really a symptom of male insecurity. After all, the women he portrays are, more or less, equals of the braceros—workers who like him are contracted to work in the labor camp cutting potatoes. However, given that the women are also pochas, any notion that Topete is only disgusted by the Chicanas because they act like men is further complicated.

Jesús Topete displays a totally unsympathetic view of pochos, both male and female, that is fervent and consistent. Soon after the women arrive at the labor camp, Topete notices that the Chicanas are reluctant to speak to the new braceros. He does not attribute this reluctance to any distrust Chicanas may feel toward the newly arrived men. Nor does Topete assume that the reason Chicanas are reticent with the braceros might actually be based on the women's embarrassment about not speaking Spanish well. Rather, Topete assumes that the Chicanas' unwilling-ness to talk to the men is a result of their hypocrisy and conceit. Yet Topete's dislike of pochos is not limited just to women. He also makes dramatic observa-tions on the pocho men who were already working there: "*De esa clase de bichos ya tenía yo algunos datos porque había dos en el campamento desde que llegamos.*"[55] (Of that kind of pest I already had some facts because there had been two of them in the labor camp since we had arrived.) One of the most obvious and principal reasons Topete dislikes pochos has to do with the kind of references that pochos make about Mexico. Topete feels appalled and offended that they, the sons and daughters of Mexicans, would speak so badly of the country of their origin.

A young man who has grown up in post-revolutionary Mexico, during a less turbulent era than the one that the parents of the pochos grew up in, it does not occur to Topete that the Mexico the pochos have heard about from their parents is a different place from the Mexico that he knows. That is, Topete does not seek to understand the pocho point of view, but rather staunchly sets up ideological barri-ers that permit him to see them only as the enemy.[56]

To sum up, Topete has a negative view of Mexican immigration to the United States because he understands that Mexican immigrants might never go back "home," that they might become permanent settlers. Such a prospect con-founds him as he is thoroughly convinced that pochos are corrupted by an impos-sible desire to be both American and Mexican. In his opinion they are neither, "*ni son una cosa ni son otra*"[57] (neither one nor the other).

In this sense, Topete's premise is similar to J. Humberto Robles's famous play *Los desarraigados* (1962).[58] Originally written in the mid-1950s during the height of bracero immigration to the United States, Robles's play dramatizes the tragic lives of families who leave Mexico for the United States—the "uprooted." The tragedy that Robles focuses on in his narrative has to do with the suffering that Mexican immigrant parents have felt about their American-born children, about having to raise pochos. When the play debuted in Mexico in 1956, it was lauded by Mexican critics because, according to them, it bravely confronted the pocho "problem," and in so doing upheld the true spirit of *mexicanidad* (Mexicanness).[59]

Chicana and Chicano Narratives

In contrast to Mexican bracero narratives, Chicana and Chicano narratives of immigration to the United States have tended to portray the immigrant experience as a positive one. They have also characteristically focused greater attention on the factors that have compelled emigration out of Mexico in the first place. Chicana/o narratives of immigration are numerous, and such novels as Ernesto Galarza's *Barrio Boy*, Estela Portillo Trambley's *Trini*, and Victor Villaseñor's *Rain of Gold*[60] have particularly explored the complex dynamics implicit in the Mexican immigrant experience.

Of particular interest when contrasting Chicana/o narrative constructs of Mexican immigration to Mexican stories is Galarza's *Barrio Boy*. Galarza's autobiographical novel focuses on the dynamics involved in the immigration process and the consequent acculturation of immigrants into their new society. Furthermore, of the many Chicano narratives of Mexican immigration that have been written since the advent of what Phillip Ortego called the "Chicano Renaissance,"[61] Galarza's autobiography best illustrates the contrast between Chicano and Mexican immigration narratives. His work presents the interaction between newly arrived Mexican immigrants and American society in a positive way, not as cultural contamination; Mexico is not romanticized as a nation nor is the United States vilified; and finally, the border crossing is not portrayed as having a traumatic, cathartic, or problematic effect on the book's protagonist.

In addition, the significance of *Barrio Boy* is that Galarza offers it as a singular representation of a historical experience that so many Mexicans have lived. In the preface to his autobiography, Galarza states, "what brought me and my family to the United States from Mexico also brought hundreds of thousands of others like us."[62] Indeed, this is also the way that *Barrio Boy* has been critically read; both Ramón Saldívar and Charles M. Tatum have observed that *Barrio Boy* speaks about a wider Mexican immigrant experience than just Galarza's.[63] Saldívar's observation that Galarza's narrative merges "historical self-explanation, philosophical self-analysis, and poetic self-expression" would seem to emphasize that Galarza's autobiography achieves a unique effect. Charles Tatum, in his essay "Contemporary Chicano Prose Fiction: A Chronicle of Misery," argues that works like Galarza's have been helpful in understanding the complexity and scope of the immigrant legacy.[64]

Of course, there are several pronounced differences between Galarza's immigrant narrative and the works written by Venegas, Spota, and Topete. The most obvious of these is that Galarza's autobiography is written in English and the others in Spanish. Also, Galarza's story is a product crafted several decades after the Mexican narratives and, with the exception of Venegas's satire, in a different country. While the Mexican narratives focus a great deal of attention on the border crossing, Galarza's text does not particularly dwell on it. To be sure, this lack of focus on the crossing has to do with the way that the border is crossed in *Barrio Boy* versus the way that it is crossed in the other stories. In Venegas's and Spota's works the crossing is necessarily emphasized because it relates a traumatic experience. On the other hand, in Topete's work the border crossing is not as prominent, because it forms a part of the greater bracero experience.

One way that Galarza's autobiography shares a close resemblance to Topete's *Aventuras de un bracero* is in the way that it is told. As autobiographies, both works base their commentary on the selected memories and anecdotes of lived experience; both of the works attempt to offer a "true" view of history based on the observations of their protagonists. Yet while Topete's story is told from the perspective of an adult who has lived and been disappointed by the immigrant experience, *Barrio Boy* is told from the perspective of a child, a curious kid who is eager to learn about life. Galarza's autobiography, moreover, is unlike Spota's and Topete's narratives in that it is much more detailed about the reasons that he and his family were forced to leave Mexico. The motivation for their departure from Mexico had nothing to do with a desire for adventure or a need to earn more money; rather, it was war—the Mexican Revolution—that uprooted them. Thus Galarza tells the story of how his mother, Doña Henriqueta, and his uncles, José and Gustavo, traveled to Sacramento, California, from the mountains of Nayarit, Mexico. The prospect that Jalcocotán, Galarza's beloved village, might be "set on fire" by one of the warring factions is what propels his family to relocate.[65] They soon realize that in order to find a safe place to live, they will have to go out of the country.

The way that Galarza and his family cross the border is important. Instead of having to sneak across the international boundary, Galarza and his family are seemingly aided by the U.S. government.[66] Surely, the image that Galarza presents of "gringo" soldiers smiling and helping refugees contrasts highly with the negative images of Border Patrol officers and the police in bracero narratives. The implication here is crystal clear: Galarza's border crossing is not only "legal," but welcomed by the "smiling" faces of Mexico's "mortal enemies."[67]

Because Galarza crosses the border "legitimately," he does not experience the kind of antagonistic relationships with Americans that Topete, Spota, or even Venegas discuss in their works. Rather, the only thing that Galarza experiences is the wonder of not knowing exactly where he is, a feeling that signals the innocent beginning of his new life in the United States. The meaning of the border for young Galarza is not based on exclusionary laws or prohibitive wire fences. Indeed, Galarza cannot even tell where Mexico ends and the United States begins; he does not feel alienated the moment he crosses the border.

As Galarza and his family proceed northward, they are better able to understand what it is that separates Mexico from the United States. Once they arrive in Sacramento, California, Galarza notes that it is religion, customs, and attitudes—that mostly separates the "us" from "them." As they had done in every city where they had stopped on their way northward, Galarza's family moves to the poor side of town. He states, "for the Mexicans the barrio was a colony of refugees."[68] Although Galarza notes that in the neighborhood people come from different places from throughout Mexico, he comes to consider the barrio as his new home. There, Galarza observes, other people live "like us." Indeed, for Galarza, the barrio is a community of families who share common experiences and conditions—a *colonia mexicana*. Moreover, Galarza points out that the new immigrants do not arrive only to be temporary residents. The new immigrants, like himself, come across the border to settle permanently in their new barrio homes. He states, "Crowded as it was, the *colonia* found a place for these *chicanos*, the name which we called an unskilled worker born in Mexico and just arrived in the United States."[69]

Inasmuch as Chicana/os feel at home in the barrio, Galarza also makes it clear that differences among the population do exist, especially among Chicanos/pochos. In Galarza's view, the pochos are the sons and daughters of prior generations of Mexican immigrants, the ones who came across the border "before the Mexican Revolution." As such, Galarza notes, pochos have become better acculturated to American society. They know the language and the customs. But Galarza also notes that "the chicanos and the pochos had certain feelings about one another."[70] Saying this about Chicanos is Galarza's way of stating that tensions between recently arrived Mexicans and already established and acculturated Mexican Americans existed. For Galarza, such tensions have arisen from a distrust that Chicanos feel about the cultural loyalty of pochos. Even though Chicanos tend not to go back to Mexico, it is clear that they maintain a sense of cultural loyalty toward their homeland and they resent that pochos do not feel the same.

To be sure, Galarza's autobiography suggests that if becoming more "American" is what turning pocho means then it can occur gradually to recently arrived immigrants as they acculturate to American society. In spite of the cultural celebrations that the *Comisión Honorífica* (Honor Commission) held, Galarza notes how recent immigrants who expose themselves more and more to different aspects of American culture attain new perspectives, selecting and integrating parts of American culture as their own. This, in fact, happens to Galarza himself.[71] Thus, what Galarza shows is that although he may remain an immigrant all his life, the fluid quality and the evolving nature of American culture allows him to go from being a Chicano to becoming a pocho.

In spite of Galarza's acculturation into American society, reminders that he and his family are Mexican immigrants arise periodically. One particular scene with such a reminder is when the ship transporting Galarza's cousins arrives at Angel Island from Mexico. When Galarza and his family go to greet their newly arrived kin, they find that because new immigration laws have taken effect, the family is unable to come into the country.[72]

What happens when the cousins attempt to come into the United States contrasts dramatically with the way that Galarza, his mother, and his uncles crossed the border. Galarza's cousins cannot cross "legitimately" into the United States. For them to remain would be "illegal." From this event Galarza learns that the American immigration system is "unfair." Yet, in spite of his suggestion to his mother that they go back to Jalcocotán with his cousins, Galarza and his family remain in the United States.

It is this choice to remain in the United States that differentiates Galarza's account most dramatically from the bracero narratives. What *Barrio Boy* suggests is that the choice that Mexican immigrants make to remain as permanent settlers in the United States is a result of the nature of their crossing into this country. As refugees, as "legitimate" immigrants, Galarza and his family do not have to hide from groups of officials who are constantly attempting to enforce "laws and orders" that prohibit their living in this country. Furthermore, as long as they remain in the barrio where other refugees have settled, they do not have to face the kind of racism that inspires immigration laws. In Galarza's words, "Only when we ventured uptown did we feel like aliens in a foreign land." [73]

Chicana Immigration Narratives

Like Galarza's autobiography, other Chicano narratives of Mexican immigration have also presented stories of immigrants who have permanently settled in the United States after crossing the border. Some of these narratives, unlike Galarza's work, have focused on undocumented crossings, but not many. Those which have, however, have tended to overwhelmingly focus on the undocumented immigrant experience of men, implying that not many women have crossed the border over the years either as documented or undocumented immigrants.

Recently, however, works like Pierrete Hondagneu-Sotelo's *Gendered Transitions: Mexican Experiences of Immigration* have argued that "perhaps the most significant recent development in Mexican immigration to the United States is the concurrent increase in undocumented settlement and the participation of women and entire families in undocumented migration and settlement.[74] Indeed, Hondagneu-Sotelo's thesis that "while Mexican men often play an important role in initiating migration, women play an important part in solidifying settlement"[75] has been corroborated not just by the personal interviews that she cites in her ethnography, but also by stories told within the increasing body of narratives written about documented and undocumented Mexican immigrant women. Such works as Helena María Viramontes's "The Cariboo Cafe," Sandra Cisneros's "Women Hollering Creek," Irene Beltran Hernandez's *Across the Great River* (1989),[76] and Estela Portillo Trambley's *Trini* demonstrate that the immigrant experience affects men differently than women. Like Hondagneu-Sotelo's study, these works show that immigration enables women to redefine traditional Mexican gender roles and to gain personal agency within a patriarchal social order. These works also illustrate what immigrant women are willing to risk.

One novel in particular that seeks to present the immigrant woman's unique perspective is Estela Portillo Trambley's *Trini*. In essence, there is a small parallel between Portillo Trambley's novel and Galarza's autobiography: both narratives discuss the many kinds of "peregrinations" that eventually lead poor Mexicans to cross into the United States. Indeed, much as a young Ernesto Galarza travels from his village of Jalcocotán across the border to a new life, so does Trini first travel as a girl of thirteen from Batopilas, her village in the mountains, to Chihuahua, to Ciudad Juárez, and eventually across the border to the United States. However, unlike Galarza's text, Portillo Trambley's novel concretely relates the unique circumstances that motivate a Mexican woman to risk becoming an undocumented immigrant. The novel covers the many tragic events that justify Trini's choice to cross the river "illegally." To be sure, the bulk of the novel covers ten years of Trini's coming into womanhood from young adulthood; it is not until she is an adult, after her husband has abandoned her, that Trini crosses the border. The border crossing itself does not seem to be too difficult for Trini. It is important to note, however, that Trini relies on a female smuggler to get her across; she is pregnant and thus reduces her risk of being sexually assaulted. Once in the United States, she immediately envelops herself in the tasks of her job. She learns to appreciate all the new marvels that she is exposed to, technological advances as well as American cultural novelties. Yet when her pregnancy becomes apparent to her American employer, she is summarily released. It is clear that Trini's Anglo employer cares only about Trini's ability to provide labor. Beyond that she is of no use. What is also significant is that Trini's *gringa* (American) employer does not want Trini to deliver her baby in the United States; the gringa actively prods Trini across the border.[77]

Back in Mexico, Trini experiences desperate times. Frustrated and worried about the fact that she is without money and about to give birth, Trini learns from a friend that any child born in the United States, regardless of whether he or she is born to undocumented parents, is automatically born an American citizen. With her older daughter in tow, she walks the streets of Juárez armed with this knowledge, becoming increasingly determined to give birth to her child in the United States. Speaking to her daughter, Trini says, "'Why not Angelita? My baby born an American citizen. I will work, buy land, and when Tonio comes back, he will be so proud of me.'"[78]

Trini's second trek across the border is more difficult than the first, as she is days away from giving birth. Reluctantly, the woman smuggler who had helped Trini across the first time repeats the process. Trini struggles to get to the church of "El Sagrado Corazón" in El Paso, the place where she has chosen to deliver her child, but after she reaches the church and delivers a baby boy, Trini runs away.

Desperately, Trini runs in the street with her newborn child, fearing that she might be deported. Then, as Portillo Trambley writes, "a Mexican woman sat next to her, waiting for the bus. She looked at Trini and the baby with interested eyes but said nothing until Trini asked, 'Where do I register my baby as a citizen?'"[79] Luckily, the woman she questions is sympathetic.[80] Against all odds, Trini manages to register her baby. Portillo Trambley writes, "Thank you, God — thank you, clerk — it was all over. Her son's birth had been registered. She walked away unsteadily, the weight of the baby in her arms, the paper held tightly in her hands."[81]

With the birth of her son, Rico Esconde, Trini is able to emigrate legally into the United States, but she does not quickly find the riches she has been looking for. Rather, she is forced once again to live among the poor. Fortunately, Trini is eventually able to find an old man who is willing to sell her his land for a dollar, as long as Trini takes care of him and buries him when he dies. Trini quickly agrees to the man's proposal and soon after the man dies Trini becomes the owner of the property.

In Portillo Trambley's account, undocumented Mexican immigration is represented as a potentially liberating process. Trini's decision to have her baby in the United States must be interpreted as an individual's determination to achieve "freedom" at any cost. Indeed, by coming to the United States, Trini takes control of her destiny, challenging the role that she is expected to play as a poor Mexican woman. Yet her self-actualization as a Mexican immigrant woman, as Hondagneu-Sotelo discusses,[82] is partly due to her husband's abandonment. By leaving her, Tonio forces Trini to become independent and to learn to provide for herself. Whereas braceros come to the United States for adventure, Trini's immigration provides her with an opportunity to escape the traditional cultural ties that oppress her. Once she has been to the United States, she, like other immigrant women, realizes that she would suffer more in Mexico.[83] Yet, like most Mexican immigrants who come to the United States, Trini finds herself yearning for the past, for what she has left behind in Mexico. Still, Trini remains in the United States because of the future, because she does not want Rico and her other American children to grow up in the kind of world she grew up in.

In contrast to Portillo Trambley's *Trini*, Sandra Cisneros's "Woman Hollering Creek" best exemplifies Gloria Anzaldúa's argument that *la mojada* (the undocumented woman) is doubly threatened in this country. Not only does she have to contend with sexual violence, but she is also prey to a sense of physical helplessness."[84] Certainly, "Woman Hollering Creek" can not be said to be about undocumented immigrant experience. The immigrant status of the protagonist, Cleófilas Enriqueta de León Hernández, is not explicitly apparent, although some aspect of her condition is disclosed when she is referred to as "another one of those brides from across the border."[85] Cleófilas's story, however, does reveal the immigrant woman's special susceptibility to abuse when she is made dependent on her husband.

"Woman Hollering Creek" is a story that on its surface seems to suggest against Hondagneu-Sotelo's argument that immigrant women prefer to settle in the United States more than Mexican men. Cleófilas is portrayed as a woman who, after believing in *telenovela* (soap opera) fantasies, is forced to accept the harsh reality that the romantic life she has always hoped for will not be achieved. The man she marries, Juan Pedro Martínez Sánchez, is a Mexican immigrant who lives in Seguín, Texas. On one of his trips back to Mexico, he courts Cleófilas and asks for her hand.

After Cleófilas and Juan Pedro get married, they travel to Texas, where Cleófilas is forced to live isolated and alone, the beautiful life she had imagined unrealized. Soon, Cleófilas and Juan Pedro have a child. It is after this happens that Cleófilas's innocence finally gives way to a more cynical view of the world. It is Juan Pedro's physical abuse that convinces Cleófilas finally to leave him.[86]

By leaving her husband, Cleófilas asserts a willingness to control her own destiny. It is another woman, a Texana by the name of Felice, who arranges to sneak Cleófilas away from her husband's tyranny. This act represents Cleófilas's coming into a new level of consciousness where survival is more important than maintaining tradition. In fact, Cleófilas's feelings about the woman who helps her escape reflect her feelings about her own action. As Cisneros writes, "everything about this woman, this Felice, amazed Cleófilas. The fact that she drove a pickup. A pickup, mind you, but when Cleófilas asked if it was her husband's, she said she didn't have a husband."[87] As Hondagneu-Sotelo has observed of immigrant women, it is the network between Cleófilas and Felice that helps Cleófilas subvert her husband's authority.[88] Thus her return to Mexico is not as much a return to her old way of life as it is a necessary transition between her dependence on Juan Pedro and freedom.

Narratives like Portillo Trambley's *Trini* and Sandra Cisneros's "Woman Hollering Creek" are significant because they offer complicated portrayals of immigration that romanticize neither Mexico nor the United States. These narratives do not primarily explore questions of class, ethnic identity, racism, or nationalism, but rather the social mechanics of gender stratification as they pertain to the experience of Mexican immigrants who come to the United States. As such, these narratives offer invaluable portraits of the kinds of realities that Mexican immigrant women and men face in their struggle to survive in the United States.

Although Chicana/o and Mexican narratives give voice to similar immigrant experiences that Mexican bracero narratives also chronicle, they tend to draw opposite conclusions about what immigration means, conclusions that justify permanent versus temporary migration to the United States.[89] In other words, discernible and distinct narrative patterns characterize the stories of immigration written by Chicanas and Chicanos versus Mexican authors. Whereas Mexican bracero narratives of immigration portray temporary immigrants in tragi-heroic terms —braceros and *ilegales* (undocumented workers) are either classical heroes or melodramatic anti-heroes—in Chicana and Chicano narratives, prominent immigrant figures such as Trini and Little Earnie tend to be those whose immigration to the United States is permanent. In other words, while Mexican narratives of immigration focus on the racial/ethnic and class struggles that Mexican immigrants experience while in the United States, Chicana and Chicano narratives of immigration concentrate their attention on the redefinition of identity, on the constant adjustments that Mexicans who are now living in the United States need to negotiate their new cultural surroundings.

The Problematics of Writing about Mexican Immigration: Hierarchies of Status

An examination of Victor Villaseñor's immigrant novel, *Rain of Gold* (1991), suggests that Chicana/o stories of immigration are quite sensitive to questions of immigrant status, that the anonymity of undocumented immigrant experience is protected not because of ethical conventions, but because exposing such status may mean revealing the author's own subjectivity to the issue. But by not addressing the legacy of undocumented immigration that Chicanas and Chicanos are a part of, Chicana/o authors risk establishing what already exists in the criticism: a hierarchy of status and power relationships where the "citizen" subject carries greater agency than the undocumented Mexican immigrant ancestor.

Specifically, there is no textual evidence that *Rain of Gold* is a story of undocumented immigration. It is, however, a factual chronicle of where and how Villaseñor's ancestors came from, a story that deeply involves the Mexican immigrant experience. The story not only focuses on events that motivated the protagonist's parents to cross the border, but also on the ordeals that they had to face as they adjusted to their new life in the United States. By not addressing his parents' immigrant status, Villaseñor seems to attribute a pejorative meaning to undocumented immigrant heritage and consequently sets up a hierarchy of status where being a citizen is valued more than being an immigrant. Such a construction of value, exercised by an author who contends, "The people in this story are real. The places are true. And the incidents did actually happen,"[90] exemplifies how the Mexican immigrant subject comes to occupy a different discursive space even within the same narratives as Chicana/o subjects. Thus *Rain of Gold* represents a good example of the way that undocumented immigrant subjects are codified into the subtexts of Chicano narratives and are kept quiet by a pattern of silences and omissions about their experience.

Rain of Gold tells the inspirational story of two immigrant families: Juan

Salvador Villaseñor's and Lupe Gomez's. The narrative depicts different episodes of Lupe's and Juan Salvador's lives, focusing on crucial and defining moments of their childhood and young adulthood. Their story is related by twenty-five chapters that are structured into five independent books, which themselves represent different perspectives of Villaseñor's parents' preimmigrant and immigrant experience.

It is because of the way that the novel is constructed that questions about immigrant status arise. Villaseñor pays a great deal of attention to crucial moments of his parents' immigrant experience; yet he leaves out the most crucial moment of that experience, the moment that defines his parents as immigrants—the border crossing.

Within the scope of the novel there exists no expression of how immigration laws affected Juan Salvador or Lupe's family. Specifically in the scene where Juan Salvador's family arrives in Ciudad Juárez and waits to cross the border, questions about the crossing experience should arise. The thousands of Mexicans that Juan Salvador sees waiting to cross the border are proof that the border had to be negotiated.[91]

In all probability, Villaseñor's family had no problems crossing the border. One of the findings that Manuel Gamio offered in his ethnographic collection of Mexican-immigration stories of the 1920s, *The Mexican Immigrant: His Life-Story* (1971),[92] was that it was precisely those immigrants who "had no trouble" crossing the border who did not dwell on the issue. The narratives that Manuel Gamio collected reveal that the only time that Mexican immigrants devoted attention to the border was when they were not permitted to cross it or when they were about to be deported.

However, because Juan Salvador's family had to wait to cross the border because there was an obstacle there, it would seem that their crossing was not an uncomplicated one. And yet a full narration of this episode is not completely offered. The significance of this ambiguity is important. Villaseñor's novel *Macho!* (1973),[93] which he interestingly published using a pseudonym, is dedicated to telling the tale of an undocumented immigrant. In that novel, Villaseñor spends three chapters narrating how the protagonist, Roberto García, crosses the border "illegally." That novel centers on a different era of Mexican immigration, but the obstacles that the protagonist faces are similar to the obstacles that Juan Salvador and his mother face when they reach the border. García, like Juan Salvador's family, has to negotiate the border as an obstacle. He, along with his partner and mentor, Juan Aguilar, enlist the aid of smugglers and sneak across the border.

In *Rain of Gold*, there are many opportunities where Juan Salvador's immigration status might have solicited some kind of commentary, either on the part of the characters or the narrator, and yet those discussions do not occur. The implication of Villaseñor's novel is that his parents' crossing and their consequent immigrant experience was one where they had no trouble with immigration authorities. In a story about immigrants, he creates ambiguity by not narrating the border crossing itself. By determining that the border crossing narration is not necessary, Villaseñor is suggesting that the only fact that matters is that the family crossed the border. Of course, suggesting undocumented status is not something that is desirable, especially when the author is talking about his own family. It is not that he is unaware of the issue, because he had no trouble at all discussing it in a historical sense in *Macho!*

Hence, this is the issue that Chicana/o critics need to engage: how do we address undocumented immigration when it has been constructed to have such a pejorative meaning, a meaning that maybe we Chicanos ourselves buy into. If we accept this meaning, then are we not accepting the structures of power that create hierarchies of status?

An example of how these hierarchies of status create stereotypes when they are not contested is presented in the novel *Fronteras*,[94] written by Maximo Espinoza in 1980. In this novel, Espinoza attempts to portray the "authentic story of illegal aliens and their hopeless struggle to survive with dignity in a dangerous world."[95] Apparently, Espinoza sought to capitalize on the increasing significance of undocumented immigration during the late 1970s and early 1980s, a time when "Mexicans again became bandits, blamed for stealing jobs."[96]

The essence of the story is effectively communicated, if not subliminally established, by the painted illustration found on the front cover of the paperback edition. At the center of the illustration stands the figure of a man whom we should assume is the "illegal" protagonist—a stereotypical image of a Mexican immigrant à la Speedy Gonzalez, complete with *huaraches* (sandals), *sombrero* (hat), a *sarape* (blanket) casually thrown over his shoulders, wearing white cotton garments common to turn-of-the-century rural Mexican *peones* (poor peasants). The figure stands with his back to the reader, in the middle of a desert plain, looking toward a distant metropolis—which we must assume is Los Angeles. The message that the illustration conveys is clear: go North and explore riches or stay in Mexico and continue to live a life of deprivation. Moreover, Mexico is symbolically rendered as a dry and desolate red-orange desert, somberly cast by dark shadows at the periphery. The American city, on the other hand, is painted as a majestic collection of skyscrapers built out of solid gold, a glowing mountain of symmetrically organized modern structures. This kind of stereotypical representation of Mexico and of its people, especially as they relate to the United States, seems a product of a narrow-minded imagination. And, sadly, the representations that are contained within the pages of the novel do not deviate too much from what's advertised by the image on the front cover of the book.

In effect, Espinoza's novel is full of stereotypical caricatures of Mexican immigrants and Chicanos. The hierarchies of status that are set up by Espinoza's novel promote the idea that undocumented immigrants and Chicanos constitute separate and distinct groups. Rodolpho Macías is the "illegal alien" who ventures into the United States only to become a victim of Baca, a predatory coyote who travels back and forth across the border ferrying "illegals." Baca, who is Chicano, fleeces Rodolpho and the other "illegals" who contract him to get them across the border.

The social order set up by the novel, however, ignores any positive interaction between Chicanos and undocumented immigrants. The idea that Chicanos may be the children of undocumented immigrants or that they may have even been undocumented themselves is not even considered. Rather, they are presented as a distinct ethnic group. But this is to be expected from *Fronteras*. After all, this is a novel that seeks to exploit the issue. In fact, the writer of the novel himself would doubtlessly be suspected by Chicana/o readers of not being Chicano at all. The references that he makes to Mexican and Chicano culture in the story are inaccurate, if not blatantly stereotypical. First, the "illegals" are represented as crude, overly macho Mexican caricatures—men whose only interest is earning dollars and bedding women. Chicanas and Chicanos are also caricatured: they are naïve barrio activists who do not understand the causes that they professedly advocate; "liberated Chicanas" with "bouncing breasts" and "tight jeans" who care only about cars; or *cholos* (gang members) whose only interest is to protect their barrios.

In spite of its many flaws, Espinoza's novel is not without merit. It represents the dangers implicit in believing that a hierarchy of status actually exists among Chicanas/os and undocumented immigrants. The novel's narrow-minded and misinformed portrayal of Chicana/o and undocumented immigrant interaction serves as a reminder of the ties that bind us—culture. While immigration status may not change for undocumented immigrants, the fluid nature of culture makes it so that some of the characteristics that Espinoza attributes to Chicanas/os ring false. His assumptions that only Chicanas/os drive lowriders, that they speak only English, and that they are the only ones who go to college and attend Chicana/o Studies courses are simplistic. His narrative also suggests that Chicanas/os have been unaffected by policies designed to combat "illegal immigration." In so doing, Espinoza's novel presents a question that must be posed when discussing Chicana and Chicano narratives: should undocumented Mexican immigrants be considered Chicana/o? Not addressing this question would negate the essential power that Chicana and Chicano narrative represents, the power to redefine "American" experience from a position of historical marginality. In essence, the voices of undocumented immigrant subjects present in Chicana and Chicano narratives should be read, understood, and discussed as a fundamental part of Chicano experience.

Postscript: The Undocumented Author Speaks

Narrative representation refers to the point of view or focus by which a story is related.[97] As such, in terms of his or her own view, the undocumented immigrant's narrative has seldom been articulated, and when it has, it has mostly been in the form of short testimonies or interviews that have been appropriated mainly to render anthropological or sociological views of undocumented immigrant culture.[98] There exists no set space—save oral discourse—where undocumented immigrant stories are routinely offered by the protagonists of those stories themselves. One notable exception is Ramón "Tianguis" Pérez's *Diary of an Undocumented Immigrant* (1991),[99] a story of an undocumented worker's experience of struggling to eke out a living as an unwanted immigrant in the United States.

Pérez's book is significant because it sheds much light on the inherent problems associated with the act of writing as an undocumented immigrant. First, the actual veracity of the autobiography cannot be verified, so there is no assurance that Pérez's testimony will be believed. Although the editors make sure to point out that "this is the true story," they also note that "this is Ramón 'Tianguis' Pérez's first book. Arte Público Press knows little more of his life than is contained herein."[100] Another problem associated with legitimizing the text as an actual undocumented immigrant representation has to do with the fact that the book has been translated. At times, the translation by Dick J. Reavis seems too literal and one suspects that some of the nuance of Pérez's observations might be lost in the process; for example, when Pérez states that "the people I encounter in the streets are all Hispanics, but meeting them doesn't give me much pleasure because a lot of them are walking around looking for work,"[101] it is clear that Pérez is alluding to *hispanos* (Spanish-speaking individuals who seem to be of Latin American origin). Pérez is not making any reference to "Hispanic" political conservatives, a connotation that the label has achieved in recent times, especially among Chicanas and

Chicanos. Although the label carries political implications that Pérez might have not intended to connote, it is, nonetheless, used in the translation.

Pérez's book tells a story that does not seek to romanticize the life of undocumented immigrants or their relationships to Chicanos, but rather attempts to assert itself in the midst of adversity. In the first section of the book, Pérez narrates his difficulty in crossing the border, as he chronicles: once when he first arrives at the border, and then after he is deported. Once in the United States, Pérez struggles to find a job, at first in Texas and then in California, having to procure such things as a false social security card. He narrates events that to most of us would seem mundane, but that to him become overwhelming obstacles.

Pérez's achievement is that he articulates key situations that enable the reader to appreciate the undocumented immigrant's "voiceless" condition. From the beginning, Pérez gives details about the immigrant's fears and aspirations. He writes, "we don't come here because we like it," [102] thus highlighting that the motivation behind the immigrant's decision to cross the border has nothing to do with a desire for amusement.[103] Pérez's confessions are emblematic not just of his own personal situation but also of the situations that other Mexican immigrants have faced. He gives descriptions of immigrants that are usually represented only by sociological treatises. He asserts, almost matter-of-factly, that his village has become dependent on undocumented immigration in order to survive.

What Pérez demonstrates is the particular way that undocumented immigrants see the world. Their actions are based on necessity, not fancy, and the way that they interrelate with others is determined by how much they are willing to reveal about themselves. Thus, undocumented immigrants are not necessarily suspicious of or hidden from everyone; they recognize each other. Moreover, undocumented immigrants, Pérez shows, help each other out, whether by lending each other money or helping each other find jobs and/or places to stay.

The Diary of an Undocumented Immigrant reveals much about what it means to live as an undocumented immigrant in the United States. It is one of the few works that chronicles the fear that immigrants have felt about the immigration law of 1986, which pales in comparison to the recent anti-immigrant legislative proposals that have been engendered by California's Proposition 187. According to Pérez, fear of the Immigration Reform and Control Act of 1986 motivated him to go back to Mexico. But he does not leave before making sure that his "voice" is heard and acknowledged. Pérez writes, "I've known several Chicanos with whom, joking around, I've reminded them that their roots are in México. But very few of them see it that way." [104] And the question is *why?* As Madrid-Barela has observed, "bracerismo (legal and illegal) is a matter of monumental difficulty. It will continue to affect and probably divide the entire Chicano community between those who call for an open border and those who call for a closed one."[105] What must be noted is that at an age when constitutional proposals are offered that would seek to deny citizenship to the American-born children of undocumented immigrant parents, it is easier than ever to imagine that undocumented immigration has never been a part of Chicano experience.

Notes

1. A recently published popular book on immigration that argues that the United States should continue to take measures against immigration such as California's Proposition 187 is Peter Brimelow's *Alien Nation: Common Sense About America's Immigration Disaster* (New York: Random House, 1995).

2. This statement appears in the preface to the book Antonia Castañeda-Shular, Tomás Ybarra-Frausto, and Joseph Sommers edited as *Literatura Chicana: Texto y contexto* (Englewood Cliffs: Prentice Hall, 1972), p. xxii.

3. This comment may be found in the introduction to Simmen's *North of the Rio Grande: The Mexican-American Experience in Short Fiction* (New York: Mentor, 1992), p. 1.

4. Juan Bruce-Novoa, "Chicano Literary Space: Cultural Criticism/Cultural Production," in *Retrospace: Collected Essays on Chicano Literature* (Houston: Arte Público Press, 1990), p. 172.

5. Kanellos makes this assertion on page 8 of his "Introducción" to Daniel Venegas's *Las aventuras de Don Chipote* (México: Secretaría de Educación Pública, 1984).

6. Nicolas Kanellos, "A Socio-Historic Study of Hispanic Newspapers in the United States," in *Recovering the U.S. Hispanic Literary Heritage*, ed. Ramón Gutiérrez and Genaro Padilla (Houston: Arte Público Press, 1993), p. 114.

7. Venegas, *Las aventuras*, p. 36.

8. Ibid., p. 23.

9. Ibid., pp. 44–45.

10. Ibid., p. 155.

11. *Don Chipote* is also a very nationalistic narrative; however, nationalism is posited as a response to the danger that Don Chipote and other Mexican immigrants face in losing their loyalty for Mexico to the United States.

12. Kanellos, "A Socio-Historic Study of Hispanic Newspapers," p. 114.

13. Kanellos, "Introducción," in *Las aventuras de Don Chipote*, p. 8.

14. Héctor Calderón's "The Novel and the Community of Readers: Rereading Tomás Rivera's *Y no se lo tragó la tierra*," in Héctor Calderón and José David Saldivar's *Criticism in the Borderlands* (Durham: Duke University Press, 1991), p. 103.

15. Ramón Saldívar, *Chicano Narrative: The Dialectics of Difference* (Madison: University of Wisconsin Press, 1990).

16. Ibid., p. 5.

17. See Barbara Harlow, "Sites of Struggle: Immigration, Deportation, Prison, and Exile," in *Criticism in the Borderlands: Studies in Chicano Literature, Culture, and Ideology,* ed. Héctor Calderón and José David Saldívar (Durham: Duke University Press, 1991), pp. 149–163.

18. See Genaro Padilla, "The Mexican Immigrant as *: The (de)Formation of Mexican Immigrant Life Story," in *The Culture of Autobiography: Constructions of Self–Representation,* ed. Robert Folkenflik (Stanford: Stanford University Press, 1993), pp. 125–148.

19. Ibid., p. 138.

20. Ibid., p. 139.

21. John J. Poggie, *Between Two Cultures: The Life of an American-Mexican* (Tucson: University of Arizona Press, 1973).

22. Padilla, "The Mexican Immigrant," p. 148.

23. José Antonio Villarreal, *Pocho* (New York: Doubleday and Company, Inc., 1959, and New York: Anchor Books, 1970).

24. Ernesto Galarza, *Barrio Boy* (Notre Dame: University of Notre Dame Press, 1971).

25. Estela Portillo Trambley, *Trini* (Binghamton: Bilingual Press/Editorial Bilingüe, 1986).

26. Arturo Islas, *Rain God* (Palo Alto: Alexandrian Press, 1984).

27. Sandra Cisneros, *Woman Hollering Creek and Other Stories* (New York: Random House, 1991), pp. 43–56.

28. María Helena Viramontes, *The Moths and Other Stories* (Houston: Arte Público Press, 1985), pp. 61–75.

29. Gloria Anzaldúa, *Borderlands/La Frontera: The New Mestiza* (San Francisco: Spinsters/Aunt Lute Book Company, 1987).

30. On the subject of what the border signifies for Chicanas and Chicanos, see José David Saldívar, *The Dialectics of Our America: Genealogy, Cultural Critique, and Literary History* (Durham: Duke University Press, 1991), pp. 149–153; and Alfred Arteaga, "An Other Tongue," in *An Other Tongue: Nation and Ethnicity in the Linguistic Borderlands* (Durham: Duke University Press, 1994), pp. 9–33.

31. Arteaga, "An Other Tongue," p. 11.

32. Padilla, "The Mexican Immigrant," p. 139.

33. Here, I take my cue from Alex Saragoza. In his 1990 essay "Recent Chicano Historiography: An Interpretive Essay" in *Aztlán* 19, 1, he warns against reductive analyses of Mexican immigration that fail to consider *mexicano* perspectives, p. 34.

34. A third paradigm that could be included here would make reference to those narratives written in English by non-Chicano authors. As a matter of fact, in his essay "Alambristas, Braceros, Mojados, Norteños: Aliens in Aztlán, An interpretive Essay" (*Aztlán* 6,

1 (1975), p. 41), Arturo Madrid utilizes three paradigmatic texts to discuss Mexican un-documented immigration. The text that Madrid cites in order to show how undocumented immigrants are represented by "Anglo" American writers is *Wetback* by Claude Garner (Notre Dame: University of Notre Dame, 1947).

35. Agustín Yañez, *Al filo del agua* (México: Editorial Porrúa, 1947).

36. Carlos Fuentes, *La región más transparente* (México: Fondo de Cultura Económica, 1958).

37. Luis Spota, *Murieron a mitad del río*, 4th ed. (México: Editorial Grijalbo, 1948).

38. José de Jesús Becerra González, *El dólar viene del norte* (Guadalajara, México: Gráfica Editorial, 1954).

39. Héctor Raúl Almaza, *Huelga blanca* (México: Academia Potosina de Artes y Ciencias, 1950).

40. Jesús Topete, *Aventuras de un bracero*, 2nd ed. (México: Editora Gráfica Moderna, 1961 reprint of 1948 ed.).

41. Magdalena Mondragón, *Tenemos sed* (México: Revista Mexicana de Cultura, 1956).

42. Herminio Corral Barrera, *Los fabricantes de braceros* (México: Editores Asociados Mexicanos, S.A., 1980).

43. María Herrera-Sobek, *The Bracero Experience: Elitelore versus Folklore* (Los Angeles: UCLA Latin American Center Publications, 1979), p. 30.

44. Spota, *Murieron*, p. 11.

45. Interestingly, like Venegas, Spota also bases his fiction on personal experiences. Much like Venegas's editorializing, Spota interjects that what he narrates is based on the authentic events he has witnessed.

46. Spota, *Murieron*, p. 41.

47. Ibid., p. 42.

48. See Leo Chavez, *Shadowed Lives: Undocumented Immigrants in American Society.* (San Diego: Harcourt Brace Jovanovich College Publishers, 1992), p. 157.

49. Spota, *Murieron*, p. 13.

50. Ibid., p. 53.

51. Ibid.

52. Ibid., p. 223.

53. Topete, *Aventuras de un bracero*, p. 6.

54. Ibid., pp. 31–32.

55. Ibid., p. 52.

56. Ibid.

57. Ibid., p. 53.

58. J. Humberto Robles, *Los desarraigados* (Mexico: Instituto Nacional de Bellas Artes, Departamento de Literatura, 1962).

59. See "Críticas y comentarios acerca de la obra," in J. Humberto Robles's *Los desarrai-*

gados (Mexico: Instituto Nacional de Bellas Artes, Departamento de Literatura, 1962), pp. 159–163.

60. Victor Villaseñor, *Rain of Gold* (Houston: Arte Público Press, 1991).

61. Phillip Ortego, "The Chicano Renaissance," *Social Casework* 52, 5 (May 1971), pp. 294–307.

62. Galarza, *Barrio Boy*, p. 1.

63. Saldívar, *Chicano Narrative*, p. 168.

64. Charles Tatum, "Contemporary Chicano Prose Fiction: A Chronicle of Misery," in *The Identification and Analysis of Chicano Literature*, ed. Francisco Jiménez (New York: Bilingual Press / Editorial Bilingüe, 1979), p. 252.

65. Galarza, *Barrio Boy*, pp. 70–71.

66. Ibid., p. 181.

67. Ibid., p. 182.

68. Ibid., p. 200.

69. Ibid., p. 200.

70. Ibid., p. 207.

71. Ibid., p. 205.

72. Ibid., p. 215.

73. Ibid., p. 239.

74. See Pierrette Hondagneu-Sotelo, *Gendered Transitions: Mexican Experiences of Immigration* (Berkeley: University of California Press, 1994), p. 2.

75. Ibid., p. xxiv.

76. Irene Beltran Hernandez, *Across the Great River* (Houston: Arte Público Press, 1989).

77. Portillo Trambley, *Trini*, p. 188.

78. Ibid., p. 203.

79. Ibid., p. 211.

80. Ibid.

81. Ibid., p. 210.

82. Indeed, on page 12 of *Gendered Transitions*, Hondagneu-Sotelo notes that male migration to the United States has, in part, accelerated the employment of women in Mexico.

83. Ibid., p. 100.

84. Anzaldúa, *Borderlands/La Frontera*, p. 12.

85. Cisneros, *Woman Hollering Creek*, p. 54.

86. Ibid., p. 47.

87. Ibid., p. 55.

88. Hondagneu-Sotelo, *Gendered Transitions*, pp. 72–74.

89. Here exist other prevailing differences between Chicana/o narratives of immigration and those written by Mexican authors. Language is a prime example. Mexican immigrant

narratives are exclusively written in Spanish while Chicana/o narratives of immigration are mostly written in English.

90. Villaseñor, *Rain of Gold*, p. xiii.

91. Ibid., p. 135.

92. Manuel Gamio, *The Mexican Immigrant: His Life-Story* (Chicago: University of Chicago Press, 1931; reprint, Chicago: University of Chicago Press, 1969).

93. Victor Villaseñor, *Macho!* (New York: Bantam Books, 1973; reprint, Houston: Arte Público Press, 1984).

94. Maximo Espinoza, *Fronteras: The Hispanic Experience* (Los Angeles: Holloway House, 1980).

95. Ibid., back cover.

96. Rodolfo Acuña, *Occupied America*, 3rd ed. (New York: Harper & Row, 1981), p. 372.

97. Wallace Martin, *Recent Theories of Narrative* (Ithaca: Cornell University Press, 1986), pp. 142–151.

98. Anthropological and sociological studies on Mexican undocumented immigration have been numerous. Besides Leo Chavez's *Shadowed Lives*, the most prominent among these studies have included Eugene Nelson, *Pablo Cruz and the American Dream: The Experiences of an Undocumented Immigrant from Mexico* (Layton, Utah: Peregrine Smith, 1975); Julián Samora, *Los Mojados: The Wetback Story* (Notre Dame: University of Notre Dame Press, 1971); and Douglass S. Massey, Rafael Alarcón, Jorge Durand, and Humberto Gonzalez, *Return to Aztlán* (Berkeley: University of California Press, 1987).

99. Ramón "Tianguis" Pérez, *Diary of an Undocumented Immigrant* (Houston: Arte Público Press, 1991).

100. Ibid., back cover.

101. Ibid., p. 54.

102. Ibid., p. 84.

103. Ibid., p. 12.

104. Ibid., p. 215.

105. Arturo Madrid-Barela, "Alambristas, Braceros, Mojados, Norteños: Aliens in Aztlán, An Interpretative Essay," *Aztlán* 6 (1975), p. 41.

3

TELLING IMAGES BRACKET THE "BROKEN-PROMISE(D) LAND"

The Culture of Immigration and the Immigration of Culture across Borders

● ● ● ●
● ● ● ●

Victor Alejandro Sorell

We do not recognize capricious frontiers on the Bronze Continent.[1]

The U.S.–Mexican border *es una herida abierta* (is an open wound) where the Third World grates against the first and bleeds. And before a scab forms it hemorrhages again, the lifeblood of two worlds merging to form a third country—a border culture.[2]

The geopolitical wound called "border" cannot stop the cultural undercurrents . . . The "artistic border" is artificial. It shouldn't be there, and it is up to us to erase it.[3]

. . . the indomitable spirit of immigrants, all with a legitimate and traditional right to traverse the land on which they live. For in the end, we are all immigrants, here on this earth for only a flash in time.[4]

Xenophobic Assaults Cast Their Sinister Pall over the Borderland: Culture and Immigration

Subjects of contentious ideological discourse, immigration and culture are inextricably linked. In the great divide between conservative behaviorism and liberal structuralism—where Cornel West locates the debate on race [5]—belongs the strident inquiry concerning immigration. Political philosopher Francis Fukuyama's discussion of immigration, resonating with the abrasive tone of conservative behaviorism, invokes the rhetoric of arch-conservative Patrick J. Buchanan and his right-wing Republican cohorts. [6] They talk of engaging in a cultural war with the object of "tak[ing] back our culture." [7] Fukuyama adds that "they dispute the economic benefits of immigration, but more importantly look upon immigrants as bearers of foreign and less desirable cultural values." [8] This xenophobic attitude "forced the inclusion of a plank in the Republican platform in 1992 calling for the creation of 'structures' to maintain the integrity of America's southern border." [9] That call to repressive action directly implicated Mexicans south and north of la frontera (the border). This chapter revolves principally around these Mexicanas/os and Chicanas/os, and the manner in which so many visual artists among them address the multifaceted issue of immigration as it impacts their lives.

Another far-reaching xenophobic plank, California's Proposition 187, emerged in the reelection campaign of Governor Pete Wilson. A so-called "initiative measure" (dubbed the S.O.S./Save Our State initiative), Proposition 187 was designed to "prevent illegal aliens in the United States from receiving benefits or public services in the State of California." [10] The proposition—which presumes to ascribe to those it chooses the dubious status of "illegals," while taking for granted the "legal" standing of others—passed by a 3–2 margin, or by 59 percent of the voters, on November 8, 1994. It became the most recent manifestation of a trend that has a protracted history. Recalling the late nineteenth century activist Jane Addams—especially Hull House, [11] the celebrated settlement shelter that she opened in 1889 in an impoverished neighborhood on Chicago's West Side—Frances Perkins, U.S. secretary of labor from 1933 until 1945, commented that Addams "discerned and revealed the beauty of the cultural life and spiritual value of the immigrant at the time when nothing was so despised and unconsidered in American life as the foreigner." [12] In 1995 that unsavory time is here again with unprecedented vengeance, presaged early in Bill Clinton's presidency in an overtly combative message of July 1993, announcing his package of immigration reforms: "We cannot and will not surrender our border to those who wish to exploit our history of compassion and justice."[13] In this climate, it comes as no surprise that a recent issue of *U.S. News and World Report* begins a brief "Outlook" piece, "Trouble on the Mexican Border," with particularly alarming and trenchant lines: "The politically charged drive to curb illegal immigration may be coming at a serious price: beatings, shootings, rapes and deaths of aliens at the hands of the U.S. Border Patrol."[14]

Just how ugly does it get? Picture a white-haired couple weeding their garden and advocating machine-gunning down a few undocumented immigrants at the border as a warning! These sinister gardeners, portrayed in *Natives: Immigrant Bashing on the Border*, a documentary film produced in 1992 by Jesse Lerner and Scott Sterling, would pluck human lives as easily as they pull weeds! Spilled blood, so vividly pictured in Anzaldúa's epigraph (one of four epigraphic inscriptions introducing this chapter), colors much of the untold story of immigration.

Affirming and Reclaiming Cultural Mestizaje

Where conservative behaviorists would demean a blending of native with immigrant cultures, finding in that *mestizaje* (mixture) a contaminated or diluted product, historian Anthony Heilbut reclaims for cultural mestizaje its rightful place. After all, what do these isolationist conservatives infer by "our culture"? Hasn't North American culture always been an amalgam of cultural strains? Do Buchanan and other reactionaries know their own history? They would do well to review the record, weighing the thoughtful observations of informed cultural historians. Robert F. Berkhofer, Jr. recognizes the incredible multiplicity of cultures of which the early Americas, their own plurality underscored, were constituted:

> The first residents of the Americas were by modern estimates divided into at least two thousand cultures and more societies, practiced a multiplicity of customs and lifestyles, held an enormous variety of values and beliefs, spoke numerous languages mutually unintelligible to the many speakers, and did not conceive of themselves as a single people—if they knew about each other at all. By classifying all these many peoples as Indians, Whites categorized the variety of cultures and societies as a single entity for the purposes of description and analysis, thereby neglecting or playing down the social and cultural diversity of Native Americans then—and now—for the convenience of simplified understanding. To the extent that this conception denies

101

or misrepresents the social, linguistic, cultural, and other differences among the peoples so labeled, it lapses into stereotype.[15]

Conservative behaviorists, one deduces, allude to an illusory, stereotypical and monolithic cultural entity of their own making.

Anthony Heilbut, in a study of the contributions to America by European immigrant artists and intellectuals, foregrounds visual artists, writers—including playwrights—and publishers under the suggestive heading, "Entrepreneurs of Images." He cites photographer Andreas Feininger's photos of New York, claiming that they "have become the definitive renderings of America's greatest city."[16] Earlier, Heilbut injects an especially far-reaching pronouncement: "Americans were trained to look at objects by foreigners, through foreign eyes."[17] Heilbut sides with Jane Addams and cultural mestizaje, underscoring how a nurturing cross-cultural symbiosis stimulates cultural efflorescence.

"Border-Crossed" Foreigners in Their Native Land

Carey McWilliams, historian and one-time editor of *The Nation*, has explained the relatively unique status of Mexicans viewed as northbound "immigrants":

> Historically Mexicans have never emigrated to the Southwest: they have simply moved "North from Mexico." They did not ask to become citizens; they were made citizens by default, under pressure, and as a result of conquest . . . Living in a region which is geographically and historically a projection of their "homeland," and having struck deep roots in this region, the Spanish-speaking are not like the typical European immigrant minority in the United States. They did not cross an ocean; they moved north across a mythical border. They were annexed by conquest and their cultural autonomy was guaranteed by a treaty. They resemble, therefore, certain suppressed national minorities in Europe, although a closer parallel would be the French-Canadians in the Province of Québec. There is this all-important difference, however, that the border between the United States and Mexico is one of the most unreal borders in the world; it unites rather than separates the two peoples.[18]

As early as 1856, in a speech delivered to the California Senate, Californio Pablo de la Guerra of Santa Barbara refers to those Mexicanos—who, in a manner of speaking, were "crossed" by a "mythical border"—as "foreigners in their own land." [19] Even earlier, in an ironic turnabout, Juan Nepomuceno Seguín—who had fought against Mexico in the Texas Revolution and served as mayor of San Antonio, Texas—joined the Texano refugees who fled to Mexico in 1842. Succumbing "to the wickedness of a few men, whose imposture was favored by their origin and recent domination over the country," [20] Seguín perceived himself as a "victim . . . a foreigner in my native land." [21] An appropriately indignant Chicana response to this unsettling marginality is embodied in Yolanda M. López's biting and eloquent offset lithograph, "Who's the Illegal Alien, Pilgrim?" (1978/81) (see fig. 3.1). Encoded with the gestural rhetorical language of artist James Flagg's celebrated World War I and World War II recruitment posters,[22] López's declamation is no less engaging or topical. Hers is an ideological confrontation aimed at recovering and reclaiming an unedited historical record. The point of her challenging interrogation is to stimulate minds and marshall militant attitudes against a xenophobic front. Others have heeded her message. Margo Vinicio González would incorporate Yolanda's print in her *ofrenda* (offering)/installation altar created in 1988 at the Hostos Community College in New York City on the occasion of a "Día de los Muertos" (Day of the Dead) observance. In May 1995 Abigail González paid homage to the same near-canonic work in "Para Servirle a Usted" (At Your Service), a mixed-media piece she contributed to "187: With or Without You," an exhibition mounted in response to Proposition 187 at Chicago's Malcolm X College.

Highlights of U.S. Immigration History, Immigrant-Artists, and the Artistic Theme of Immigration

The late Cynthia Jaffee McCabe, curator of painting and sculpture at the Smithsonian Institution's Hirshhorn Museum and Sculpture Garden, "originated the idea . . . and assumed . . . major responsibility for [the] preparation and presentation" of the exhibition "The Golden Door: Artist-Immigrants of America, 1876–1976." [23] This brief acknowledgment by Abram Lerner, the Hirshhorn Museum's director, cannot begin to do justice to the courageous curatorial vision that gave such long-overdue and substantive attention to immigrant-artists. The artists were subsumed within three periods, grouped chronologically according to dates of arrival in North America. The earliest all-male contingent arrived between 1876 and 1929 and included Alexander Archipenko, Marcel Duchamp, Mark Rothko, Eero Saarinen, Ben Shahn, Joseph Stella, and Max Weber, all major figures in the history of U.S. art and architecture. The second group of artists immigrated between 1930

Figure 3.1. Yolanda M. López, "Who's the Illegal Alien, Pilgrim?" (1978/ 81), offset lithograph. Resisting conventional readings of U.S. history, López demands a much-needed review of the "silent" record.

and 1945: Josef Albers, Walter Gropius, George Grosz, Jacques Lipchitz, Agnes Martin, Ludwig Mies van der Rohe, and László Moholy-Nagy numbered among the newly settled master artists. The final host of artists represented in the exhibition relocated between 1946 and 1976, and included Max Beckmann, Christo, Chryssa, Naum Gabo, Marisol, and Lucas Samaras.

What this landmark exhibit did not do was advance the theme of immigration itself through a majority of the artwork it presented. Only occasional pieces resonated with nuances of the subject, seemingly underscoring Lerner's own bias that "such provocative social and historical issues [do not belong] in the domain of a museum of art." [24] Notable exceptions were Arnold Genthe's turn-of-the-century photographs of Chinese immigrants; Joseph Stella's drawings of Italian immigrants dating from the same period; as well as his collages of 1938, incorporating newspaper reports from the *New York Daily News* concerning the Nazi deportation of Polish Jews; and a couple of Ben Shahn's striking paintings on the subject of Nicola Sacco and Bartolomeo Vanzetti, Italian immigrants and avowed anarchists charged and indicted in 1920 for their alleged robbery and murder of a paymaster in Massachusetts. From Shahn's series entitled "The Passion of Sacco and Vanzetti" (1931–32), consisting of twenty-three small gouache paintings and two large mural-like panels, the Hirshhorn show featured a small gouache of Vanzetti shown seated, and a large moving panel portraying the ashen-hued, martyred immigrant-anarchists in their coffins.

Notwithstanding the paucity of imagery explicitly concerned with immigration, the exhibition catalog prepared by McCabe more than redeemed the show's limitations by its inclusion of a one-hundred-year chronology from 1876 until 1976, subdivided into the areas of "General History," "U.S. Immigration History," and "Fine Arts History." [25] Early on, it referred readers to two photographers not included in the exhibition but critically important for their documentation of immigrants. A citation for the year 1890 named Danish-born Jacob A. Riis and referred to the publication of his indignant book, *How the Other Half Lives*, which exposed and indicted the living conditions of the very poor—including scores of immigrants—in New York's abysmal tenements, later providing the basis of social reform.[26] Under the year 1905, sociologist Lewis W. Hine was mentioned for his photographs addressing conditions at Ellis Island and in the tenements, factories, and mines of working America. The chronology added that the term "picture story" was first used in connection with Hine's pioneering photojournalism, which for him "represented a form of concrete evidence for his university studies." [27] The very title of an exhibition held in 1942 in New York City, "First Papers of Surrealism," invoked an immigrant's first citizenship papers.

The chronology's coverage of key dates and happenings in U.S. immigration history affords the present study an expansive and comparative backdrop. Reviewing this tumultuous history, one finds virulent xenophobia before and after the founding of Hull House. The Chinese Exclusion Act of 1881 was directed against Chinese laborers; renewed indefinitely in 1902 (a year also marked by a record number of deportations), the act wouldn't be repealed until 1943. Barely five years after Addams and Ellen Gates Starr founded Hull House, the Immigration Restriction League, begun in 1894, sought the reduction of southern and eastern European immigrants. In 1903, a year after the renewal of the Chinese Exclusion Act, Emma Lazarus's legendary and compassionate poem, "The New Colossus" (written in 1883), was engraved on a bronze plaque and affixed to the Statue of Liberty's pedestal. In that same year, the Committee on Immigration, which was formed by five Jewish societies, planned a massive protest in New York, prompted by the increasing deportation of "aliens," and amidst continuing allegations of discrimination, irregularities, and improprieties committed by immigration offi-cials. How hollow French sculptor Frédéric-Auguste Bartholdi's Lady Liberty and her poetic evocations would become over the years is part of the ensuing narrative in this essay.

No less tenacious and pernicious than the supporters of the Chinese Exclu-sion Act were those who supported protracted efforts to enact a literacy bill. First sponsored in 1896 by Senator Henry Cabot Lodge of Massachusetts, the bill pro-vided for the exclusion of any immigrant not able to read forty words in any lan-guage. Vetoed through 1915, the literacy requirement was finally incorporated into the Immigration Act of 1917 along with a call for the exclusion of peoples from most of Asia and the Pacific. Twelve years earlier, in 1905, the Japanese and Korean Exclusion League had been formed in San Francisco, followed a year later by the establishment of the Bureau of Immigration and Naturalization under the Depart-ment of Commerce and Labor, and in 1907 by the congressional formation of the Dillingham Commission to investigate immigration. In 1920, the so-called "red scare" reached its height, and raids initiated by U.S. Attorney General Alexander Palmer against alleged radicals and subversives filled Ellis Island with "deportable aliens." The Quota/Johnson Act of 1921 had the intended effect of reversing the trend of immigration by southern and eastern Europeans. Some three years later, the Immigration Act of 1924 (known also as the Quota Act and the Johnson-Reed Act) was enacted on May 26 as a permanent restrictive quota law that failed to distinguish between immigrants and refugees. In 1929 the National Origins Quota System became fully operative, severely limiting the total number of immigrants. A year later, in the face of the severe Depression, President Hoover initiated a provi-sion—to become known as the Likely Public Charge Clause of the Immigration Act of 1917—denying visas to all "aliens" not possessing considerable sums of money. "Your poor," welcomed by Lazarus in her poem, were suddenly and officially unwelcome beneath the "mighty woman with a torch . . . Mother of Exiles." Between 1931 and 1932, immigration fell while deportation climbed. Two to three years later, in that space within the second "window of opportunity" noted for artists in McCabe's exhibition, approximately 1,100 refugee artists and architects arrived in the United States. In 1936 the National Coordinating Committee (later to become the National Refugee Service) formed to coordinate and help fund various agencies assisting immigrants. The year 1940 was a pivotal one for immigration law with the introduction of the Alien Registration Act and the Nationality Act. The former required fingerprinting and registration of all "aliens" within or seeking to enter the United States. The latter codified and unified most naturalization laws in the country. Furthermore, authority over the Bureau of Immigration and Naturalization was transferred to the Department of Justice at the suggestion of President Roosevelt to ensure "more effective control over aliens." On the one hand, 1943 was an auspicious year for the repeal of the Chinese Exclusion Act, and on the other hand, it was notorious for the violent, race-motivated "zoot-suit riots" in southern California. Not unexpectedly, restrictive immigration legislation—recalling congressional actions at the turn of the century targeting anarchists, epileptics, the "insane," and "professional beggars"—was enacted during the fifties, first through the Internal Security Act (1950) with its expansion of provisions for the exclusion and deportation of "aliens who are potentially dangerous to the national security," and later through the Immigration and Nationality Act (the McCarran-Walter Act) of 1952. That act continued and enlarged upon qualitative restrictions, while a 1954 amendment to the act provided for the expatriation of persons convicted of offenses under sections of the U.S. code relating to rebellion or insurrection, seditious conspiracy, or advocating the overthrow of the government. Interestingly, the act itself claimed the elimination of race and sex as bars to immigration. Curiously, McCabe's chronology was conspicuously silent regarding "Operation Wetback," instituted in 1954 to curb rising "illegal immigration."[28] Her documentation did, of course, take into account the U.S. Senate's adoption of the Civil Rights Act of 1964. McCabe closed with a reference to a 1975 investigation by the Justice Department into the employment of "illegal aliens" in the United States. Journalist Peter Brimelow's chronology in *Alien Nation* ushers his readers into the nineties through Proposition 187.[29] He cites the Refugee Act of 1980, characterizing it as the "first explicit recognition of refugees as a permanent, distinct immigrant stream"; the Immigration Reform and Control Act of 1986, offering "amnesty for many illegal immigrants"; and the Immigration Act of 1990,

Figure 3.2. Guillermo Pulido, "Ballad of the Wetback" (1979), mixed media. Inspired by a *corrido norteño*, a narrative folk ballad popular in south Texas, Pulido inscribes the lyrics on *La Luna*, one of the *lotería* game cards depicted. Courtesy of the artist.

which "further increases legal immigration, [and] institutes [a] small immigration lottery for countries squeezed out by [the] workings of [the] 1965 system."[30]

The discussion that follows—one largely hinging on the iconography and semiotics of immigration as read in the work of Chicana/o and Mexicana/o artists—will have occasion to refer back to the Hirshhorn's invaluable chronology. The Hirshhorn show was supported in part by a subvention from the Balch Institute for Ethnic Studies. Nine years later, in 1985, the Balch would mount its own exhibition, "The American Experience: Contemporary Immigrant Artists,"[31] guest-curated by McCabe herself, which spoke about immigration quite overtly, as the inclusion of "Ballad of the Wetback" (1979), a mixed media work by Mexican-American artist Guillermo Pulido, bore witness (see fig. 3.2). Textual references to *mojados* (wetbacks), *ilegales* (illegals), and a *corrido del mojado* (folk narrative ballad of the wetback), coupled with a partially concealed Mexican flag and *lotería* (game of chance) card invoking *la muerte* (death), all reinforce the lyrical suggestiveness of the title, but withhold what other artists would show as the more tangible signs of suffering endured by "illegal immigrants."

The Iconography and Semiotics of Immigration: An Omnibus of Telling Images

Immigration has long loomed large in the "lived realities"[32] of Chicanas/os and Mexicanas/os alike. This specter, as Carey McWilliams would remind us, has prevailed since Mexicans "moved north across a mythical border . . . were annexed by conquest and their cultural autonomy was guaranteed by a treaty."[33] What McWilliams was alluding to was the Treaty of Guadalupe Hidalgo. Some 147 arduous years later, the treaty's legacy is indeed one of conflict, to borrow Chicano historian Richard Griswold del Castillo's apt characterization.[34] As for the border, it's anything but a "mythical" fabrication in the nineties. Quite to the contrary, it can lacerate with the sting of a razor. The chain link border fence separating San Diego from Tijuana assumes metaphoric function in Terry Allen's public performance project, "Across the Razor," realized between September and October 1994 under the auspices of "in Site 94."[35] The Santa Fe–based artist fitted two vans with roof-mounted platforms that accommodated as many as five people. Driven along the fence on both sides of *la frontera*, the "SITE" vans literally carried the voices of people standing atop the vehicles speaking, reciting poetry, and singing. Projected through microphones, sometimes to the accompaniment of musicians, the performers readily commanded public attention. A translator's presence insured that these calls and responses were understood. Evidently, Allen keenly appreciated the potential for language to heal the "wounds" Anzaldúa and Guillermo Gómez-Peña lament in their writings. Unrestricted by the physicality of the razor, or fence, the sounds transcended nationalities and geopolitical spaces, arguably erasing the border's existence, consistent with Gómez-Peña's exhortation in his introductory epigraph to this chapter. The irony that language cuts both ways, that it can wound as well as heal remains a not-too-subtle subtext in Allen's rhetorical strategy. Las Comadres, a San Diego/Tijuana–based multicultural women's collective, also strives for rapprochement at the border through the catalytic and cathartic possibilities inherent in language. More often than not, a border focus defines the drama of immigration.

Like Las Comadres and Terry Allen, a significant proportion of the visual artists about to be considered likewise bracket the border as they focus on issues

109

of immigration. Collectively, they conceive of la frontera as a near template, layering that basic and ubiquitous building bloc(k)—a "master stencil/trope"—with other related narratives. So described, this type of palimpsest border document is analogous to the experiential maze the immigrants themselves live through in the "broken promise(d) land" north of the border. Congruent with this density, the artists' iconographic and semiotic approaches are not merely satisfied with explicit commentary, but so often are given to allegorical twists and turns.

The range of narratives governing immigration and admittedly tied to the border encompasses a cornucopia of seemingly freestanding and self-contained indices. The triad of geography, land, and ecology is a natural extension of the border. Migrant workers or farmworkers (*campesinos*) and undocumented workers (also referred to variously as "illegals" and "illegal aliens") also fit within the parameters of the border envelope. The Immigration and Naturalization Service (INS), "the law," the police, clandestine acts of surveillance, and authoritarian brutality are similarly contained. Lastly, culture, language, religion, identity, patriotism, human rights, race, class, and gender are those more inclusive rubrics frequently inscribed with the force of a thumbprint on the face of the border, their respective imprints stamped at once on the "flesh" of immigration. That "skin" bears yet another and obverse "tattoo," that of deportation—or repatriation, as the authorities would have it more genteelly put.

The master stencil/trope of the border does not invite simple analysis, nor is it easily divided into discrete categories or themes. Rather, the palimpsest would be best likened to a true fresco surface where the imagery of the painted mural is bonded to its physical ground not as a superficial layer, but as part and parcel of the ground itself. Consequently, the iconographic and semiotic story of immigration unfolds as a multifaceted account composed of inextricably linked narratives. That is to say, reading any one narrative is tantamount to reading all the narratives at once.

Overwhelmingly, the images enlisted below indict U.S. immigration policies, notably the latest manifestation in the form of Proposition 187. However, to maintain that no artist ever equivocates or elicits equivocation on the subject is certainly to overstate the case. Even humor can color the occasional image. Not unlike the Hirshhorn and Balch exhibitions, the projects mounted by the Border Art Workshop (Taller de Arte Fronterizo), documented in two catalog-like publications,[36] and "La Frontera/The Border: Art About the Mexico/United States Border Experience,"[37] a groundbreaking collaborative project of the Museum of Contemporary Art in San Diego and the city's Centro Cultural de la Raza, have mapped what previously had been little charted. The border has emerged as a remarkably charged expressive zone, with artists negotiating its troubled waters through a plethora of barbed images.

Artists Respond to the Language of Immigration: A Duel of Words and Images Waged across Borders

In the absence of a crisp thematic framework, discourse becomes a viable means for organizing the core segment of this essay. From the Treaty of Guadalupe Hidalgo to Proposition 187, immigration policies directed at Mexicanas/os and Chicanas/os have been proposed and enacted through codified spoken and written language. Revealingly, the actual language of that legislation, and, for that matter, the mere fact that the legislation is linguistically rendered, is arguably among the least scrutinized aspects of immigration vis à vis culture.

What Allen and Las Comadres have in common with so many other like-minded artists engaged in addressing issues of immigration is their discursive approach involving a deliberate conflation of verbal and nonverbal imagery. That the proverbial picture is worth so many hundreds of words foregrounds a long-standing relationship between words and images. Together, that picture is worth a host of words, and those words that would be pictures become so much more persuasive than either medium could be standing alone. Given that the goal of these artists is ultimately to inform public opinion and foment sentiments similar to their own, is it any wonder that they would marshall an arsenal of pictures and words wedded together as Yolanda M. López has? What better means through which to undermine the discursive foundation of immigration policy than a visual culture at once discursive and trenchant? These rhetorical questions find an answer in the premise that the duel of words and images waged across borders involves the audacious and creative cooptation of the dominant culture's systemic codes.

THE ARTISTS SURVEYED

Beyond Terry Allen, Las Comadres, Abigail González, Margo Vinicio González, Yolanda M. López, and Guillermo Pulido, some seventy-seven other individual artists, artist groups, and their collaborators will be surveyed. Named alphabetically, they are Mireya Acierto, Lalo Alcaraz, Felipe Almada, Carlos Almaraz (with the Third Street Gang), Carmen Amato, Aaron Anish, David Avalos, Eric Avery, James Avila, Judith Baca, Santa Contreras Barraza, Antonio Bernal, Border Art

Workshop (BAW/TFA), Robert C. Buitrón, José Antonio Burciaga, Cristina Cárdenas, Barbara Carrasco, Yreina Cervántez, Enrique Chagoya, Esther Cinet (TGM), Carlos Cortéz-Koyokuikatl, Alfredo de Batuc, Amador de Lira, Aurelio Díaz, Miguel Gandert, Rupert García, Richard Godinez, Mauricio Gómez (TGM), Jesús Gómez G., Guillermo Gómez-Peña, Isela Guerrero (TGM), Ester Hernández, Emily Hicks, Louis Hock, Graciela Iturbide, Luis Jiménez, Eduardo Juárez (TGM), Andrew Kong Knight, Richard Lou, Jesús Macarena-Avila, Ralph Maradiaga, Cheech Marín, César Augusto Martínez, Amalia Mesa-Bains, Genaro Molina, Malaquías Montoya, Florencio Morales, Sylvia Orozco, Rubén Ortíz, Amado Peña, M. Esther Tapia Picón, Johanna Poethig, Juan Hector Ponce, "F. P.," Armando Rascón, Marcos Raya, Pedro Rodríguez, Elvia Rodríguez-Ochoa, Roberto Salas, Lillian M. Salcido, Robert Sánchez, Gilbert Sánchez-Luján, Juan Sánchez R., Carlos Santístevan, Michael Schnorr (with MECHA), Domingo Segura, Ernest Silva, Elizabeth Sisco, José Cruz Soria, Eloy Tarcisio, Eloy Torres, Michael Tracy, Rudy Treviño, Norma Urenda (TGM), Eugenia Vargas, Alex Webb, and René Yañez.

A DUEL OF WORDS AND IMAGES

The Amerindian protagonist in Yolanda M. López's rhetorically titled "Who's the Illegal Alien, Pilgrim?" angrily crumples the papers imprinted with "immigration plans." The language of this unjust legislation is no longer legible, having been rendered symbolically silent. It no longer matters. In Armando Rascón's "Artifact with Three Declarations of Independence" (1991), three textual panels constitute the lower register of his mixed-media installation (see fig. 3.3). In the context of his piece, language functions not only as an ingredient but as the one ingredient of paramount and profound significance. Reading from left to right, the complete text for "El Plan de Delano" appears as the first panel. The central panel is inscribed with the Plan of La Raza Unida formulated on October 28, 1967, in the border town of El Paso, Texas.[38] The right-most panel reproduces Chicano poet Alurista's eloquent preamble[39] to one of El Movimiento's most influential cultural statements, "El Plan Espiritual de Aztlán."

Delano, a town in California's San Joaquin Valley, became the focal point of César Chávez's organizing of agricultural labor and of the subsequent grape strike from 1965 through 1970. The Plan of Delano was a manifesto and public declaration issued in March 1966 by farmworkers who marched to the state capital in Sacramento to "dramatize the inequities suffered by farmworkers."[40] Snippets of language from this plan are highly revelatory:

Figure 3.3. Armando Rascón, "Artifact with Three Declarations of Independence" (1991), mixed media. Rascón's complex imagery reminds readers and viewers that a defiant Chicana/o rhetorical strategy conflating words and images is highly charged and resonant. Photograph by Ben Blackwell, courtesy of the artist.

gathered in Pilgrimage . . . in penance for all the failings of Farm Workers as free and sovereign men . . . the propositions we have formulated to end the injustice that oppresses us . . . our sweat and our blood have fallen on the land to make other men rich . . . forced migration . . . subhuman conditions . . . We have suffered unnumbered ills and crimes in the name of the Law of the land. . . . the basic brutality of stoop labor . . . They have imposed hungers on us, and now we hunger for justice. We draw strength from the very despair in which we have been forced to live. WE SHALL ENDURE! . . . We seek the support of all political groups, and the protection of the government, which is also our government. . . . At the head of the Pilgrimage we carry the Virgin of Guadalupe because she is ours, all ours, Patroness of the Mexican people.

Overall, the text is inscribed with a strident religiosity, one circumscribed by the farmworkers' "pilgrimage," their "penance," and their abiding faith in "La Guadalupana." These are also people who identify with the land and who have experienced forced migration and the brutality of stoop labor. Admittedly drawing strength from the very despair in which they have been forced to live, these obviously patriotic farmworkers still acknowledge the government as their government. The farmworkers are decrying the system — especially the so-called "law of the land" — but are attempting to change that flawed system through its own rules.

"Strong enforcement of all sections of The Treaty of Guadalupe Hidalgo" is a demand under point six of "El Plan de La Raza Unida." This invocation of the treaty negotiated between Mexico and the U.S. in February 1848 to end the Mexican–U.S. War also serves as an admonition in good faith to those who would violate the terms of that agreement. That there was ample provocation for such cautionary advice is made clear under point seven: "We are outraged by and demand an end to police harassment, discrimination and brutality inflicted on La Raza." Such language from El Paso suggests the strong possibility that this kind of mistreatment is inflicted on immigrants at the border crossing.

Alurista's combative preamble to "The Spiritual Plan of Aztlán" (delivered by fellow poet Rodolfo "Corky" Gonzales on March 31, 1969, on the occasion of the first National Chicano Youth Conference held in Denver, Colorado, under the auspices of Gonzales's Crusade for Justice) is a clarion call to Chicanas/os to gather in solidarity under a nationalist banner: "the brutal 'Gringo' invasion of our territories . . . We, the Chicano, inhabitants and civilizers of the northern land of

114

Aztlán, from whence came our forefathers, reclaiming the land of their birth . . .
Aztlán belongs to those who plant the seeds, water the fields, and gather the crops,
and not to the foreign Europeans. *We do not recognize capricious frontiers on the
Bronze Continent.* With our heart in our hands and our hands in the soil, We
Declare the Independence of our Mestizo Nation . . . "[41]

Here is this essay's foremost epigraphic inscription alluding to the "capricious" construct referred to as the Mexico–U.S. border and a hubris-filled paean
to another construction, Aztlán.

Its textual density noted, Armando Rascón's work reasserts its visual essence.
Surmounting the three "Declarations of Independence," the artist has assembled
twelve found photographs. In that format, the work appeared in the exhibition
"Mistaken Identities," co-curated by Abigail Solomon-Godeau and Constance
Lewallen. Writing about the installation for the catalog, Solomon-Godeau describes the images: "Assembled here are twelve 'found' photographs, framed as
found, including dust and marks of age and neglect. With the exception of the four
portrait snapshots, the pictures consist of familiar stereotypes of 'Mexicanness'—
the bullfight, the 'native' market, the grizzled campesino, the richly adorned seño-
rita, the Zorro-like silhouette, and so forth." [42] With considerable acuity, she then
relates these pictures to the words in the Declarations, and, in turn, to the viewer's
experience of that conflation:

> Counterpointed in Rascón's installation is, on the one hand, the im-
> age world of cultural stereotype—what could be called the Gringo
> imaginary—mingled with modest, vernacular examples of self-
> representation (such as the snapshot portrait of the campesino
> couple)—and on the other, the actual process of political articula-
> tion and political/cultural self-definition. It is the space between
> these two representational "sets" that can be said to constitute the
> viewer's share. This space operates as a kind of discursive ellipsis,
> dividing the domain of conventional and stereotypic representation
> (in which the Chicano or Mexican exists as object) from the dec-
> larations of political agency, in which the participants collectively as-
> sert their identity as subjects.[43]

Rascón's complex and variegated verbal and nonverbal landscape reads like a
web of interlocking narratives creating what this author called a "palimpsest border
document." The frontera template is conspicuous enough as a discursive element.
Of the triad of geography, land, and ecology, the former two are also discursively

present, if pictorially ambiguous. Migrant workers, or campesinos, are represented in both image and word. The law, the police, and authoritarian acts of brutality are textually inscribed. Culture, religion, identity, patriotism, human rights, race, and class are like so many colored threads running through this relatively monochromatic work. With respect to gender, there is little doubt that the male artist was privileged in the work's conceptualization, but the female presence in several of the photographs and the known fact, although seldom stated, that Chicanas have always had a voice in El Movimiento's course, leave no doubt that Rascón's declarations are gender-balanced in their inclusivity. Oddly enough, the work is almost devoid of the rich texture of linguistic code switching—with little evidence of bilingualism—yet the work remains essentially discursive.

A counterpoint to Rascón's installation is Antonio Bernal's untitled mural painted in 1968 for the headquarters of the Teatro Campesino/Farmworkers' Theater in Del Rey, California. The two-panel in situ painting addressed the Chicana/o's pre-Columbian past, Mexican legacy, and ongoing struggle to guarantee civil and human rights. A figure from the recent past, New Mexico's land grants activist, Reies López Tijerina, is portrayed holding a document identified as "Tratado de Guadalupe Hidalgo," the mural's only trace of verbal language.[44] Brief as it is, this titular reference in Spanish to the Treaty of Guadalupe Hidalgo functions not unlike the "discursive ellipsis" Solomon-Godeau finds in Rascón's installation. Once mentioned, the viewer should understand that the full text of the treaty as ratified—including the original text of Articles IX and X, as well as the Protocol of Querétaro—is there to be educed and read. Indeed, that densely legalistic text is usually silently elicited, the guiding assumption or presumption being that all readers must surely be familiar with the language and contents of the treaty. The fact of the matter is that the opposite is more likely to be the case. Who, for example, among the readership can recall the references in the document to "Our Lord," or to "Almighty God, the author of Peace"? What of the treaty's actual, descriptive title: "Treaty of Peace, Friendship, Limits and Settlement between the United States of America and the Mexican Republic"?[45] Article V prompts one to ask just how far-reaching and sincere these claims to peace and friendship were, given that a reference to the border, or "the Boundary line between the two Republics," sets the tone for that article. Setting limits seemed the more pressing issue. Those charged with mapping "the Boundary line with due precision" were to "meet at the Port of San Diego, and proceed to run and mark the said boundary in its whole course to the mouth of the Río Bravo del Norte." Rather elastic property and citizenship rights are expressed under Article VIII. The original version of Article IX commented at greater length on religious freedom than the more abbreviated and ratified version. Article X, stricken out by the U.S. Senate, concerned land grants. Interestingly, it may well be that language that was not elided betrayed as much, if not greater insincerity. Where Article XXII talks of the "fate of prisoners of war" in relatively benign terms, what such treatment looked like in truth is strikingly visualized in a lithograph of 1848, "Los Azotes dados por los Americanos" (Lashes Given by the Americans), attributed to Abraham López. The work "depicts American troops lined up in a public square as one American soldier whips a Mexican who is bound to a street lamp."[46] Such was the punishment of Mexicans "who were caught engaging in guerrilla activities."[47] On November 3, 1847, some three months before the treaty was signed, a correspondent for the *New Orleans Picayune* described in harsh racist language just such a violent incident that occurred in Mexico City: "This afternoon . . . a greaser was whipped in the plaza. He had attempted to kill one of our soldiers, and was sentenced to receive one hundred lashes. . . . Nearly ten thousand Mexicans were in the plaza, and as soon as the whipping commenced they began to throw stones. About a dozen of our dragoons, however, charged upon the mob, when they dispersed in all directions. The greaser was then whipped and taken back to the guard house."[48] How loudly that "discursive ellipsis" speaks through Bernal's mural! The Treaty of Guadalupe Hidalgo thus betrays a certain hollowness, that of a broken treaty from the "broken-promise(d) land."

The curatorial juxtaposition of two related works by Luis Jiménez, "Crossing the Río Bravo," a fiberglass sculpture from 1989, and "El Chuco/El Paso," an unstretched painting in acrylic on canvas dating from 1993, in the exhibition, "Art of the Other México: Sources and Meanings,"[49] is analogous to this chapter's juxtaposition of works by Rascón and Bernal (see fig. 3.4). Jiménez's loosely painted landscape with a pronounced Río Bravo as both word and image serves as a discursive counterpoint to his totemically conceived sculpture depicting a man carrying a woman and child on his back and shoulders. Devoid of any verbal language of its own, the sculpture moved art historian and curator Madeleine Grynsztejn to describe it as "a sort of 'Chicano-ized' Flight from Egypt."[50] The backdrop of the painting is inscribed with the reference to the river invoked in the Treaty of Guadalupe Hidalgo, and some ten other lines of text with the makings to compose a near litany for immigrants: "border crossing," "mojados" (wetbacks), "pollos" (undocumented persons),[51] "aliens," "coyote" (contractor),[52] "cholo" (mestizo), "¿derechos humanos?" (human rights?), "Juariles" (Juárez, México), and "El Paso."

Although Bernal is the sole artist in this survey who so blatantly injects the

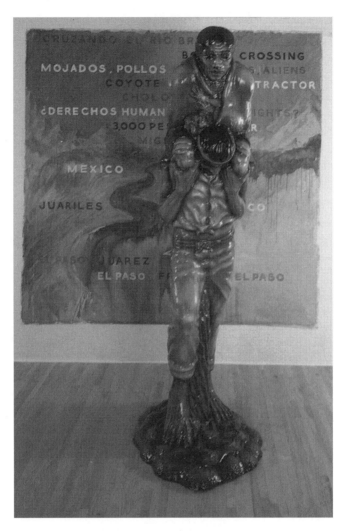

Figure 3.4. Two images in one photo: Luis Jiménez, "Crossing the Río Bravo" (1989), fiberglass sculpture, and "El Chuco/El Paso" (1993), un-stretched painting in acrylic on canvas. The cold legality of immigration policy contrasts with the profound human drama that unfolds every time someone crosses the border by land or water. Photograph courtesy of Mexican Fine Arts Center Museum, published by permission of the artist.

pivotal treaty as icon and sign, vestiges of Guadalupe Hidalgo—linguistically considered or ideologically gauged—are, in this writer's opinion, discernible elsewhere. Rudy Treviño's "George Zapata" (1973; mixed media on canvas) is a wonderfully seductive melding of two legendary icons: George Washington's likeness with a textual caption borrowed from U.S. paper currency is repeated three times paired with Emiliano Zapata's famous portrait derived from a photograph in the Archivo Casasola.[53] Zapata is armed and on guard against a Washington temporarily "put on ice." With a touch of humor, Treviño seems to be saying that Mexicans must always be on guard and wary of U.S. promises. They can melt or go up in steam as the presence of both water condensation and a cloudlike projection might imply. Lastly, the intentional and seemingly interchangeability of names, George for Emiliano, and Zapata for Washington—duly noting the added allusion through the latter to the geographic seat of U.S. power—begs the question of the border as an arbitrary and "capricious" construction, giving some currency to Carey McWilliams's already challenged notion of a "mythical border." Two works by fellow Tejano (Texan) artist, César Augusto Martínez, also come to mind in this context. "Forma Goyesca sobre la frontera" (Goyaesque Form over the Border), done in 1991 in mixed media on metal and wood, and "Unstable But Somehow Hopeful Climate Along the Border" (1992), also a mixed media execution, are home to spectral emanations of various types. A titular allusion to Goya, the distinguished nineteenth-century Spanish painter and printmaker, infuses the former with a note of pessimism—an aspect often endemic to Goya's work—while the latter smacks with the optimism of its own given title.

Yet, the "Goyaesque" coyote or wolflike phantoms and reddish line (an allusion to the Río Bravo/Grande where blood has been shed?) are illuminated by *trompe l'oeil* votive candles with Don Pedrito Jaramillo[54] and other guardian saints pictured on their printed labels. Furthermore, a rainbowlike form describes its own auspicious arc in the background. In the second composition, one largely inscribed with the "language" of abstraction, something unnamed seemingly hovers menacingly overhead, above the meandering river border.

This threat is certainly greater than the unstable climate denoted by the clouds and downpour of rain. In both instances, the specter of the treaty is an historical fact, or an actual imprint in light of Madeleine Grynsztejn's observation concerning Martínez's paintings. She sees them as "secular vehicles for the healing of personal and communal discords emanating from the border's unique problems and predicaments."[55] Votive candles in Don Pedrito's name, however, are hardly secular trappings, underscoring instead a folk spirituality, one nurtured in God-

conscious folk. The god repeatedly mentioned in the treaty—a near signatory—
might well preside over Martínez's *paisajes fronterizos* (border landscapes).

Felipe Almada, a Tijuana-born-and-based artist who died in 1993, brought
into high relief the conflictual legacy of the Treaty of Guadalupe Hidalgo. His mixed
media installation, "The Altar of Live News," (1992) has the look of bricolage, as
though a tinkerer assembled it. But Almada's choices were quite deliberate. A tentative sentence fragment, "Casi te deceo" ("I almost wish for you," although the
Spanish rendering for the verb would be *deseo*), entered in a cursive hand atop the
altar, might be read as one Mexican's equivocal position with respect to the United
States itself, or to certain things available in the United States. That verbal inflection is visually expressed in the incorporation of Bart Simpson and a giant ham-
burger (both are of the plaster cast variety that can be purchased in Tijuana[56]) in
the installation. Aside from the nod to U.S. popular culture, and in particular to
the dubious role that television plays in promoting that cultural fare, Almada reminds viewers of a truly important fact. Among the newspaper cutouts he has
appended to the altar's lower register, one is headlined, "Tratado Trilateral de Libre
Comercio" (Trilateral Treaty of Free Commerce), bringing home the unpalatable
reality that while Canada, Mexico, and the United States were entering into negotiations for the free trade of goods across their boundaries, such negotiations had
not fostered a more liberal attitude toward immigration. In retrospect, the opposite
has happened. A new treaty, the North American Free Trade Agreement (NAFTA),
has only served to compound the ills of the earlier treaty. South of the border, an
insurgency movement, the Zapatista Army of National Liberation (EZLN), has
been organized in the state of Chiapas, while north of la frontera, Proposition 187
has surfaced as the newest incarnation of xenophobia.

In his denunciation of Proposition 187, Enrique Chagoya of northern California targets Governor Wilson. Chagoya, himself an immigrant who left Mexico
City in 1977, chose amate paper—a ground obtained from the Mexican fig tree
and the same type used in Amerindian codices—to paint "The Governor's Nightmare" (1994) (see fig. 3.5). Done in acrylic and oil, this 4-x-6-foot statement must
be entertained first and foremost as one textual document commenting on another.
As with Almada's work, this painting is at once informed and animated by U.S.
popular culture, a subject with which Chagoya was well versed, having experienced
North American comic books and Hollywood films in Mexico.[57] Curator of the
exhibition "Enrique Chagoya: Borders of the Spirit," Steven A. Nash of the M. H.
de Young Memorial Museum, provides an elegant explanation of the painting and
its message of indignation:

Figure 3.5. Enrique Chagoya, "The Governor's Nightmare" (1994), acrylic and oil on amate paper. In a pungent satirical manner, Chagoya disarmingly appropriates and deploys the enemy's arsenal while defending those whom his artistry champions. Photograph courtesy of M. H. De Young Memorial Museum, San Francisco, and Gallery Paule Anglim.

In this large work, the stereotypical association of Mesoamerican culture with human sacrifice is transposed into the modern political arena of anti-immigration sentiment and legislation. Mickey Mouse, the North American, is facetiously hog-tied and served up, well-seasoned, on a platter with jalapeños, echoing distantly the Catholic icon of a sacrificial Christ at the upper left. A band of "primitive" and voracious Indians looks eagerly toward their next victim. If Chagoya has exaggerated the horrific quality of his original ancient images—and he concedes that he has—it is only to express better the ugly issues of racial stereotyping and xenophobia that are so strong in U.S. private views and public policy today. Chagoya's sometimes bitter, sometimes humorous, but always engaging montages of imagery and associations propose a communal internal voyage. As he puts it, "in a world which has masses of people who move, we are talking about a spiritual experience in everybody. Everybody is an immigrant of some kind.⁵⁸

121

Beside Nash's resonant commentary, this writer would cite two short frag-
ments from the first section of the text of the proposed law advanced as Proposition
187. These "findings and declarations" by "The People of California" state "that
they have a right to the protection of their government from any person or persons
entering this country unlawfully." [59] Transposing this language at face value into
Chagoya's work, it is tempting to read the painting's miasmic aura as the artist's
intentional nonverbal riposte to the proposed law's claims. It is as if Chagoya's work
were confirming Pete Wilson's worst nightmare: a scenario where one unfounded
stereotype deserves or begets another. What Pete Wilson and his supporters put
forward in the public transcript—the text of the proposed law—is being used
against them through the hidden transcript in the painting, which speaks subver-
sively to those ideologically opposed to the public transcript.[60] Should the reader
find an element of theatricality in all of this, one might imagine any one of Chagoya's painted protagonists coming to life as "El Mojado Peligroso" (The Dangerous Wetback) [61] as portrayed in 1979 by Guillermo Gómez-Peña—and confront-
ing Pete Wilson on stage!

Underscoring illegality, the Proposition also states that "The People of California . . . have suffered and are suffering economic hardship" by virtue of illegal
aliens entering this state." [62] So incisive is Nuevomexicano poet Jimmy Santiago
Baca's barbed poem "So Mexicans Are Taking Jobs from Americans" [63] that it renders rhetorically speechless this hypocritical piece of legislation. What economic
hardships do exist are borne by the poor, the very Mexicans whom the poem says
are "trying to cross poverty to just have something." [64] To cross poverty is tantamount to crossing the border. But, in the "broken-promise(d) land," there are no
signposts leading the immigrant out from an impoverished "lived reality." As visual artists David Avalos, Louis Hock, and Elizabeth Sisco demonstrated in 1988,
the city of San Diego is a chimerical place where, if luck is on their side, undocumented workers might find menial employment as dishwashers and hotel chamber-
maids. A more likely outcome, however, is that they will be arrested by the border
authorities. Those dismal options are portrayed in the silkscreened poster "Welcome to America's Finest Tourist Plantation" (see fig. 3.6). The photographic
mural was displayed on one hundred San Diego Transit System buses during January 1988 to coincide with football's Super Bowl XXII. In an interview with Louis
Hock, art historian and critic Robert L. Pincus relates that he was told that the
trio of artists "wanted to reinterpret commercial space, which reaches a broad
popular audience." [65] Avalos would add that the work was to be understood as an
"advertisement for itself." [66] What ensued was a public debate, conducted through

Figure 3.6. Elizabeth Sisco, Louis Hock, and David Avalos, "Welcome to America's Finest Tourist Plantation" (1988), silkscreen, San Diego Transit bus poster. The artists render with brilliant conviction the notion that places aren't always what they seem. Photograph by Elizabeth Sisco.

featured and guest editorials and letters to the editors of the local papers, revolving around the role of the "illegal immigrants" in the local economy, as well as the validity of the poster itself.[67] The same three artists initiated another project in 1993 to have the public acknowledge that "illegal" workers are taxpayers. During the months of July and August of that year, the artists handed out a total of $4,500—$1,250 of which came from the National Endowment for the Arts as part of a substantial grant awarded to San Diego's Museum of Contemporary Art for a series of projects concerned with border issues—at locales where undocumented workers congregated.[68] Pincus describes the process and purpose of the project:

> Each willing participant would sign a sheet and receive an envelope containing ten dollars and a statement outlining the intention and themes of "Art Rebate/Arte Reembolso." In bold letters, the sheet declared, "This ten dollar bill is part of an art project that intends to return tax dollars to taxpayers, particularly undocumented taxpayers. The art rebate acknowledges your role as a vital player in an economic community indifferent to national borders."[69]

Pincus is quick to point out that "the artists couldn't have taken the side of these workers at a more auspicious moment" in light of Governor Pete Wilson's "get tough on Mexican immigrants" policy, which he launched in August 1993.[70] On the heels of that repressive action, coupled with the perception of reactionaries that the artists' rebate was nothing but a "handout" to "undocumented workers leeching off the U.S. economy,"[71] how could anyone not anticipate that the imposition of legislation of the ilk of Proposition 187 was likely to happen sooner or later? Indeed, it is sobering to consider just how heinous certain actions can potentially become. Lawyer, writer, and educator Donna A. Demac reports on an INS-concocted scenario included as part of a 1986 report entitled "Alien Terrorists and Undesirables: A Contingency Plan." That scenario called for "new detention sites to be identified by the military for the imprisonment of persons of targeted nationalities."[72]

Genaro Molina's color photograph of campesina Maria Rulis's near-disembodied hands—with nearly all her fingers wrapped in duct tape to prevent cuts when she strips olives from their branches—becomes emblematic for this writer of economic hardships present even with a job. Despite the tape, Maria's fingers are still raw by the end of a day's work in Corning, California.[73] To whom of those subscribing to the language under Section 1 of Proposition 187 would she relinquish her task? Who among them would begrudge her such painful toil? Her injured hands speak volumes. They prick our collective conscience.

The plight of migrant workers and immigrants as a whole is communicated by another "speaking hand" painted in the monumental mural "Tome Conciencia" (1987) at the One-Stop Immigration and Educational Center on Whittier Boulevard in Los Angeles (see fig. 3.7). Appearing palm-up with eyes, nose, and open mouth animating the splayed fingers, the rhetorical hand speaks beneath the mural's commanding title entered on a red and white field that at one and the same time is derived from and parodies the Coca-Cola logo.[74] But the mural exhorts one to "drink conscience," not Coke. That satiric note resonates again in two images of Superman, recalling Almada's and Chagoya's works. Norma Urenda, Isela Guerrero, Eduardo Juárez, Mauricio Gómez, and Esther Cimet (the mural's authors and team members of el Taller de Gráfica Monumental/Monumental Graphics Workshop, headquartered in Xochimilco, Mexico) also inject iconographic, semiotic, and textual elements foregrounding history and civil and human rights. A likeness of Ricardo Flores Magón, prominent Mexican journalist and political leader, is depicted at sidewalk level, and a textual reference to his imprisonment in Leavenworth is dated 1922, the year he died there.[75] Following Magón's gaze, the viewer tracks a trail of blank sheets of paper terminating in a prediction that reads, "El presente es de lucha. . . . El futuro es nuestro" (To struggle is [our lot] in the present. . . . The future is ours). Are the Maria Rulis's of the present being promised a propitious future? Not yet! Directly above the favorable promise, the artists depicted the Statue of Liberty's face and crown. To the left of that, and seemingly within one of the crown's windowlike recesses shown enlarged for visual effect,

Figure 3.7. Norma Urenda, Isela Guerrero, Eduardo Juárez, Mauricio Gómez, Esther Cimet (members of the Taller de Gráfica Monumental),
"Tome Conciencia" (1987), mural in Los Angeles. Parodying U.S. con-
sumerism's great appetite, a group of Mexican public artists admonish
their audience north of the border to imbibe historical truths and to
quench the thirst for greater justice. Photograph by Robin J. Dunitz,
courtesy One-Stop Immigration and Educational Center.

three snippets of text appear: "Raza Sí / Migra / Los Derechos Plenos de los Trabajadores Indocumentados" (Yes to Raza / [No][76] to the INS / The Full Rights of
Undocumented Workers). Enmeshed within the text are some youths carrying a
placard emblazoned with a screaming face. Is the scream directed at the "Mother
of Exiles," whose torch, as this essay has already shown, does not burn equally
bright for everyone?[77] To be sure, she rings hollow for the undocumented
worker—arguably the painted narrative's denouement—in the act of climbing a
barbed wire fence. The elusiveness of that *indocumentado's* "full rights" punctuates
Flores Magón's line of vision like an exclamation mark at the end of a declarative
statement.

Being thwarted before the Statue of Liberty recalls art historian Albert
Boime's characterization of this symbol as a "hollow icon."[78] She carries that
stigma in many satirical works, two of which, like "Tome Conciencia," are also

murals involved with immigration. Juan Hector Ponce, a native of El Salvador, spent six years in Mexico before moving to Los Angeles. His 1992 mural "Immigrant at El Tigre Market" (Tiger Market) depicts the Statue of Liberty as a mirage, forcing one immigrant to dig through a dumpster for cans. In "To Cause to Remember" (1992), San Francisco artist Johanna Poethig has painted Liberty as a fallen idol,[79] deprived of her torch, with chains at her feet. Strangely, though, Emma Lazarus's comforting words above and below her image seem somehow to want to place her back up on her pedestal. Chains are a poignant throwback to the bondage of slavery, a modern version of which the late Carlos Almaraz and Third Street Gang members address in their denunciatory mural, "No Somos Esclavos de la Migra . . ." (We Are Not Slaves of the Immigration Service . . .), painted in 1974 in the barrio (neighborhood) of East Los Angeles. Abandoned by Liberty, these undocumented workers are shown bound with barbed wire and chains. "Ya Basta" (Enough), the mural shouts to low wages and general exploitation of undocumented immigrants threatened daily with deportation. Mural historian Alan W. Barnett speaks to the painting's uniqueness: "The vehemence of the caricature is something that only Chicanos have dared in murals. Almaraz and a few others, following Orozco, have used the distortions of cartoons to create a monumental rhetoric of denunciation."[80]

In 1973, Rupert García printed "¡Cesen Deportación!" (Halt Deportation!), a small silkscreen with its textual denunciatory challenge inscribed in yellow, menacingly large barbs rendered in black, insect-like in their delineation, animating three strands of taut wire, and a sanguine field underscoring the often violent nature of deportations (see fig. 3.8). The late Ralph Maradiaga's "Dolor" (Hurt/ Pain) of 1979, another small silkscreen conceived as a *trompe l'oeil* triptych, is a synecdochic portrayal of the Passion of Christ (through thorns, blood, and the sacred heart with burning cross) and, on a human scale, the immigrant's suffering (through cacti, barbed wire, and blood). A diminutive but thoroughly captivating silkscreen by Malaquías Montoya, "Undocumented" (1981), quite literally stops the would-be immigrant in his tracks as he collides stingingly with a barbed wire fence. The word "UNDOCUMENTED" cuts obliquely across the limp body. An acrylic on canvas painting of 1986 by José Antonio Burciaga, "Amor Indocumentado" (Undocumented Love), depicts a crucified, though still active figure, subtended and nearly overshadowed by a sacred heart, barbed wire fencing, copious blood, and a partial U.S. flag. Yet one more fascinating installation, employing actual wire fencing and a painted reference to barbed wire, is David Avalos's "Border Fence as Moebius Strip." A Mö[e]bius band, or strip, is the nonorientable surface

Figure 3.8. Rupert García, "¡Cesen Deportación!" (1973), silkscreen. This barbed poster was produced for CASA (Centros de acción social autónoma/Centers for Autonomous Social Action) in Los Angeles, a group dedicated to helping undocumented immigrants and affecting immigration policies. Photograph by M. Lee Fatherree. Courtesy of the artist; Rena Bransten Gallery, San Francisco; and Galerie Claude Samuel, Paris, France.

obtained from a rectangular strip by twisting it once and then gluing the two ends. (Refer to *McGraw-Hill Dictionary of Physics and Mathematics* New York, 1978, p. 634). It is this character of nonorientability that Avalos exploits so brilliantly in two floor inscriptions below the wire fencing shaped as a Mö(e)bius band: "You try to cross the border but you never reach the other side"/ "You cross the fence, then realize you're still on the same side." One must conclude that the border is merely a construction of the imagination or, to quote from the installation's wall text, "The Border is an International Fiction."

In 1979, under the aegis of the Bay Area Committee on Immigration, Malaquías Montoya silkscreened a singularly indignant poster, "Abajo con la Migra" (Down with the Immigration Service), portraying a martyred immigrant impaled

127

on Liberty's crown. Behind her image as butcher—she threateningly wields a butcher's knife in place of the usual torch—appears a barbed wire barrier. The poster, calling for "an end to deportations," also advertised a showing of the film *The Alien Game*. Ten years later, Malaquías rendered his painting "Human Rights" (1989) in oilstick on canvas. In it, a seeming vestige of Lady Liberty's face and crown—an image which, admittedly, also brings to mind a Native American in headdress—occupies an unobtrusive corner below a stenciled human rights invocation, superimposed, in turn, on a fragmented U.S. flag that shares space with an immobilized, bound figure. What emerges is a generalized portrait of Liberty denied, or the painter's reminder to viewers that there remains a pressing urgency to safeguard the human rights of historically disenfranchised peoples.

Liberty literally turns her back on a detained immigrant being frisked by a border agent as depicted in David Avalos's "Donkey Cart Altar" (1985), a life-size parody of a Tijuana tourist photo backdrop. Painted with arms upraised, the immigrant's allusion to Christ is readily noted. Within reach of his hands, two plastic statuettes of Liberty, her back to the viewer, occupy their own shallow brackets from which arm *milagros* (charms) are suspended. That staggered or stepped arrangement with its insistent upward thrust is consistent with an altar's configuration. As with Montoya's composition in "Abajo con la Migra," a barbed wire fence appears as part of the tableau immediately behind the detainment scene. That seizure and search drama has been acted out over a much protracted period, as Alex Webb's 1979 documentary photo "U.S.–Mexico Border (San Ysidro, CA)" testifies.[81] A far worse and tragic consequence for those crossing the border is depicted by Avalos on the other and rarely seen side of the "Donkey Cart Altar." There, one encounters a portrait of Francisco Sánchez, a youngster shot to death by the Border Patrol on December 8, 1980. The artist has placed upright flashlights where votive candles might otherwise have been. Parodying the movie character, Rambo, Avalos would later do a cartoonlike depiction of the Border Patrol, titling it "Dumbo" (1986) and adding a textual legend: "They sent him on a mission where he could not fail. Shooting kids." It was also during 1986 that the artist, wanting to contribute to "Streetsites," an annual exhibition of temporary public art, installed his Cart[82] in the plaza fronting a downtown San Diego federal building. What unfolded was documented by Robert L. Pincus:

> The artist believed his contribution to Streetsites might provide debate, but it gained notoriety for a different, unexpected reason: U.S. District Court Judge Gordon Thompson, Jr., had it removed, labeling

it a security risk. One story quoted Thompson to this effect: "We didn't know if some kook would get into this chicken-wire-and-box arrangement in the middle of the night and plant some bomb." The American Civil Liberties Union joined forces with Avalos and Sushi to seek damages, though the process ended unsuccessfully when the Supreme Court denied an appeal of a Circuit Court of Appeals ruling.[83]

The audacious and tenacious strategies of David Avalos find their match in the inspired artistry of Ester Hernández. "Libertad" (Liberty), her now-canonic etching of 1976, reshapes the Statue of Liberty into a figurative Amerindian stele, captioned "Aztlán"[84] and supporting on the palm of an extended hand the artist herself, engaged in her reconstructive carving. A provocative riposte to this last deconstruction might be what this writer interprets as a visual construction of Liberty.

In the opening scenes of Cheech Marín's brilliantly written and directed "rasquache"[85] film, "Born in East L.A." (1988), a stunning "woman in a green dress" is seen advancing toward the viewer—with James Avila's "Untitled" (1985) mural functioning as a backdrop—along a trajectory that recedes from the camera in a straight axis to a point in the mural where unfurling U.S. and Mexican flags intersect. That line she walks evokes the border. Late in the film, the same female is seen again, her right arm upraised, in a gesture or posture of Liberty herself. Doubtlessly, the film asks the thoughtful viewer to equivocate concerning this venerable symbol.[86]

At this juncture, Proposition 187 reemerges through a focus on Liberty. At the San José Center for Latino Arts, el Movimiento de Arte y Cultura Latino Americana, Inc. (Movement of Latin American Art and Culture / MACLA) mounted a juried[87] exhibition entitled "Artists Respond to Proposition 187." Running from June 7 through July 15, 1995, the show featured twenty-five selected individual artists, one artists' group, and one guest artist. In their "Curatorial Statement," the Curatorial Committee states that "the artists have reacted to this event in our political history with anger, outrage, cynicism, sorrow, compassion and defiance."[88] Artist Andrew Kong Knight brings all of the sentiments the curators identify. His uncompromising print, "Give Me Your Tired, Your Poor" (1994), incorporates within a caption these compassionate titular words from Lazarus's poem, "The New Colossus." Printed more conspicuously are two declarative, exhortative statements: "DEPORT KING WILSON / VOTE NO 187." Governor Wilson, wearing royal ermine and crowned like a king or Lady Liberty, manipulates the victims

129

of 187 as if they're pawns in a chess game being played on a game board over which the earlier mentioned caption is superimposed. Appropriately, two strands of barbed wire and something resembling a curved blade appear overhead, almost mimicking the threat of a guillotine. Nothing approaching Enrique Chagoya's "hidden transcript" would seem iconographically or semiotically probable in such an explicit and overt context.

Contrastingly, guest artist René Yañez encodes that exact probability in the title of his mixed media installation, "Ideas Are Empowerment" (1995). Against a retaining wall, Yañez has arranged a small central altar to the all-important patron saint of Chicanas/os and Mexicanas/os, the Virgin of Guadalupe. To the left and right of this image, he has interspersed text and images—including the Statue of Liberty, Christ, and the barbed epithet, "Fuck 187"—printed posterlike on violet, white, and yellow stock. A banner extending below the central altar reads: "NO A LA 187 / NO TO 187." The apparent religiosity of la Guadalupana belies her aggressive/militant aspect promoted in recent years by strident Chicanas bent on disavowing and undermining the icon's traditional, institutionally grounded connotation of feminine passivity.[89] That sort of feminist Chicana activism clearly illustrates the point this work's title strives to make. Furthermore, according to the "Curatorial Statement," this installation "is a work in progress that calls for the community to respond to Proposition 187 and its repercussions on our society."[90] That is, "Ideas Are Empowerment" calls for a "Post-187 State Strike" on Monday, October 16, 1995, "to measure the economic impact that our community will have in our state."[91] The public is urged by the artist to fax their ideas to MACLA, and thus empower themselves by contributing to the "unfolding" installation.[92]

Recovering the "economic hardship" clause with which the discussion of Proposition 187 began leads one to consider another cluster of related works. The image of Maria Rulis is vividly remembered in connection with mural subjects by Michael Schnorr (and crew) and Judy Baca. The former's sixty-five-foot-high pylon painting, entitled "The Undocumented Worker" (1980), was executed in San Diego's Chicano Park. The artist raised funds from MECHA (Movimiento Estudiantil Chicano de Aztlán) student groups around the country. Decoding surrealistic and folkloric imagery, Alan Barnett explains that "the mural is to be read from bottom to top as the struggle of migrants to seek a livelihood in an inhospitable foreign country . . . there is first the need to elude the helicopter and monsters of la migra."[93] Subtending the allegorical pictures is a bilingual textual panel. Judy Baca speaks to the deplorable living and working conditions awaiting migrant laborers in her "Pickers" scene from the four-panel acrylic on plywood "Guadalupe Mural"

(1990) in Leroy Park, Guadalupe, California. A cauliflower picker in the work's foreground looks out of the composition with a heavy weariness that interrogates the onlooker. It is the same haunting gaze Santa Contreras Barraza registers in "Los Migrantes" (Migrants), a delicately drawn pencil rendering of 1973 in which a father and child are shown resting momentarily; that Amado Peña's "Migrante" (Migrant) exudes in a diminutive serigraph of the seventies, inscribed "Migrante, hermano de la Tierra/hijo de la Desesperación" (Migrant, brother of the Earth/ son of Desperation) and that Carlos Cortéz-Koyokuikatl captures in his 1984 woodcut, "De la tierra somos" (We Are of the Earth), in which the work's title is further punctuated by the emphatic, "¡No Somos Ilegales! (We Are Not Illegals!).

These migrants' toil finds a measure of redemption in the double-edged humor of Lalo Alcaraz's 1993 cartoon, "La Cucaracha" (The Cockroach), which appeared in POCHO [94] magazine. About to walk away with his food tray, a McDonald's customer has something extracted from his order by an attendant who tells him, "I'm sorry but you can't have this lettuce and tomato because they were unlawfully picked by 'Illegal Aliens!'" Abigail González, who was cited much earlier for her recent tribute to Yolanda M. López's iconography, had occasion to aim some barbs of her own at McDonald's in the context of Proposition 187. Contributing "At Your Service" (1995) to the exhibition, "187: With or Without You," she helped fulfill the main objective for that group effort: "to expand the knowledge about the complexity of Proposition 187 and its effect." [95] Her explanation for incorporating the McDonald's logo and associated imagery is worth quoting in full, notably because it reminds everyone of the real or "silenced" victims of the "economic hardship" clause in the proposition:

> I have a great deal of McDonald's paraphernalia in this piece because I had heard through my sister-in-law that after the issuance of Proposition 187, McDonald's and Taco Bell had come out with public advertisements for the Proposition. I think that this is really ironic because many of the people I have seen working there are immigrants. Their motion made me angry because they know that they sometimes hire people who have crossed over illegally, but they turn the other way because they know that only a few other legal people would work for such low hourly wages. My hope is that my work will make the viewers think about economic and social injustices. [96]

"Illegal" or "legal" status seems not to matter much in Sylvia Orozco's intriguing acrylic on canvas painting, "Legal Migrants/Illegal Migrants" (1979). An elegantly attired immigrant carrying luggage walks away from the viewer toward a barbed wire barrier. Inscribed within that same space is a poem authored by the artist:

> Legal Migrants
> Illegal Migrants
> Alien Migrants
> flow on the border
> wetting the country with sweat
> border patrol guards the migratory stream
> looking for deportable aliens
> ignoring their status [97]
> a proportion of all leave
> *cargando sueños, esperanzas, aspiraciones*
> [carrying dreams, hopes, aspirations]
> exported C.O.D.

Seemingly uncertain of what lies ahead, or equivocating on his own status, the figure looks back. The artist's point is that, notwithstanding one's immigrant status as measured by the authorities, if you're Mexican you're still discriminated against.[98] But humble gardeners who daily cross the border to earn a livelihood — one of whom seems oblivious to Miguel Gandert's camera catching him in the act of shaving before his journey sometime in 1995 — can become the homeowners as another photographer, Robert C. Buitrón, shows in the image of Albert and Edna, the "Suburban Ethnics" (1981). They pose casually but proudly before their home, garden and lawn mower.

A mexicana like Dolores Del Río, or a mexicano like Anthony Quinn, achieved celebrity status and was paid homage by fellow artists. In 1984/90, Amalia Mesa-Bains erected/reconstructed a flamboyant "Ofrenda" (Offering) altar to Del Río who, in one of her many roles, played opposite Henry Fonda in John Ford's *The Fugitive*, based on Graham Greene's novel, *The Power and the Glory*, set in Mexico during the anticlerical reforms of the twenties and early thirties.[99] In 1990, Alfredo de Batuc and his collaborators painted a large portrait mural on Hollywood Boulevard in Del Río's memory. Amidst floral bouquet offerings and an extensive textual legend, her role in *The Fugitive* is visually referenced. Anthony Quinn is magnificently portrayed on a monumental scale — befitting his considerable talents — by Eloy Torres. Recognized as *Zorba, the Greek*, or *The Pope of Broadway* —

titles Torres gives his work—Quinn seems about to dance off the very L.A. wall on which he's painted.[100]

These triumphal stories in the sun are so exceptional that they soon fade into the shadow of Amado Peña's desperate migrant and Sylvia Orozco's anxious immigrant. María Rulis's hurt turns to the kind of desperation Cristina Cárdenas makes so palpable in her exquisitely conceived "El Colgado 'por la ilusión ingrata de ganar dó(l)lares'" (Hanged 'due to the frustrated dream of earning dollars') of 1992 (see fig. 3.9). That delusion of economic profit is inscribed in cursive script, written in black acrylic at the foot of the textured, brown amate bark paper, the same indigenous material used by Chagoya. Above the verbal caption, a fragmented wire fence, its sharp projections resembling a briar of thorns, directs the viewer's gaze vertically to the truncated, flag-entwined legs of the hanged, bleeding victim memorialized in the work's title. Related to this splendid *memento mori*, which speaks for all "crucified" undocumented workers, are a host of other denunciatory images. While Cárdenas's martyred subject might have taken his own life, other subjects are the victims of circumstances circumscribed by dangers seen and un-seen. "Red Asphalt" (1989), a mixed media installation by Michael Schnorr and Elizabeth Sisco, reflects on the tragic theme of undocumented workers killed on the highway while crossing "the razor." Pursuant to these accidental deaths, California has found it necessary to erect road signs warning drivers. Such CAU-TION/CUIDADO warnings—the printed text running above the silhouettes of a migrating family of three—are incorporated in "The Reading Room" from "La Vecindad/Border Boda" (The Neighborhood/Border Wedding), an exhibition mounted by Las Comadres (Midwives) in 1990.[101] The magnitude of these count-less tragedies, however, seems understated by virtue of the very smallness and infrequency of these roadside warnings.

Availing herself of the prominence and grander scale of the Spectacolor in New York's Times Square, Barbara Carrasco electronically "shouted" her indigna-tion concerning the deadly effect of pesticides on agricultural workers. "Pesticides" (1989) was realized as a computer animation in fourteen parts, done under the auspices of the Public Art Fund. Late in 1988, Robert Sánchez began conceptual-izing his "Encinitas Gardens" project, another powerful indictment of pesticides and other deadly chemicals to which migrants are exposed. Issued first as a textual document, "Encinitas Gardens" was a deliberately duplicitous solicitation made to "laborers with documents (authentic or forged) . . . [to] gather the most beautiful flowers . . . [in] an open airy workplace, stunning white water views, warm

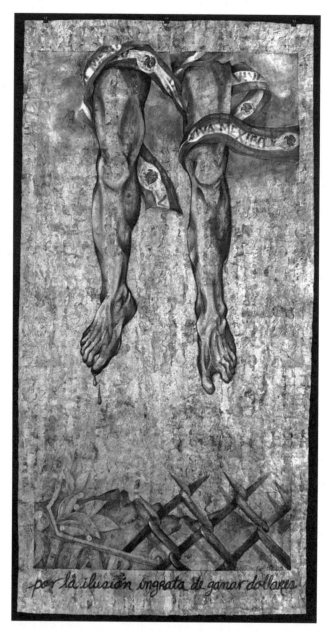

Figure 3.9. Cristina Cárdenas, "El Colgado 'por la ilusión ingrata de ganar dó(l)lares'" (1992), gouache and crayons on amate paper. Cruel fate and harsh reality dash the expectations drawing immigrants to the "broken-promise(d) land." Photograph by Dominic Oldershaw, courtesy of the artist.

fabulous sunsets, the surroundings of a rich contemporary lifestyle — golf, lagoon, and ocean. An absolute delight." [102] The double-speak continues: "We don't care how you come, by foot, through tunnels, stacked in vans or trucks, just get here quick before our multimillion dollar flower industry dies in the dirt. We ask that you hide from our agents and spies, leave your luggage at home, speak only our language, live under the ground, absorb all the pesticides and chemicals that keep our crops so healthy and bright." [103]

The forged documents alluded to by Sánchez in his double-edged solicitation are punishable as a crime under Section 2 of Proposition 187. A *retablo* (votive painting) in oil on metal by Juan Sánchez R., dated November 20, 1990, portrays the artist/petitioner praying to the "Lord of the Conquest" to intercede in his behalf "para solucionar un problema para arreglar unos papeles de importancia de E.U.A." (to resolve a problem of arranging some papers of importance in the U.S.A.). [104] Without such papers, deportation is a foregone conclusion, as Marcos Raya hints in his large acrylic painting, "Twenty-Five Years of Mural Painting in the Mexican Barrio" (1995). Bracketing the particular barrio in Chicago where he lives and works, Raya juxtaposes a "no to 187" sign with the exhortation, "cesen deportación" (halt deportation). Sections 7 and 8 of Proposition 187 exclude "illegal aliens from Public Elementary and Secondary Schools" and "from Public Postsecondary Educational Institutions." Artist Mireya Acierto decries Section 7, in particular, in a narrative sequence of three black and white photographs collectively titled, "The Power of Education" (1995). Reading from right to left, the first image presents a group of five gleeful, optimistic children lined up school fashion. The second photo depicts five more students, seated and sullen, perhaps aware of their impending dilemma. The last picture in the series captures six youths standing police-lineup fashion, having been driven, it would seem, to take desperate measures as a direct consequence of their educational deprivation. Augmenting her visual rhetoric, the artist entreats the audience further with verbal commentary: "Education is such a powerful thing. Have I made my point?" [105]

Affirming Acierto's onerous premonition, this essay brings to a close the ongoing discussion of Proposition 187. The essay as a whole will not close but will leave a door open to future immigrants. That strategy revolves around Richard Lou, a Mexican-Chinese experimental artist, his work, and a shameful pattern in the fabric of U.S. immigration history. Recall the Chinese Exclusion Act of 1881, aimed at Chinese laborers and not repealed until 1943. It ignominiously stood some sixty-two years! By virtue of his dual ancestry, Lou stands twice victimized,

Figure 3.10. Carlos Santístevan, "Breaking Barriers" (1970), brass welding wire. Santístevan weighs the U.S. flag's multivalent symbolism, especially in view of his father's and grandfather's expulsion at gunpoint from their own land. Photograph by Dave Buresh, courtesy of the artist.

most recently by Proposition 187. His answer to this pattern of injustice is "The Border Door" (1988), a functional free-standing door he erected a quarter mile east of the Tijuana International Airport, at the decrepit border fence site itself. Entry was made possible only from the Mexican side, facilitated by 134 detachable keys Lou hung on that entrance as an invitation to those wanting "to cross the

.border with dignity." Eventually, the Border Patrol would remove this symbolic "golden door."[106]

Not unrelated to Lou's work is the wire construction "Breaking Barriers" (1970) by long-time Colorado-based activist/artist Carlos Santístevan (see fig. 3.10). Inspired by his own family's history of immigration, the artist conflates "the design of the U.S. flag with that of a prison door." In the pie, one observes a conspicuously active figure, shaped out of brass welding wire, prying apart the bars of this flag/prison door, reminding the viewer that rhetorically resonant notions of "one continent" and "one people" are often little more than empty rhetorical expressions.

Conclusion

This essay has striven to survey a truly representative number of Chicana/o and Mexicana/o visual artists, artist groups, and their collaborators—including non-Latinas/os—concerning their respective visions of immigration as expressed in a host of media. The telling images bracketing the "broken-promise(d) land" have spanned some three decades, between the 1960s and the 1990s. A crazy quilt pattern of narratives, verbal and nonverbal, emerged. The dense interweaving and superimposition of themes precluded either strict linear analysis or neat categorization. Despite its strident efforts at inclusivity, the essay fails to address the issue of Mexican immigration to Canada or special areas or issues of concern concomitant to immigration. For example, Guillermo Gómez-Peña and Emily Hicks of the Border Art Workshop collaborated on a site-specific performance, entitled "Tijuana–Niagara" (1988), at the U.S.–Canadian border. Also, Eugenia Vargas, Chilean by birth and residing in México, collaborated with Michael Tracy and Eloy Tarcisio on a processual performative project, "The River Pierce: Sacrifice II, 13.4.90" (April 1990), to underscore the multivalent meanings surrounding the Río Grande. Not only is it an instrument of the INS used to divide nations and peoples, but it is also an environmentally threatened source of life.[107]

Notes

1. "El Plan Espiritual de Aztlán," adopted at the Chicano Liberation Youth Conference hosted by the Crusade for Justice in Denver, Colorado, in March 1969, in *Aztlán: An Anthology of Mexican American Literature*, ed. Luis Valdez and Stan Steiner (New York: Vintage Books, 1972), p. 403.

2. Gloria Anzaldúa, *Borderlands/La Frontera: The New Mestiza* (San Francisco: Spinsters/Aunt Lute, 1987), p. 3.

3. Guillermo Gómez-Péna, "A New Artistic Continent," *High Performance: A Quarterly Magazine for the New Arts Audience* 9, 3 (1986), pp. 27–28.

4. José Antonio Burciaga, *Spilling the Beans: Lotería Chicana* (Santa Barbara: Joshua Odell Editions, 1995), p. 37.

5. Cornel West, *Race Matters* (Boston: Beacon Press, 1993).

6. Francis Fukuyama, "Immigrants and Family Values," in *Arguing Immigration: The Debate over the Changing Face of America*, ed. Nicolaus Mills (New York: Simon & Schuster, 1994), pp. 151–168.

7. Ibid., p. 151.

8. Ibid.

9. Ibid., p. 152.

10. Text of Proposition 187, the proposed ten-section law authored by California Assemblyman Dick Mountjoy.

11. Historian Louise Año Nuevo Kerr identifies the Hull House area of the West Side as one of three neighborhoods which recruited them. L. Año Nuevo Kerr, "Mexican Chicago: Chicago Assimilation Aborted, 1939–1954," *Ethnic Chicago*, ed. Melvin G. Holli and Peter d'A. Jones (Grand Rapids, Mich.: William B. Eerdman's Publishing Co., 1984), p. 270.

12. From book jacket for Jane Addams, *Twenty Years at Hull-House* (New York: NAL Penguin, Inc., 1981).

13. Ted Conover, "The United States of Asylum," *Arguing Immigration*, p. 191.

14. Gerald Parshall, "Outlook/U.S. News," *U.S. News and World Report*, 24 April 1995, p. 10.

15. R.F. Berkhofer, Jr., *The White Man's Indian: Images of the American Indian from Columbus to the Present* (New York: Alfred A. Knopf, 1978), p. 3.

16. Anthony Heilbut, *Exiled in Paradise: German Refugee Intellectuals in America, from the 1930s to the Present* (New York: The Viking Press, 1983), p. 217.

17. Ibid., p. 216.

18. Carey McWilliams, *Brothers under the Skin* (Boston: Little Brown and Co., 1964), pp. 119–120.

19. David J. Weber, ed., *Foreigners in Their Native Land: Historical Roots of the Mexican Americans* (Albuquerque: University of New Mexico Press, 1973), pp. vi, 148.

20. Ibid., p. 178.

21. Ibid.

22. Peter Paret et al., *Persuasive Images: Posters of War and Revolution from the Hoover Institution Archives* (Princeton: Princeton University, 1992), pp. 52, 70. The authors point out that Flagg designed forty-six posters, including the famous "I Want You," during

W.W. I. It would appear that Flagg's own source for "I Want You" was a British poster of 1915 entitled "Who's absent? Is it you?," featuring an imperious John Bull pointing a finger at the would-be recruit or soldier. López has apparently infused elements from both into her design.

23. A. Lerner, "Preface and Acknowledgements," in Cynthia J. McCabe, *The Golden Door: Artist-Immigrants of America, 1876–1976* (Washington, D.C.: Smithsonian Institution Press, 1976), p. 10.

24. Ibid., p. 9.

25. Ibid., pp. 45–102. The subsequent review of U.S. immigration history is drawn largely from this chronology.

26. Tim N. Gidal, *Modern Photojournalism: Origin and Evolution, 1910–1933* (New York: Collier Books, 1973), p. 10.

27. Ibid.

28. Peter Brimelow, *Alien Nation: Common Sense about America's Immigration Disaster* (New York: Random House, 1995), p. xi.

29. Ibid., p. 152.

30. Ibid. p. xiii.

31. Cynthia J. McCabe et al., *The American Experience: Contemporary Immigrant Artists*, exhibition catalog (New York and Philadelphia: The Balch Institute for Ethnic Studies, 1985).

32. "Lived reality" or "*la realidad vivida*" is a phrase borrowed from Spanish philosopher José Ortega y Gasset. Introduced in the provocative essay "*La deshumanización del arte*" (The Dehumanization of Art) under the heading "*Unas gotas de fenomenología* (A Few Drops of Phenomenology), the phrase refers to *el punto de vista humano* (the human point of view) shaped by the experiences life affords one. In other words, each individual's "lived reality," or personal point of view toward a blanket reality, is the product of her or his own unique experiences. More succinctly put, the phrase embraces both the objective world in which an individual lives and that individual's subjective reading of it. See José Ortega y Gasset, *La deshumanización del arte y otros ensayos estéticos* (Madrid: Revista de Occidente, S.A., 1970), pp. 27–32.

33. Carey McWilliams, *Brothers under the Skin*, pp. 119–120.

34. Richard Griswold del Castillo, *The Treaty of Guadalupe Hidalgo: A Legacy of Conflict* (Norman, Okla.: University of Oklahoma Press, 1990).

35. Sally Yard, ed., *Guide to in Site 94: A Binational Exhibition of Installation and Site-Specific Art/Una Exposición Binacional de Arte-Instalación en Sitios Específicos* (San Diego: Installation Gallery, 1994), pp. 48–49. Also see "in Site 94" supplement to the *San Diego Daily Transcript* (20 September 1994), p. 16. A very short video documentary (done by KNSD/Channel 39) airs public opinion, from both sides of the fence, about Allen's project. The fence is praised by one onlooker with his remark "good fences make good neighbors."

Another voice is heard to say that Governor Pete Wilson is a "racist." As for Allen himself, he is quoted as saying that the purpose of the project was to "give people a voice" and that it was "about human beings communicating with one another." The notion of language crossing or overcoming borders is also an intrinsic part of Ernest Silva's Site project, "Cora's Rain House," which afforded the exchange of stories written during rainy weather and is told by children occupying two houses Silva built, one in San Diego and another in Tijuana. "ESL" (English as a Second Language), another Site project, involved many scenarios orchestrated by members of the Border Art Workshop (BAW/TAF) in an effort to convey the complexity of language vis-à-vis the border region. That language can hold one hostage is one possible reading. Language fluency or lack of it can certainly typecast an individual, as Guillermo Pulido's "Ballad of the Wetback" (1979) portrays, characterizing the subjects of the work as non-English speakers. This writer is grateful to Sharon A. Reo and Danielle Reo for their kind and most timely assistance with important written and visual materials.

36. Jeff Kelley, ed., *The Border Art Workshop* (BAW/TAF) 1984–1989: A Documentation of Five Years of Interdisciplinary Art Projects Dealing with U.S.–Mexico Border Issues (A Binational Perspective) (San Diego: BAW/TAF, 1988); and Edgardo Reynoso et al., *Border Art Workshop, 1984–1991: A Continuing Documentation of Seven Years of Interdisciplinary Art Projects Surrounding Issues of the U.S./Mexico Border* (San Diego: BAW/TAF, 1991). This writer is particularly indebted to Susan Yamagata of BAW/TAF for her graciousness and generosity in providing invaluable written and visual resources.

37. Kathryn Kanjo et al., *La Frontera/The Border: Art about the Mexico/United States Border Experience* (San Diego: Centro Cultural de la Raza and Museum of Contemporary Art, 1993). This writer extends heartfelt thanks to Patricio Chávez for his gift of the catalog, and to Kathryn Kanjo for forwarding splendid visuals and written materials.

38. See Juan Gómez-Quiñones, *Chicano Politics: Reality & Promise, 1940–1990* (Albuquerque: University of New Mexico Press, 1990), pp. 128–138.

39. That Alurista was the author of this preamble is an attribution made by artist and co-contributor to the "Spiritual Plan of Aztlán," Emanuel Martínez. See V. A. Sorell, "The Persuasion of Art/The Art of Persuasion: Emanuel Martínez Creates a Pulpit for El Movimiento," in *Emanuel Martínez: A Retrospective*, ed. Teddy Dewalt (Denver: Museo de las Américas, 1995), p. 27.

40. Gómez-Quiñones, *Chicano Politics*, p. 105.

41. *Aztlán: An Anthology of Mexican-American Literature*, ed. Luis Valdez and Stan Steiner (New York: Vintage Books, 1972), pp. 402–403.

42. A. Solomon-Godeau, "Mistaken Identities," in *Mistaken Identities* (Seattle: University of Washington Press, 1993), p. 62.

43. Ibid., p. 63.

44. For an extended discussion of this mural, refer to V. A. Sorell, "Articulate Signs of Resistance and Affirmation in Chicano Public Art," in *Chicano Art: Resistance and Affirma-*

tion, 1965–1985, ed. Richard Griswold del Castillo et al. (Los Angeles: Wight Art Gallery/ UCLA, 1991), pp. 143–144.

45. A most telling designation for México as "the United Mexican States" appears in Article XVII. For this and other citations from the treaty, see Richard Griswold del Castillo, *The Treaty of Guadalupe Hidalgo*, pp. 179–202.

46. Martha A. Sandweiss et al., *Eyewitness to War: Prints and Daguerreotypes of the Mexican War, 1846–1848* (Fort Worth, Tex. and Washington, D.C.: Amon Carter Museum and Smithsonian Institution Press, 1989), pp. 353–354.

47. Ibid.

48. Ibid. The correspondent's letter, signed "C. C.," appeared in the 19 December 1847 issue of *Picayune*.

49. For a thorough review of this exhibition, see V. A. Sorell, "Citings from a Brave New World: The Art of the Other México," in *New Art Examiner (The Independent Voice of the Visual Arts)* 21, 9 (May 1994), pp. 28–32 and 56–57.

50. Madeleine Grynsztejn, "La Frontera/The Border: Art about the Mexico/United States Border Experience," in *La Frontera/The Border*, p. 35. The source for this scriptural inflection may well have been another of Jiménez's own pieces, "Border Crossing with Halos" (1990), done in oil stick on canvas. Three other works, all entitled "Border Crossing," are also related: a drawing in crayon on paper and a polychrome fiberglass sculpture, both dating from 1986, and a lithograph with chine collé of 1987. See Ellen Landis et al., *Man on Fire/El Hombre en Llamas: Luis Jiménez* (Albuquerque: The Albuquerque Museum, 1994), pp. 146–149. Another work that contains an element highly suggestive of a halo, headdress, or aureole is the piece designated "Land" from the three-part "Pancho Trinity" (1993) sculptural grouping, rendered as painted urethane-coated styrofoam figures, by California-based Chicana artist Judy Baca. Notably, that element is Baca's representation of a fragment of border fencing. Refer to Amalia Mesa-Bains et al., *Art of the Other Mexico: Sources and Meanings* (Chicago: Mexican Fine Arts Center/Museum, 1993), pp. 106, 140.

51. A variant of *pollo* (literally "chicken") is *chivo* (literally "goat"). Author Ramón "Tianguis" Pérez attributes the use of the latter referent to "the odor we exude from lack of bathing facilities and clean clothing." See his wonderfully engaging *Diary of an Undocumented Immigrant* (Houston: Arte Público Press, 1991), p. 16. Someone who helps undocumented persons across the border is referred to in Caló, the argot of the Pachuco, as a *pollero*. See Harry Polkinhorn et al., compilers, *El Libro de Caló: The Dictionary of Chicano Slang* (Encino, Calif.: Floricanto Press, 1986), p. 50.

52. Interestingly, in Caló a "coyote" is defined as a crooked businessman or a treacherous person, qualifications perfectly consistent with the profit motive driving this "contractor" to smuggle the undocumented across the border. The emphasis on the Río Bravo in Jiménez's work under discussion serves as an important reminder that the border crossing being invoked here is defined by the river itself. That fact also explains why the woman

and child are supported on the man's back, suggesting that the water poses an added danger to them. A similar crossing through water is portrayed by Yreina Cervántez in her very evocative L.A. mural dedicated to Dolores Huerta, "La Ofrenda" (The Offering) of 1989. "Countless deaths by drowning . . . when attempts are made to cross the border north to supposed safety," Madeleine Grynsztejn writes, are memorialized, among other recollections of conscience, by artist and physician Eric Avery in his installation of molded paper woodcuts, "Family Oars" (1989). See La Frontera/The Border, pp. 32 and 140. Two photographers, Carmen Amato and Miguel Gandert, have each documented "poller(a)os" who help those "polla(o)s" crossing by water. "River Runner" (1995) and "Mujer Pasamojados" (1991) are two such black and white images by the latter and the former, respectively.

53. Refer to V. A. Sorell, "The Photograph as a Source for Visual Artists: Images from the Archivo Casasola in the Works of Mexican and Chicano Artists," in The World of Agustín Víctor Casasola: Mexico, 1900–1938, ed. Rebecca Kelley Crumlish and V. A. Sorell (Washington, D.C.: The Fondo del Sol Visual Arts and Media Center, 1984), pp. 16–27.

54. A highly venerated folk healer (1829–1907) from south Texas. See The Faith Healer of Los Olmos: Biography of Don Pedrito Jaramillo, compiled by the Brooks County Historical Survey Committee (Falfurrias, Tex.: Brooks County Historical Society, 1990); and Eliseo Torres, The Folk Healer: The Mexican-American Tradition of Curanderismo (Kingsville, Tex.: Nieves Press, n.d.).

55. Grynsztejn, La Frontera/The Border. p. 37.

56. Such figurines also play a prominent role in "Los Vendedores de Tijuana," an installation piece by artist Roberto Salas reflecting on the street vendors of Tijuana and their plaster wares. Salas refers fondly to these peddlers as "monumental shamans of kitsch." See in Site 94 Guide. pp. 162–163.

57. Steven A. Nash, "Enrique Chagoya: Borders of the Spirit," in a flyer by the same title published by the M. H. de Young Memorial Museum in San Francisco, 14 September– 27 November 1994.

58. Ibid. Chagoya's own words are echoed in this essay's ultimate epigraphic inscription by Chicano author José Antonio Burciaga. For similar perceptions about the ubiquity of migration/immigration, refer to Iain Chambers's highly stimulating book, Migrancy, Culture, Identity (London: Routledge, 1994), and Edward Said's invaluable essay, "Reflections on Exile," in Out There: Marginalization and Contemporary Cultures, ed. Russell Ferguson et al. (Cambridge, Mass., and New York: The MIT Press and the New Museum of Contemporary Art, 1990), pp. 357–366.

59. Proposition 187: Text of Proposed Law, an initiative measure submitted to the people in accordance with the provisions of Article II, Section 8 of the Constitution. See "California Ballot Pamphlet" for the General Election, 8 November 1994, prepared by Tony Miller, acting secretary of state.

60. The conceptual framework of hidden and public transcripts as discursive sites is

formulated by political scientist James C. Scott. See his *Domination and the Arts of Resistance: Hidden Transcripts* (New Haven: Yale University Press, 1990).

61. See G. G. Peña, *Warrior for Gringostroika: Essays, Performance Texts, and Poetry* (St. Paul, Minn.: Greywolf Press, 1993), p. 70. On the issue of alleged "criminal conduct," Professor Norma Cantú provides a wonderful insight on just how pernicious racist and xenophobic attitudes are and the degree to which they can influence public opinion. Given time, they can even become the attitude of the very people being victimized. Donna García, photographed at work in the fields by Lillian M. Salcido, seems amused about how she — succumbing to the biased opinion of others, who routinely maligned migrant workers — commented one day to her own husband, her fellow migrant, that the "mishap" he was talking about was probably the fault of "those migrant workers." His own response to her says it all: "Mama, we are migrant workers." See N. E. Cantú, "Living on the Border: A Wound That Will Not Heal," in *1993 Festival of American Folklife*, ed. Peter Seitel (Washington, D.C.: Smithsonian Institution Press, 1993), pp. 26–29. This writer wishes to thank his friend, folklorist Olivia Cadaval, director of the Borders Program (Festival of American Folklife) at the Smithsonian Institution's Center for Folklife Programs and Cultural Studies, for having thoughtfully sent him a copy of this stimulating publication. Not unrelated to Cantú's example is the purpose behind a mixed media installation Elvía Rodríguez-Ochoa mounted on the occasion of the Malcolm X College exhibition (revolving around Proposition 187), which she co-curated. Her "Mi Ter Ror Izmo" (My Ter Ror Ism) of 1995 was done "in response to the way groups of people become generalized and demonized in media, and thereby in many people's minds." Refer to "Artist's Statement." Such implicit appropriation and manipulation of mass media images from both Mexico and the United States, with respect to immigration and other issues, also lies at the heart of Rubén Ortíz and Aaron Anish's videotape project, "How To Read Macho Mouse" (1991).

62. Proposition 187: Text of Proposed Law.

63. See *Unsettling America: an Anthology of Contemporary Multicultural Poetry*, ed. Maria Mazziotti Gillan and Jennifer Gillan (New York: Penguin Books, 1994), pp. 115–116. It is noteworthy to add that one of Santiago Baca's books of poetry is entitled *Immigrants in Our Own Land*.

64. Ibid., p. 116.

65. R. L. Pincus, "The Invisible Town Square: Artists' Collaborations and Media Dramas in America's Biggest Border Town," in *But Is It Art? The Spirit of Art as Activism*, ed. Nina Felshin (Seattle: Bay Press, 1995), p. 33. The interview with the three artists was originally published under the title "Bus Artists Driving Home a Point," in the *San Diego Union*, 9 January 1988.

66. Ibid.

67. Ibid.

68. Ibid., pp. 35, 47–49.

69. Ibid., pp. 47–48.

70. Ibid., p. 48.

71. Ibid., p. 49.

72. D. A. Demac, *Liberty Denied: The Current Rise of Censorship in America* (New Bruns-wick, N.J.: Rutgers University Press, 1990), pp. 82–83.

73. This photograph is from Molina's "Fields of Pain/California's Migrant Farm Work-ers Series." See *FotoFest '94: The Fifth International Festival of Photography*, ed. Liz Branch (Houston: FotoFest, Inc., 1994), p. 29.

74. A more probable source for both the mural's title and Coke logo is Chicano author and painter José Antonio Burciaga, who conceived his "Tome Cultura" concept around 1975, and which he used as the title to one of his books. See *Drink Cultura: Chicanismo* (Santa Barbara: Joshua Odell Editions/Capra Press, 1993).

75. For a stimulating discussion of Ricardo and his two brothers, Enrique and Jesús, all of whom were leaders in the early movement against President Porfirio Díaz of México that led to the Mexican Revolution of 1910, see James D. Cockcroft, *Intellectual Precursors of the Mexican Revolution, 1900–1913* (Austin: University of Texas Press, 1976).

76. Another instance of discursive ellipsis. A mural in Chicago, "Prevent World War III" (1980), includes a passage by Aurelio Díaz et al., entitled "Raza Sí/Guerra No" (Yes to Raza/No to War), in which placards echo the mural's own title, conflating the INS and the police, and calling for an end to the federal Immigration and Naturalization Service.

77. Two recent studies devoted to the Statue of Liberty—one of which culminated in an exhibition observing the monument's centennial—address the monument from a vari-ety of perspectives, including its symbolism for immigrants. Refer to Wilton S. Dillon and Neil G. Kotler, eds., *Making a Universal Symbol: The Statue of Liberty Revisited* (Washington, D.C.: Smithsonian Institution, 1994), and Pierre Provoyeur, June Hargrove et al., curators, *Liberty: The French-American Statue in Art and History* (Cambridge, Mass.: Harper and Row, Publishers, 1986).

78. A. Boime, *Hollow Icons: The Politics of Sculpture in Nineteenth-Century France* (Kent, Ohio: Kent State University Press, 1987). His "Excursus on the Statue of Liberty" is quick to point out that the statue's original title was "Liberty Enlightening the World," p. 113.

79. Toppled monuments have their own history. Within the context of the visual arts, possibly most celebrated of these is the Vendôme Column (in the Place Vendôme, Paris) commemorating Napoleon. Interestingly, Gustave Courbet and other artists petitioned the French government, demanding the removal of the monument "on the ground that [it] is devoid of all artistic value, tending by its expression to perpetuate the ideas of war and conquest inherent in the imperial dynasty but rejected by the feelings of a republican na-tion." The Column was demolished on 16 May 1871. See Georges Boudaille, *Courbet: Painter in Protest* (Greenwich, Conn.: New York Graphic Society, 1969), pp. 118–123. Few would argue with Bartholdi's artistry, but his statue's symbolic reputation has become somewhat tarnished over time. Barbed wire, like the Statue of Liberty or the U.S. flag, can

become an ubiquitous icon/sign in works addressing immigration. Certain of these works are discussed in the narrative of the essay, while others are cited here.

80. A. W. Barnett, *Community Murals: The People's Art* (Philadelphia: The Art Alliance Press, 1984), p. 181.

81. Carole Naggar and Fred Ritchin, eds., *Mexico through Foreign Eyes/Visto por ojos extranjeros, 1850–1990* (New York, 1993), p. 187. Pedro A. Rodríguez portrays another apprehension/arrest by the INS in his acrylic on particle board painting of 1979, "La Migra II" (Immigration Service II). Arms upraised, with hands clasped behind the neck or atop the head, two would-be immigrants are being escorted to what more than likely is a deportation compound. The frequency with which such events take place would explain the near-anonymity of the detainees and their captor as painted by the artist.

82. The choice of a prominent and public downtown site underscores an affinity this writer finds between Avalos's Cart and "The Homeless Vehicle," conceived by Krzysztof Wodiczko to raise public awareness of the plight of the homeless during 1988 and 1989 in and around New York City and Philadelphia. See Kyoichi Tsuzuki, ed., *ArT Random/ Krzysztof Wodiczko with David Lurie: The Homeless Vehicle Project* (Kyoto, Japan: Kyoto Shoin International Co., Ltd., 1991). Of course, one can argue that there can be a natural connection between homelessness and immigration. It is "the homeless" who are "tempest-tost" in Emma Lazarus's poem, "The New Colossus," enshrined in the Statue of Liberty. See Dan Vogel, *Emma Lazarus* (Boston: Twayne Publishers, 1980), p. 158.

83. R. L. Pincus, "The Invisible Town Square . . . ," pp. 36–37. The highly suspicious circumstances surrounding the removal of Avalos's work resonate with frightening intensity and irony today, as an Anti-Terrorist Bill comes before the U.S. Congress. That legislation would essentially give the INS boundless latitude to target immigrants for deportation and worse. Refer to "Firing Line Debate," aired on PBS/Channel 11 (Chicago), 1 September 1995.

84. The fanciful imagination of Gilbert Sánchez-Luján navigates whimsical vehicles between places unknown and Aztlán. In his silkscreen, "Returning to Aztlán" (1984), and the later mixed media piece, "Powered by the Heart" (1985), the migrations would seem to be flights of fancy rather than of fact.

85. For a thoroughly engaging discussion of this concept, refer to Tomás Ybarra-Frausto, "Rasquachismo: A Chicano Sensibility," in *Chicano Art: Resistance and Affirmation*, pp. 155–162.

86. A most interesting yard shrine artist, Florencio Morales, had immigrated to Los Angeles from Mexico and lived there until his death. In his loving and sincere "Valentine's Day" message in the form of a yard shrine, he may indeed have meant, as author Amy V. Kitchener maintains, "to express his love for both of his countries." The installation includes a heart flanked by U.S. and Mexican flags. Refer to A. V. Kitchener, *The Holiday Yards of Florencio Morales: "El Hombre de las Banderas"* (Jackson, Miss.: University Press of Mississippi, 1994), p. 64, plate 32. Where individual viewers might equivocate about which

flag, if either, each identifies with, Morales seemingly remains loyal to his motherland, while simultaneously taking a patriotic stand as an immigrant.

87. The jurors were Dorothy Burkhart, Rupert García, and Long Nguyen.

88. "Curatorial Statement," typescript. This writer is most grateful to Jaime Alvarado, executive director of MACLA, and his gracious staff for their assistance and materials provided.

89. Folklorist José Limón speaks to these very points in his essay, "La Llorona, the Third Legend of Greater Mexico: Cultural Symbols, Women, and the Political Unconscious," in *Between Borders: Essays on Mexicana/Chicana History*, ed. Adelaida R. Del Castillo (Encino, Calif.: Floricanto Press, 1990), pp. 399–432. In an etching and aquatint of 1975, the incomparable Ester Hernández portrays an aggressive Guadalupana. "La Virgen de Guadalupe Defendiendo los Derechos de los Xicanos" (The Virgin of Guadalupe Defending the Rights of Chicanos) delivers a martial arts kick in behalf of her equally militant fold. That la Guadalupana can also "strike" a geographic chord is evident in photographer Graciela Iturbide's engaging image of a Guadalupana tattooed on a cholo's back—he being shown within the context of an open although highly abbreviated landscape—and tellingly titled "The Frontier, Tijuana" (1990). Perhaps, the cholo's identity as a mestizo—and in more modern times as a member of a Pachuco gang—assigns him, almost by definition, a liminal, marginal, or border locus.

90. "Curatorial Statement," typescript, MACLA.

91. "The Post-187 State Strike" is addressed to "all Latinos, Chicanos, Mexicanos, Salvadoreños, Nicaraguenses, Portorriqueños, Chilenos, Hispanics, Asians and sympathizers," and asks that they "not go to work or school, or shopping . . . [that they] not leave home." Refer to Statement issued by the "Artist/Media Post-187 State Strike Coalition," copy obtained through MACLA.

92. "Curatorial Statement," typescript, MACLA.

93. A. W. Barnett, *Community Murals*, pp. 295–297.

94. Pejorative term used especially by Mexicans to refer contemptuously to Chicanos whose Spanish lacks fluency and who have adopted Anglo-American customs and dress.

95. Curatorial Statement issued by Elvia Rodríguez-Ochoa and Jesús Macarena-Avila, exhibit curators, one-page typescript. Initially, the show ran at Chicago's Malcolm X College from 5 May through 31 May 1995. A second showing was held between 15 September and 6 October 1995, at Chicago's Roberto López Gallery. This author is deeply appreciative of the help he received from both curators as well as Ms. Lizzette Richardson, director of the Latino Center at Malcolm X. An additional point deserves mention: the "S.O.S." computer-generated printed button, designed and produced in 1995 by Jesús Macarena-Avila to promote the show, was "to represent," through its wide distribution, "a make-believe election." Hidden transcripts may abound. The "S.O.S." abbreviation could and more than likely does refer to the "Save Our State" initiative, as Proposition 187 has been characterized in California, or it can signal an international distress call, or even

invoke the noted poem by the same title, a wonderfully spirited call and response piece, authored by African American poet Amiri Baraka.

96. Artist's "Statement About (Her) Work," Malcolm X College. Related to this verbal and non-verbal statement issuing out of Chicago is Richard Godinez's markedly evocative oil on canvas painting, "Setting the Table" (n.d.) done for the MACLA show. Derivative of Norman Rockwell's well-known, popular painting, "Freedom from Want" (1943), a work depicting a Thanksgiving meal presided over by grandparents serving their children and grandchildren, Godinez's work foregrounds struggling farmworkers, rendered sharply in hues of red and brown, thus transforming—although quoting and retaining elements from—the often-reproduced prototype. Rockwell's painting was the third in a series he did under the serial title "The Four Freedoms." The other works are "Freedom of Speech," "Freedom of Worship," and the fourth, "Freedom from Fear." That "Freedom from Want" was painted when war-time rationing was in force must have made it all the more effective (see *102 Favorite Paintings by Norman Rockwell*, with an Introduction by Christopher Finch, New York: Crown Publishers, Inc., 1978). Rationed food, or the lack of food altogether, is implicit in Godinez's reference to poor farmworkers.

97. Sixteen years later, curtailment of legal immigration as well as the escalation of surveillance and penalties against "illegal" immigration were at issue in bills proposed by GOP Senator Alan Simpson of Wyoming and Republican Representative Lamar Smith of Texas. See David Bowermaster, "The Immigration Battle: Closing the Golden Door," in *U.S. News and World Report* 119, 12 (25 September 1995), p. 42. Tellingly, this same issue's thematic cover story reads: "One Nation, One Language?/The Battle over English in America."

98. Telephone conversation with the artist 13 July 1995.

99. See Arthur G. Pettit, *Images of the Mexican American in Fiction and Film*, ed. Dennis E. Showalter (College Station, Tex.: Texas A&M University Press, 1980), p. 149.

100. Barbara Carrasco's controversial mural, "The History of L.A., A Mexican Perspective" (1981–83), also highlights Mexicans in the film industry, incorporating their portraits and interweaving celluloid with human hair, the latter functioning as a dominant formal motif in the mural.

101. Eighteen artist-members of Las Comadres contributed to this installation. Marguerite Waller, one of the eighteen, has also written an excellent critical essay about this work, commenting at length on the catalytic and cathartic possibilities inherent in language as the group strives for rapprochement at the border. See M. Waller, "Border Boda or Divorce Fronterizo?" in *Negotiating Performance: Gender, Sexuality, and Theatricality in Latin/o America*, ed. Diana Taylor and Juan Villegas (Durham, N.C., 1994), pp. 67–87.

102. J. Kelley, ed., *The Border Art Workshop (BAW/TAF), 1984–1989*, pp. 80–81. Sánchez's verbal piece is dated 11/22/88. In 1989, he would execute a mixed media installation piece, "Encinitas Gardens." See David Joselit, "Living on the Border" in *Art in America* 77, 12 (December 1989), p. 122.

103. Ibid.

104. See Jorge Durand and Douglas S. Massey, *Miracles on the Border: Retablos of Mexican Migrants to the United States* (Tucson: University of Arizona Press, 1995), pp. 146–147. This extensive study was preceded by the authors' *Doy gracias: iconografía de la emigración México–Estados Unidos* (Guadalajara, JA, México: Programa de Estudios Jaliscienses/Universidad de Guadalajara, 1990). The later compilation is an important scholarly contribution to immigration studies. Besides Juan Sánchez R., another artist/petitioner known only as "F. P." gives his thanks for having had the requisite papers to reenter México. Several other artists/petitioners (notably José Cruz Soria, Amador de Lira, Domingo Segura, M. Esther Tapia Picón, and Jesús Gómez G.) all give thanks to their intercessors for their respective safe border crossings on land and by water (pp. 128–133, 136–137, and 190–191).

105. "Artist's Statement," Malcolm X Show.

106. Lou's own poignant thoughts surrounding his work were broadcast by the artist and Guillermo Gómez-Peña on "Crossroads," a program on National Public Radio. See "The Border Door," in *The Border Art Workshop, 1984–1989*, pp. 46–47.

107. See Joan Christophel, Graciela Iturbide et al., "Texts/Photos," *The River Pierce: Sacrifice II, 13.4.90* (Houston: The River Pierce Foundation/Rice University Press, 1992).

4

THE CELLULOID IMMIGRANT

The Narrative Films of Mexican Immigration

o o o o
o o o o

David R. Maciel and María Rosa García-Acevedo

Mexican undocumented emigration to the United States is the single most complex and difficult issue currently facing these two countries. The controversy concerning Mexican undocumented workers in the United States includes economic, political, legal, social, cultural, and even moral considerations. Mexican migration has, in fact, become one of the salient political issues of the 1990s.[1] The question has intensified in the political discourse of both countries and has received considerable attention from the academic community, policy makers, and the printed and mass media.

Although there exists a growing important body of scholarly studies on the subject, it is the media that, by far, have been the most influential in setting the agenda of the political debate and in molding public opinion in the United States and Mexico. The printed and visual media coverage and representation of the issues surrounding Mexican immigration have been greatly responsible for the current rise in xenophobia and anti-immigrant sentiment in the United States.[2] In Mexico, media portrayals of the immigrant experience have contributed toward the move for political action on the subject. Among the visual media, cinema is the one that has been singularly influential because of its consistency and popularity in addressing the theme of Mexican immigration.

For decades cinema has been the leading popular form of amusement.[3] To a large degree, this is due to the fact that in most industrialized societies, movies are one of the most inexpensive means of entertainment. Films have a broad appeal to many age groups. For the most part, movies provide a highly entertaining means for escapism; many people flock to the theaters to get away from their everyday problems.

Yet, as has been well documented, cinema is much more than simply an art or plain entertainment. In the modern world, cinema has acquired important social, cultural, and even political functions through its popularity and mass consumption. Films have in many ways become larger than life. They are critical manifestations of popular culture and mass entertainment and are attended by large segments of contemporary society.[4] Audiences worldwide clamor to be entertained, educated, distracted, absorbed, stimulated, or just diverted.[5]

Moreover, movies act as a potent source of informal education and ideas. As such, their content is never free of value judgments or individual biases. Their messages, themes, images, and ideology have a definitive societal impact.[6] In many instances, the viewing public forms its judgments, opinions, and even values on the basis of images, ideological constructs, and representations fabricated by the silver screen.

Mexican migration has been a dominant cinematic theme on both sides of the U.S.–Mexico border from the early decades of the century to the very present. Just as the process of Mexican emigration to the United States encompasses the entire twentieth century, so do representations and images of Mexican immigrants in the silver screen have an equally long history. The majority of immigration films do not necessarily provide narrative elements that contribute toward a more insightful understanding of the complexity of Mexican migration; nonetheless, films on immigration do reveal national idiosyncracies. According to one scholar, the elements films reflect about a particular society "are not so much exploit credos as psychological dispositions — those deep layers of collective mentality which extend more or less below the dimension of consciousness."[7] As such these films are an important measure of national attitudes on Mexican emigration to the United States, for as a noted scholar has demonstrated, "recurrent screen motifs reflect the needs and fears of the entire nation."[8]

The cinematic productions of both Mexico and the United States on immigration have included numerous commercial features, independent films, and documentaries; because of limitations of space, this chapter omits a discussion and analysis of the documentaries, although they are important, often well-crafted artistically, and certainly in need of scholarship. This chapter, then, will concentrate on narrative full-length feature films. These films can be subdivided by country of origin, subgenre, production formula, and the historical period in which they were produced and screened.

In Mexico alone, close to one hundred full-length "immigration movies" have been produced and distributed in the Americas.[9] The films have included works by many of Mexico's most distinguished filmmakers such as Miguel Contreras Torres, Alejandro Galindo, David Silva, Pedro Armendáriz, Julio Alemán, Hector Suárez, Ernesto Gómez Cruz, María Novaro, Patricia Reyes Spíndola, Mario Almada, and Gonzalo Vega.

Mexican immigration films clearly merit scholarly inquiry and analysis. They were and are widely viewed. The importance of cinema in Mexico has been profound. In fact, up until the late 1950s, motion pictures were the most important artistic form of popular entertainment in Mexico.[10] Mexican cinema has been of equal significance in the United States, particularly from the late 1930s to the 1960s. In that historical period, throughout the Southwest and other areas with large Latino populations, an extensive chain of theaters operated that showed Spanish-language films exclusively (almost all Mexican) on a year-round basis.[11]

As subjects of research, Mexican films that focus on the Mexican immigrant experience in the United States open a wealth of avenues for academic study. Aesthetically, these productions display the origins, technical and artistic aspects, process, and maturity of filmmaking in Mexico. As historical documents, they constitute essential sources for an understanding of the construction of Mexican policies, popular attitudes, and general perceptions toward their compatriots north of the Río Bravo. In addition, these films are an important chapter in the complex and dynamic relationship between Mexico and the Chicano community.

Hollywood immigration films are equally significant because of their origin, ideological constructs, and popularity. The American film industry, the largest and most powerful one worldwide, distributes more films than any other national cinema.[12] Hollywood features are the most widely viewed motion pictures in almost every country in the world. Because of the films' mass consumption, American cinema is highly influential. The Hollywood style has set the standard for popular films both thematically and artistically. Film genres such as westerns, slapstick comedies, thrillers, action, and melodrama have inspired and influenced filmmakers around the world.[13]

In American cinema, major stars of the past and of today such as Tom Mix, Hopalong Cassidy, Lloyd Bridges, Charles Bronson, and Jack Nicholson have performed in immigration films. Because of their audience and ideological messages, Hollywood immigration films are critical documents for academic study.

One other cinematic perspective on immigration emerged in the 1970s and has continued to the present: Chicano cinema. Although producing fewer films than other cinemas, Chicano cinema has, nonetheless, made significant contributions to this genre. Several Chicano narrative films have offered important and moving portrayals of the Mexican/Latino emigrant experience. Measured by artistic creativity and approximations to social reality, they are the most accomplished of the three cinematic perspectives.

As stated earlier, our study focuses on feature films that deal exclusively with Mexican undocumented immigrants in the United States. All three distinct cinematic immigration perspectives—Mexican films, the Hollywood style, and Chicano cinema—receive extensive commentary and analysis. Each, in turn, with its own set of characteristics, representations, and discursive elements, is placed in a cultural and social history construct. Research for this chapter was conducted in a threefold manner: a careful examination of primary and secondary materials, a contextual analysis of immigration genre films (over one hundred films were carefully screened and deconstructed), and extensive interviews with prominent members of the filmmaking community in the United States (principally in Los Angeles) and in Mexico City.

The conceptual mode of analysis applied in this discussion of films is the study of "genre," defined as a "category, kind, or form of film distinguished by subject matter, theme, or techniques." [14] Genre films, then, are features that are imitations of other ones. Such films follow a similar pattern or formula. Basic common ingredients found in genre narratives include setting, plot (conflict and resolution), recurring images, and interchangeable cinematic techniques. [15] Foremost is the fact that genre films "are commercial films which through repetition and variation, tell familiar stories with familiar characters in familiar situations." [16] In addition, they deal with the relationship between groups of films as well as with the societies in which they are produced and the cultures in which they are shown. Genre films are almost exclusively popular movies, compared to art films, which generally serve a specific taste or viewing public. In the words of a recent critic, genre films are "pure emotional articulation, fictional constructs of the imagination, growing essentially out of group interests and values." [17] Structurewise, the plot is the single most critical aspect of the genre film. In other words, what matters most in these films is the story itself. The narration, therefore, is linear with a clear beginning and an equally clear ending.

Classic genre films are a fairly simple and unsophisticated art form oriented toward a mass audience. By their very nature, genre films simplify film viewing.[18] Since the narratives are well-known and easily recognized by the audience because of their repetitiveness, genre films make viewing easier for the spectator and, to a large degree, more enjoyable.[19]

Genre productions are no less significant than other cinematic art forms. They have their own purpose and share the following objectives: (1) they attempt to relieve fears created by social and political conflicts; (2) they aid in discouraging action about such conflicts; (3) they produce satisfaction rather than action, as well as pity and fear rather than organization; and (4) most important, they contribute toward the perpetuation of the status quo.[20]

It is also important that genre films, at times, have addressed social issues. Salient questions that film genre analysis stresses are: What makes a particular film genre popular? What elements make it survive and persist? How does a genre film relate to society? What is the political/ideological influence of the film? What effects does the genre film have on the societal and individual psyche? What actual or imaginary events does the film allude to? And how does the genre film represent the historical experience?[21]

Moreover, recent genre film studies stress the importance of acknowledging and understanding the milieu and background of the work through its relationship with history, popular culture, and politics.[22] These conceptual modes of genre studies are remarkably applicable to this discussion and analysis of immigration films. Genre films dealing with Mexican immigration to the United States are repetitive and rely on previous productions; emphasize the arrangement of actions (plot); have a close relationship with history, society, and politics; have been popular; and have been distinct from other film genre.

The Quest for El Dorado[23] in the Cinema of Mexico, 1922–1970

Mexico's concern for its population in the United States dates as far back as the Texas Rebellion of 1836 and continues to the very present. This interest and attention has manifested itself in diplomatic, political, educational, and cultural efforts.[24]

Within Mexican cultural modes, the cinema has been particularly instrumental in depicting Mexico's views and interpretations toward its diaspora in the United States. Numerically, Mexican cinema has more features on immigration than any national cinema. Over a hundred narrative films have been produced and screened in Mexico on this specific theme. There exist two very distinct periods of immigration films in Mexico: from 1922 to the late 1960s, and from the mid-1970s to the present.

While the films of this first period vary in structure, ideological constructs, artistic worth, style, and narration, they nonetheless encompass the following general characteristics: (1) All of these productions have strong didactic messages. The most common is that if you emigrate to the United States, only heartache, disappointment, and oppression await you. (2) Related to the previous point is that most of these films end in tragedy. The migratory experience is consistently portrayed negatively. (3) The main characters for the most part return to Mexico. Very few of the principals ever choose to stay permanently in the United States, and those few Mexican immigrants who do reside north of the Río Bravo often speak of and long for a return to their native country. (4) Mexican cinematic preoccupation with this theme responds to internal issues, cycles of Mexican emigration to the United States, and the country's foreign policy vis-à-vis the United States. (5) Many of the leading Mexican filmmakers, throughout the early decades of the twentieth century, have participated in such productions. (6) This film genre includes comedies, musicals, melodramas, and action features. (7) This is the only Mexican cinematic cycle that has yet to run its course. While melodramas and musicals, for example, had their high point in earlier years and have all but disappeared, immigration films continue to be produced and to captivate the imagination of Mexican filmmakers (a case in point is the 1994 production *El jardín del Edén*).

The initial cycle of Mexican immigration genre films parallels and responds to the political, social, and cultural processes of the first three decades of this century. Besides reflecting the historical trends of the period, Mexican immigration narratives exhibit the dramatic turnabout in Mexico's attitudes and policies toward its compatriots north of the Río Bravo.

This attitudinal shift would follow a process originating in the 1840s and culminating in the 1920s. Observing the experiences of the Mexican-origin population in Texas after its secession from Mexico in 1836, officials in Mexico knew their fears about the fate of the Mexican community were well founded. In the wake of the defeat by the United States (1846–1848) and the loss of 50.2 percent of its national territory, Mexico, through the terms of the Treaty of Guadalupe Hidalgo, attempted to pressure for just treatment toward "el México perdido." The Mexican government demanded that this treaty of peace include specific articles protecting the property and well-being of the Mexican population who chose to remain in what was now U.S. territory.

However, in spite of the promises and guarantees of "all the rights of citizens of the United States according to the principles of the constitution" to those Mexicans who chose to stay, little was delivered. Throughout the nineteenth century, numerous examples exist of Mexican protest on behalf of those that stayed in the lost land, over events in the Southwest. Mexican newspapers such as *El Siglo XIX* and *El Monitor Republicano* carried news and editorials on the situation of the Mexican community north of the Río Bravo. Mexican attitudes toward their compatriots in the nineteenth century were for the most part positive, sympathetic, and nationalistic.[25] The situation unfortunately began to change with the advent of the new century.

In the late nineteenth century, Mexican workers in significant numbers began to emigrate to the U.S. Southwest in search of better economic opportunities. With the onset of the Mexican Revolution (1910–1917) and the ensuing economic crisis in the country, Mexican emigration intensified dramatically. In spite of the fact that Mexico could not employ its entire labor force, making it an economic necessity for Mexican workers to seek jobs elsewhere, bitter feelings developed toward those who abandoned *la patria*.[26]

As more people left Mexico and settled in the United States, the resentment among Mexicans grew. Writings, *corridos* (folk ballads), and other popular manifestations voicing strong nationalistic sentiment equated the process of emigrating to the United States with traitorous acts or turning one's back on the country.[27]

Mexican filmmakers, highly influenced by the political and ideological climate of the times, would transpose the pervasive attitudes toward those that emigrated to images on the screen. The first production that dealt with the Mexican immigrant experience in the United States was the 1922 silent film *El hombre sin patria* (The Man without a Country)—produced, directed by, and starring Miguel Contreras Torres. This pioneer motion picture clearly reflected Mexican attitudes and concerns about its emigrants.

The film recounts the misadventures of Rodolfo, a young upper-class Mexican who is leading a wasteful and frivolous life. After numerous conflicts with his father, he is finally kicked out of home and disinherited. He opts to follow the example of others and emigrate to the United States. Since initially he has funds, his early stay in the United States is a continuation of his previous escapades in Mexico. However, soon his money runs out, and he begins to experience the cruel realities of what it is like to be Mexican in the United States. Various discriminatory practices and degrading employment patterns make up the greater portion of the film. The low point is reached when he kills a racist and evil foreman in self-defense. Fearing for his life, a now not-so-young Rodolfo returns to his homeland, reconciling with his family and beginning to make amends for the past. The production ends on a happy note with the main character—now a mature, hardworking, patriotic Mexican—finding true love and following a proper path of life.[28]

El hombre sin patria was far from the best feature in the long and distinguished film career of Miguel Contreras Torres. Yet the movie is seminal because it was not only the earliest Mexican production on the subject of immigration, but also the first Mexican motion picture that was shot on location in the cities of Los Angeles and San Diego. The film was so well received by the general public that Contreras Torres, years later, released a second version of the same film, this time a "talkie."[29]

The ideological message of *El hombre sin patria* is direct: if you emigrate to the United States, nothing but racism and oppression await you. As difficult as your situation might be in Mexico, you still will have family warmth, familiar surroundings, and the satisfaction of working toward the building of post-revolution Mexico. The title of the feature is consistent with Mexican attitudes toward those compatriots that have left for the United States and thus have no real homeland or roots.

The didactic message of dissuasion conveyed by *El hombre sin patria* followed official emigration policies of the period. Reports were widely distributed by Mexican authorities and their consulates in the United States about rights violations and mistreatment directed toward immigrants.[30] However, such efforts were not successful in curtailing massive migration. In fact, it has been estimated that from 1890 to 1930 more than one million Mexicans crossed the Río Bravo in search of "El Dorado."[31]

It would not be until 1938 that Mexican cinema would again address a similar theme, with the film *La China Hilaria*. This minor feature is one of the precursors to the ranchera cycle. Rancheras are musical comedies situated in a rural setting. They are among the most popular and enduring of the Mexican film genres, but they would not find their way and full popularity until *Allá en el Rancho Grande* (It Happened on the Rancho Grande, 1939). *La China Hilaria* narrates the story of a rural Mexican worker by the name of Isidro who decides to migrate to the United States to seek better employment. His goal is to find work, save money, and return to his home to marry his sweetheart Hilaria (thus the name of the film). Isidro works long hours thinking only of the day he will return to his beloved Hilaria. Since he presumed that all was as they agreed, he does not communicate with his loved one. After a long wait and without receiving any news from Isidro, Hilaria relocates and begins a successful career singing in local palenques (fairs).

Two men court Hilaria. Although she is taken with one, she remains faithful and waits for Isidro. Time passes and his stay in the United States begins to change Isidro. When the prodigal son finally returns, he is now married. Predictably, Hilaria, after recuperating from her broken heart, ends up with her one true love, and the film closes with a happy ending.

Similar to *El hombre sin patria*, this production highlights the changes in the character of a Mexican after a prolonged stay in the United States. The point is made that Isidro's values and moral fiber were diminished by prolonged exposure to North America. The one other memorable aspect of *La China Hilaria* is the appearance of the great future star Pedro Armendariz in one of his first starring roles.

The next Mexican productions on this theme would incorporate national concerns on the latest chapter of emigration to the United States—the Bracero Program. Signed in 1942 between Mexico and the United States, it permitted large-scale recruitment and contracting of Mexican workers to work in the United States in order to meet labor needs in times of war. Yet the program spurred illegal immigration, since many that wanted to work in the United States were either not contracted or did not fall within certain regulatory measures of the program.[32]

One production on the Bracero Program is Alfonso Patiño Gómez's *Pito Pérez se va de bracero* (Pito Pérez Becomes a Bracero, 1947). The film attempted to combine two important elements: the lovable picaresque main character of the celebrated novel, *La vida inútil de Pito Pérez*, and the Bracero Program. José Rubén Romero, one of the major novelists of the Mexican Revolution, imaginatively revived the tradition of the Spanish picaresque novel and adapted it with great success to the time and place of post-revolutionary Mexico. His *pícaro* (rogue) travels through the country, interacting with a wide spectrum of society and its institutions. Through acute observations and biting dialogue, the novel satirizes and denounces many of the social ills and governmental shortcomings of the period. The main character of the novel, Pito Pérez, gained great acceptance and became an icon of Mexican popular culture.[33] It is, therefore, not surprising that filmmakers would envision the same character having an equal success on the silver screen, particularly if his setting was in the context of a rising national concern, Mexican immigrant workers in the United States.

The cinematic narrative follows the improbable misadventures of Pito Pérez, who, after a series of misfortunes in Mexico, joins a group of prospective braceros as they make their way to the United States. Upon crossing, Pito Pérez and the group begin laboring as fieldworkers. Finding this type of employment exhausting and hazardous, he searches for easier and better-paying work. His next escapade is as a dishwasher in a dance hall, where he meets the heroine of the story. Later in the film, it is learned that she—along with the owner of the dance hall and other accomplices—is in the business of illegal trafficking of Mexican workers to the United States. Violence erupts when police move in. The main leaders are wounded and captured. Pito Pérez is incarcerated because of guilt by association. His blond friend, the dance hall girl, and his benefactor, who remained aloof from the sting, pay the fine and he is deported. The film closes with Pito Pérez returning to his native Mexico having learned his lesson and vowing to never return to the United States.

All the charm, freshness, and relevant social satire which the original Pito Pérez character exhibited in the novel—thus gaining much popular acclaim—was not present in this opportunistic and little-thought-out production. *Pito Pérez se va de bracero* was not particularly creative, well conceptualized, or even properly cast.

In *Soy mexicano de acá de este lado* (I Am a Mexican from This Side of the Border, 1951) the theme of the *pocho*[34] and the bracero are combined by the veteran director Miguel Contreras Torres. The title of the film highlights its principal ideological message. Through the two main characters, a Chicano born in Texas but now residing in Mexico, and a former bracero, striking differences between the Chicano and Mexican communities are accentuated.

Implied by the title of the film is that citizens on the Mexican side of the border are authentic Mexicanos, whereas those on the other side are not really Mexicanos any longer but pochos. This theme is clearly conveyed by Freddie, the pocho character, in a lengthy sequence in which he outlines the condition and plight of the Chicano community. He stresses issues of lost identity, cultural values, and traditions of Chicanos. The effectiveness of such moments is lost, however, in the long and erratic melodrama.

Soy mexicano de acá de este lado exhibits the patriotic traits of director Contreras Torres by stressing nationalism and the enduring Mexican traditions and values, but little else. The film's main problem is the lack of a defined story or character. From the onset to the finish, the film narration moves in multiple directions. Too many themes were attempted without any of them ever really being developed.[35]

Acá las tortas (This Is the Place for Tortas, 1951) continues merging the theme of immigration with the concept of the pocho. Here, "pocho" is even applied to the son and daughter of a Mexican couple who own a small restaurant that specializes in *tortas* (Mexican sandwiches). The son and the daughter, upon returning to Mexico after completing studies in the United States, display American influences and appear to be followers of North American traits and mannerisms. The film makes the statement that pochos are not just Chicanos that were born or reside permanently in the United States, but all those Mexican immigrants who live there temporarily and behave in an Americanized manner when they return to Mexico. In *Acá las tortas*, the point is made even on food choices. The son redeems himself toward the end of the production by rejecting non-Mexican dishes and promising to join his parents in continuing to sell tortas.

The film *Acá las tortas* displays all the variations of Mexican concerns of the dangers of Americanization of the country. The solution, according to the film-makers, is to accentuate Mexican values and nationalism for youth—the most susceptible to foreign influences. The "American way of life" and U.S. traditions are portrayed in a static negative vein. A strong value judgment is made: "lo mexi-cano" is the only positive direction for Mexico; "lo gringo" only corrupts and degrades Mexican society and traditions.[36]

Throughout the early decades of the twentieth century, Mexican officials and educators were quite distressed with the possible loss of *mexicanidad* by the Mexican-origin population in the United States. It is important to note that Mexi-can consuls were officially given the task to promote and foster each and every aspect of mexicanidad by any means possible. There is much evidence that histori-cally documents this ongoing effort. Consuls in a multitude of U.S. cities organized patriotic festivities and other events aimed at retaining the spirit of mexicanidad.[37]

In 1954 Mexico premiered an impressive film, *Espaldas mojadas*, directed by the respected Golden Age director Alejandro Galindo (see fig. 4.1). *Espaldas moja-das* opens with a view of Ciudad Juárez, while a narrator informs the viewer that "on this side of the Río Bravo it is still Mexico, where Spanish is spoken and songs are sung to the Virgin of Guadalupe. . . . On the other side of the Río Grande, as the gringos call it, are skyscrapers and it's where everyone owns a car." A country, continues the narrator, that "forty years of movies have presented as a place where everyone is happy."[38]

Rafael, the main character, has just arrived in Ciudad Juárez from the city of San Luis Potosí. He has been working as a tractor driver in the region known as El Mante, but had to leave because of a conflict with a powerful landowner. The incident involved the son of this prominent and influential individual. Rafael is fearful of reprisals of this *cacique* (a local strongman). Rafael travels to the Mexican border hoping to cross into the United States. When he goes to a bracero hiring hall, he tries to get work as a tractor driver but is promptly and unceremoniously informed that for Mexicans on the other side there is only one kind of work—as

Figure 4.1. Original movie poster for the classic Mexican film *Espaldas mojadas*. Courtesy Filmoteca Nacional/UNAM.

a field hand. The real problem, though, is that Rafael has no "working papers" or passport that would enable him to work legally in the United States.

Margarita, a bar waitress, befriends Rafael; she directs him to Frank Mendoza, a *coyote* (term used to denote those who are in the business of smuggling undocumented workers to the United States). Mendoza works for a Mr. Sterling and specializes in getting *espaldas mojadas* across the border. That same night, Rafael and a group of migrant workers attempt to cross the Río Grande, but tragedy strikes. Surprised by the U.S. Border Patrol, some in the group are killed or wounded by the *migra*. A newly made friend, Felipe, is mortally wounded, and as a last gesture he gives Rafael all his money and asks him to cast his body into the river so that it will float back into Mexico. Rafael, back in Ciudad Juárez, is advised to seek out Sterling, who is in the business of hiring undocumented workers on a large scale for agricultural and railroad work. Upon meeting Sterling and discussing his plight with him, Rafael is offered work on *el traque* (the railroad).

After a stint in this occupation, Rafael leaves due to a fight with Sterling over his unethical treatment of workers. Along the way he meets up with Luis. At a roadside cafe, he encounters a waitress by the name of María del Consuelo, whom he had briefly met after crossing the border. When a policeman comes in, she hides Rafael as the cop utters the classic line, "You seen a Mexican with a brown leather jacket? Looks more like a wop than a Mexican."[39] María del Consuelo saves Rafael from being apprehended by the law. She also vents her frustrations with the oppressive North American system as she tells Rafael of her unhappiness: "I'm not Mexican, I'm a Pocha. The Mexicans don't like us and the Gringos look down on us."[40]

Alejandro Galindo is the Mexican film director who best captures the agonizing and difficult situation of Chicanos vis-à-vis their country of origin that has forgotten them and the North American institutions and discriminatory practices that victimize them. Through María del Consuelo's dialogues, Mexican viewers of *Espaldas mojadas* were exposed for the first time to a sensitive, well-informed, and complex cinematic Chicano character. Her character portrayed the rejection and exploitation that Chicanas/os are subjected to on both sides of the border.

Rafael is much attracted to María del Consuelo. After courting her, Rafael asks her to marry him and she agrees. They plan to meet in Ciudad Juárez to marry and settle there. The irony of the plot is that Rafael tries to re-enter Mexico the same way he left, crossing the Río Bravo—this time through a hail of bullets that "rains" on him from Sterling and the U.S. authorities. He then encounters and is detained by the Mexican Border Patrol. Having lost his identification papers, Rafael is treated by the Mexican police as an *indocumentado* and they initially refuse to admit him into the country. A dialogue ensues in which Rafael pleads his case by saying that he is a Mexican national and wants to get back into the country. The officer tells him that there are many people with swarthy skin—pochos, Greeks, Italians. "When will you people realize," continues the officer, "the trouble that you cause by crossing illegally. Have you no dignity?" "Dignity?" asks Rafael angrily. "We're hungry, that's the reason."

After giving the Mexican official a brief rundown on the things that are wrong with Mexico, Rafael pleads to be allowed to stay. It works; he is released and continues on his way to find María del Consuelo in Ciudad Juárez. At the cabaret where he meets her, he runs into Sterling. Rafael and others proceed to take revenge on Sterling for the deaths of many of their friends by giving him a severe beating. It is suggested that Sterling not be killed there but that he should be taken to the river and dumped in. Forced to swim across the river, Sterling is shot to death by U.S. Border Patrol officers as he attempts to reach the shore.

Leaving the scene of the killing of Sterling, a member of the group comments to Rafael, "Neither you nor we killed him. It was he who stupidly tried to swim to the other side." Trying to make a fresh start, Rafael, María del Consuelo, and Luis decide to move on, and they depart to the interior of Mexico, having had more than their fill of being *mojados*.[41]

Espaldas mojadas is by far the single best Mexican commercial production on the subject of immigration. The production departs from the genre to become more of a director's art film. This movie's powerful impact is due to its hard-hitting look at the socioeconomic problems of Mexico, the hopelessness of existence for some sectors of the Mexican population, the need for many Mexican workers to emigrate to the United States as a safety valve, and even the condition of the Chicano community on the U.S. side of the border. The acting, directing, and plot are all exceptional.

Another important film is *Los desarraigados* (The Uprooted, 1958), an early Mexican attempt at a sensitive portrayal of the immigrant experience. The story focuses on a typical family that left Mexico shortly after the Revolution of 1910 and emigrated to the United States. As the title indicates, their existence on foreign soil is a tragic one. The two eldest sons are killed fighting for the Allied cause in World War II. Even with hard work and efforts at accommodation in the United States, family harmony is absent from the home. The parents face severe intergenerational conflicts with their two remaining sons and a daughter. The elder son, Joe, is a struggling reformed alcoholic who lives in constant fear of returning to his old habit. Jimmy, the youngest, comes under the influence of bad company, winds up peddling drugs, and is ultimately arrested and jailed. The daughter, Alice, rejects her heritage and runs away from home, attempting assimilation as a solution to her personal crisis.

After such tragedies, the tide begins to change. The parents finally sense a fulfillment of their dreams through their children. Alice returns home repentant and wishing to start again; Joe promises to travel to Mexico to be with his new love, a woman from there whom he recently courted; and Jimmy is released from jail under bond with the assurance that he will leave his life of crime. The Pacheco family, at last, has some hope for the future.

Overall, the film is disappointing and does not achieve its full potential. The identity questions which are central to the story are never fully addressed realistically or with much depth. In spite of the fine cast—which includes Jose Elías Moreno, Pedro Armendariz, Sonia Furió, Lola Tinoco, and Ariadne Walter—and a script based upon a well-written play, the film fails to convey its meaning in a convincing manner. Again, the main theme in this film is the human cost of leaving Mexico and emigrating to the United States. In a fatalistic manner, the children of the family have followed the wrong paths. The implicit message is that the "American way of life" is to blame for this situation.[42]

A decade later, comedian and singer Eulalio González, "Piporro," addressed bracero/immigrant themes in two well received popular films, El bracero del año (The Bracero of the Year, 1963) and El pocho (1964). González established a unique precedent in recent Mexican cinema, being an actor who not only would be the star of the films, but would serve as director, screenwriter, and producer.[43]

In El bracero del año, "Piporro" stars as a typical would-be migrant worker. Natalio Reyes Colas (Piporro) crosses illegally with a group of others in search of work in the Texas agriculture fields. After numerous escapades, all in a lighthearted vein, he is selected by his peers as "the bracero of the year." As a prize, our hero asks for and is granted his green card. He flies to Los Angeles where he is further rewarded by being honored with a parade and festivities in his honor. Finally Natalio returns to Mexico and to his girl whom he had left behind. As the narrative shows, El bracero del año is a very far-fetched and silly Mexican immigrant success story. Many critics have questioned the ideological premise of treating such a serious and dramatic issue as a humorous farce.

El pocho (1964) is Piporro's most significant contribution to such film themes and perhaps best captures Mexican perceptions about the Mexican-origin community in the United States in the 1950s and early 1960s. Certain fundamental issues of the U.S.–Mexican border such as identity, music, language, and the complex and at times ambivalent situation of Chicanos/Mexicans in a border context are addressed in this film.

The movie El pocho was filmed entirely in the twin border cities of Ciudad Juárez and El Paso, giving authenticity to the film. The plot revolves around events in the life of José Guadalupe García, played by Piporro. García, a clerk in an El Paso drugstore, is an orphan whose parents drowned trying to cross the Río Grande illegally into the United States. He grows up in El Paso, going by the name of Joe Garsha, the name that he received at the orphanage. Despite the fact that he has been strongly influenced by United States culture and values, his mexicanidad is very much present, although initially his cultural loyalty is doubted. The movie opens with José Guadalupe García trying to assimilate into United States society by speaking only English and acquiring an Anglo girlfriend. However, he soon encounters overt discrimination, even to the point where his girlfriend's brother and friends beat him up solely because he is Mexican and dating an "American" girl. This episode dramatically changes Garcia's feelings toward his newly adopted country.

He reacts in the only manner that he knows how: he crosses the border into Juárez. Trying to court a young Mexican woman newly arrived from Guadalajara (played by the noted singer and film star Lucha Villa), he is ridiculed and rejected by her. To add insult to injury, he is accosted by a group of locals who proceed to give him the beating of his life for being a pocho and courting a Mexican woman.

The movie closes with García jumping into the Río Bravo, mourning the fact that the one true home for the Chicano is right there in the middle of the river, neither here nor there. His rejection by both American and Mexican society puts José Guadalupe in the unenviable position of many Chicanos along the border.[44]

As a film, El pocho is weak. In his multifaceted role of producer, screenwriter, director, and principal actor, Eulalio González does not succeed on all levels. El pocho closed the cycle of Mexican cinema that focused on questions of mexicanidad of the Mexican-origin population in the United States. The 1970s and beyond would begin a different direction of the interpretation of Mexican immigrants by the narrative films of Mexico.

The Control of Our Border According to Hollywood

On the theme of immigration, Hollywood has followed a path distinct from the Mexican experience. Unlike other cinematic themes that have reflected creativity and diversity in American cinema, in the question of immigration genre films the Hollywood style has opted for a static and rather conventional format.

On the whole, Hollywood genre films on immigration share certain particular characteristics: (1) They cover a lengthy historical period of production, from the silent-film period to the present. (2) American immigration films follow one basic discursive formula, a modified version of the western in which the hero struggles valiantly against gangs involved in the trafficking of undocumented workers, always defeating them at the end. (3) Although these films are supposed to deal with the theme of Mexican immigration, in reality the immigrant experience is always vague and the least developed aspect of the film. (4) Hollywood immigration movies are, without an exception, a vehicle for a traditional action story for the principal star, be it Tom Mix or Jack Nicholson. (5) They have a clear policy message: the importance of the control of our southern border and the need to institutionalize a campaign against the smuggling of undocumented workers to the United States. (6) Hollywood immigration films reveal U.S. preoccupations and concerns with the immigration issue on U.S. soil; the roots and causes of Mexican immigration and the substantial contributions of Mexican immigrants to the U.S. economy are never addressed in much detail. (7) These movies do not offer any alternative solutions to Mexican undocumented immigration. (8) Almost without exception, women are totally secondary as characters; there is, then, a serious lack of important or interesting gender representation. (9) For the most part, Hollywood immigration films can be classified as B movies (that is of secondary billing and of low budget). (10) Hollywood films are the least-developed in narration or character development of the three cinematic perspectives on immigration.

The Hollywood style used on immigration films offers an important look into the blend of art, politics, and commercialism in the United States. Certain immigration films have proved moderately successful at the box office. Even more critical, they reinforce widely held beliefs and reflect the political and ideological ambiance of the time of production in the United States. What follows is a chronological assessment of Hollywood immigration films from their origins to the present.

Her Last Resort (1912) is perhaps the first American film on the theme of Mexican immigration. This unusual and sympathetic portrayal of the plight of Mexican workers has the protagonist crossing the Río Grande in search of employment after exhausting all possibilities in Mexico. Yet after he enters the United States, all he encounters is discrimination and exploitation.

The film's narrative develops as follows: On his way back to Mexico, after reaching the breaking point with constant oppression, the protagonist heroically saves the life of a rancher who has suffered a serious accident. The same rancher, ironically, had earlier denied him employment and had run him off his land. Asking for no compensation for his noble deed, the protagonist continues his trip home. Upon his arrival, he discovers that his wife had stolen a cow from an American rancher to get milk for their infant son. A posse arrives and, in spite of his wife's confession, is about to hang the man, when in the nick of time, the rancher that had been rescued earlier arrives and saves the day. To fully repay his debt, the rancher provides stock as gifts and a permanent job to the protagonist. The film thus closes on a happy note.[45]

The Mexican (1914) is the single other silent immigration film. Legendary western star Tom Mix acts in and directs this melodrama that traces the story of a Mexican worker who crosses the border seeking employment to feed his starving family. While working under oppressive conditions, he is badly abused and physically harmed. The Mexican seeks revenge upon his assailants by burning their fields and ranch houses. In the middle of this, he comes upon the daughter of one of the ranch owners who had done him harm earlier. The young woman had been bitten by a rattlesnake and become gravely ill. The Mexican, putting aside his vendetta, acts quickly and is able to save her life. In appreciation, the rancher rewards the Mexican worker by permanently providing for him and his family in Mexico. Another happy ending with redemption and justice emerging in the conclusion.[46]

By this time, Mexican-origin characters had primarily become another type of institution in early American cinema—the convenient villain. From the earliest productions on, Mexican archetypical characters appeared consistently in films as villains, cowards, and buffoons.[47]

Contrary to this, these two initial U.S. immigration genre films break from tradition by representing Mexican immigrant characters in a positive light, but, nonetheless, do so in a condescending way and leave little doubt as to the implied superiority of the Anglo who has to save the Mexican from his fate.[48]

In addition, *Her Last Resort* and *The Mexican* reflect the immigration issues of the times with the silent cinematic discourse of the period. By the 1920s, Mexican immigrants in the Southwest had increased by the thousands.[49] These immigrants had become an essential part of the economic and social life of the U.S. border cities and in such other cities as Chicago, Los Angeles, San Antonio, and Tucson. Although the Mexican immigrants were instrumental in helping build the U.S. Southwest into an economic powerhouse, their numbers and origin caused concerns about the possible social and cultural consequences on American institutions of this most recent and extensive immigrant group. In this environment, scholars, educators, and social workers were sent to study "the Mexican problem" in the Southwest.[50]

Years later, U.S. filmmakers would once again merge a political and social concern with artistic creation, producing a number of films whose main themes derived from aspects related to the Bracero Program (1942–1964).

Border Patrol (1943) builds on the immigration genre in this period. The ever-popular western genre and one of its great early stars, "Hopalong Cassidy" (William Boyd), combine this narrative format with the theme of illegal Mexican immigration. The narrative of this film has the Texas Rangers (Hopalong Cassidy being one) in a struggle to the death against a vicious gang that is importing illegal Mexican aliens to the United States and farming them out to the highest bidder.

As in a typical western, in *Border Patrol*, the heroes face grave adversity. They are initially captured by the villains, tried in a "kangaroo court," and sentenced to

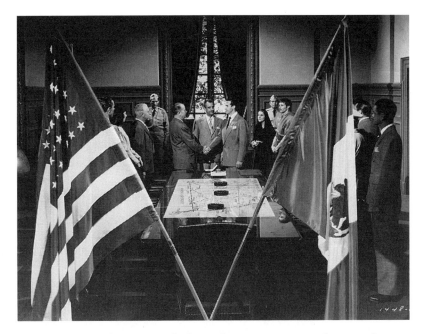

Figure 4.2. The signing of a law enforcement agreement between the United States and Mexico in a scene from *Border Incident*. © 1949 Loew's Inc.; courtesy National Screen Service Corp.

death. As expected, just before the executions, the pendulum shifts; they manage to escape and turn the tide against the villains, eliminate the gang in a climactic and predictable shoot-out, and thus save the poor indocumentados. Once again, the "valiant" Texas Rangers defeat the evil smugglers.[51] What irony is presented here. The Texas Rangers coming to the aid of Mexicans is incredible; the historical reality documents totally the opposite. For the Mexican-origin population of Texas, the Texas Rangers were always "los diablos texanos."

Border Incident (1949) was the next production on the theme of immigration (see fig. 4.2). This social problem movie is important for various reasons: it was produced by a large Hollywood studio, MGM, and directed by the respected Arthur Mann; the film was generally devoid of the negative stereotyping of Mexicans common to the Hollywood cinema of previous decades; the plot showed a certain knowledge and sensitivity toward Mexican emigration to the United States; and, for once, Mexican-origin actors were cast in feature roles.

The story centers upon the plight of Mexican migrant workers who, unable to secure work permits under the Bracero Program, cross the border illegally to toil in the agricultural fields of California's Imperial Valley. The laborers are constantly exploited by a brutal gang. Often the workers are robbed, and some are even murdered on their return trip home. United States and Mexican immigration officers, played effectively by George Murphy and Ricardo Montalbán, are assigned to uncover and apprehend all those involved in the murders on both sides of the border. Disguised as a worker, Montalbán is successfully able to infiltrate the gang, while Murphy poses as a fugitive who possesses stolen bracero permits. As the story unfolds, the abuses and sufferings of the undocumented workers are vividly detailed in hard-hitting scenes.

Upon uncovering the workings of the ring and its members, an intricate capture is planned. However, before the plan is carried out, Murphy's true identity is discovered by the villains. He is tortured and brutally murdered. The same fate almost strikes Montalbán and his coworkers, but they put up a courageous struggle until the authorities arrive and capture all of the gang members.

The film is effective, well made and one of the—if not the—best Hollywood immigration films ever. Ricardo Montalbán and George Murphy deliver solid performances, and they are supported by an equally good secondary cast. The filming was done in an actual border location in the San Joaquin Valley. The director, Arthur Mann, develops the narrative convincingly in a semidocumentary format. Suspense and interest are maintained until the final scene. Clearly, *Border Incident*, because of its political message and the care taken in the development of its theme and characters, can be classified as one of the very best social problem films of the decade.[52]

In *Illegal Entry* (1949), once again the narrative revolves around a well-organized band of smugglers that are illegally transporting Mexican undocumented workers to various work areas in the United States (see fig. 4.3). A crack government agent, played by Howard Duff, is given the task of bringing to justice these criminals involved in the trafficking of human contraband.

While the theme of Mexican immigration is supposed to be central to the film, as has been so often the case in this genre features, the Mexican workers are the least represented in the film. Their plight is alluded to only marginally and they remain as invisible subject matters of the narrative. After the usual escapades and twists in fortune, the movie closes with the expected conclusion: the hero, with the help of the central female character, is able to defeat and capture the entire smuggling gang. Justice prevails once again, and one more illicit cartel is eliminated.[53]

Figure 4.3. A mounted Border Patrol officer faces crime on the border in *Illegal Entry*. © 1949 Universal Pictures, Inc.; courtesy National Screen Service Corp.

The 1956 film *Wetback* has Lloyd Bridges playing the part of a fishing boat captain who, in search of clients and work, falls innocently into the clutches of a ring of clever smugglers who take undocumented workers through sea routes to various points in the United States. As the narrative unfolds, officials of the immigration department continue on the trail of these criminals for some time, and they recruit Bridges to help catch the smugglers in the act and thus bring them to justice.

After various turns of the unbelievable and repetitive plot involving secret agents, double-crosses, sea chases, romances, and the expected downfall of the crooks, justice again triumphs and the movie closes with the main character and the female lead sailing off happily into the sunset. One other border, the sea, is safe again and under control.

In spite of its title, in *Wetback*, the theme of immigration is, as usual, the least developed aspect of the film. No single immigration question is touched upon in any detail. Altogether, *Wetback* is an inconsequential, mediocre action film that is reminiscent of Lloyd Bridges's television series *Sea Hunt*. The script, direction and acting performances are all typical of a classic B movie.[54]

Borderline (1980) was the first major contemporary Hollywood genre film on the theme of Mexican immigration (see fig. 4.4). It stars the international action-film favorite Charles Bronson as the hero. He plays a compassionate and honest cop, chief of a Border Patrol office near the San Diego–Tijuana border. The protagonist does his job well, although he does not particularly like what he sees or has to do—which is, by his own account, capture and deport hardworking individuals who just seek a decent job.

The plot is an update of the typical "hero of the West in search of the killer of a colleague and close friend" story. When a truck loaded with undocumented workers is routinely stopped by a veteran Border Patrol officer, instead of surrendering, the head of the smuggling gang shoots the officer and a young Mexican witness in cold blood. The narrative revolves around a cat-and-mouse game between Bronson and the killer. Before the final scene and duel on the border, in which the outcome is as predictable as in any western, other characters are introduced in caricature form: the smuggling ring (the real villains), the defenseless victims (the undocumented workers), the good guys (the Border Patrol), and the leader of the gang (a deranged killer, a former Vietnam veteran, now using all his military training for profit and evil).

The intentions of *Borderline* are essentially good; the film shows a genuine sympathy for the exploitation of Mexican undocumented workers. Yet the lukewarm social message is entirely lost. The dilemma of Mexican immigration is never really addressed in any fashion. The ambiguity is reflected throughout by the dialogue. Bronson asks one of his men, "How can you bust people for trying to better themselves?" However, at the close of the film, statistics appear stating that over a million undocumented Mexican workers in the early 1980s were apprehended and deported, and that more than that number escaped detection and apprehension and are currently residing and working in the United States.

Borderline, as could be expected, was filmed with the full cooperation of the U.S. Border Patrol. Many agents, in fact, participated as extras and as technical advisors. Its implicit message is that the Immigration and Naturalization Service needs more resources and stricter immigration legislation to carry out its mission of controlling our borders, particularly the one with Mexico.[55]

The characters in the movie are all secondary to the hero and the villain.

Figure 4.4. Charles Bronson stars as a U.S. Border Patrol officer whose best friend is slain during an illegal alien smuggling action across the U.S.–Mexico border, a ruthless act that spurs Bronson to devise a trap for the powerful organization dealing in misery and millions of dollars in *Borderline*. © 1980 Associated Film Distribution.

The undocumented workers, the supposed subject matter of the story, are the least developed and least known aspect of the film. They have no faces, no names, no personal histories, motivations, or feelings. The reasons for their ordeal or circum-stances are never revealed or addressed. There are countless stories that *Borderline* could have told or developed, but unfortunately, the filmmakers were content to

Figure 4.5. Jack Nicholson in the role of a Border Patrol officer appre-
hending María (Elpidia Carrillo) in *The Border*. © Universal City Studios,
Inc.

use a contemporary issue to exploit the star quality of Charles Bronson, hoping
the combination would pay off commercially. To a certain degree it did.

  Similar to *Borderline* in certain aspects and quite different in others is *The
Border* (1982), directed by Tony Richardson and starring Jack Nicholson (see
fig. 4.5). This movie is Hollywood's most recent contribution to the immigration
genre. *The Border* is nothing more than a vehicle for the acting talent and star power

of Jack Nicholson. The narrative and the supporting actors are all secondary to a typical Nicholson characterization of contemporary man—at odds with the values and corruption of the system—who has to make a choice between good and evil, accommodation or resistance, complacency or turmoil.

The narrative develops around Nicholson, a Border Patrol agent, who is assigned to El Paso where he joins a former best friend, also a Border Patrol officer. After several raids and apprehensions, Nicholson learns that many border agents, including his friend and the chief, are in business with the contractors and coyotes to smuggle certain indocumentados into the United States. Nicholson ultimately rebels against his corrupt colleagues when killing is involved. Symbolically, he states that this is the line (the border) he will not cross.

In the course of the story, he meets María (Elpidia Carrillo) and her brother, both undocumented Mexicans who face constant ill-treatment and oppression. When María's baby is abducted and her brother is shot by a coyote and dies, Nicholson lashes out in revenge. María, in disbelief of her newly acquired champion, asks him why he helps her. The Nicholson character just answers, "I guess I got to feel good about something I do."[56] The predictable climactic gunfight at the border ensues and the equally expected triumph by the hero occurs. The film closes with Nicholson crossing to Mexico with the rescued baby to join the virtuous María and live in bliss.

The Border, despite fine performances by Jack Nicholson and the supporting cast and solid directing, is highly routine and stereotypical. The villains are all totally bad and corrupt, with only a single motivation, money. The women are either pure, kind, innocent, and helpless like María, or sexual ornaments interested only in immediate gratification, like Nicholson's wife. The undocumented workers in Borderline are objects as well and not real characters. Nowhere in the film do we learn anything about the Mexicans, not even about María or her brother. Their plight is never addressed. Whatever social message was intended is again obscured by the superficiality of the characters and the plot. In spite of the fact that the performances and direction of The Border exceed Borderline, its faults and overall purposes are similar. In The Border, the Border Patrol officers are represented as thugs, violators of civil rights, and morally corrupt.

It is evident, though, that the questions and concerns over Mexican undocumented immigration have gained enough public attention for Hollywood and its principal studios like Warner Brothers to produce films on the subject and cast superstars in the films. Important also is the fact that The Border and Borderline have received wide circulation in the United States in the movie circuit and through

173

cable television. Because of the popularity of the stars, the two films are the most wide-reaching Hollywood statements on the issues of Mexican immigration to date. In Mexico, however, these movies were not allowed to be screened in theaters. Government officials found the films degrading to Mexico and enforced a law which stipulates that no cultural or media production offensive to the country shall be exhibited in movie theaters.[57]

Since *The Border*, Hollywood has not premiered any additional major film addressing the immigrant experience. Yet, given the existing current national concern with immigration, it seems likely that it is only a matter of time before American cinema will return to the theme of immigration. Based on previous trends, the films to come will possibly be more of the same.

"Braceras y Mojados" in Contemporary Mexican Cinema, 1970–1996

From the 1970s throughout the 1980s and into the 1990s, immigration genre films inundated the silver screen in Mexico.[58] These contemporary productions are part of a very distinct period of immigration films in Mexico. The reasons for the resurgence of the genre of immigration films are varied and include political, economic, and cultural factors. By the 1970s, Mexican undocumented immigration in the United States had become a major issue in U.S.–Mexican relations because of the increasing numbers. Mexican policy-makers began to respond to national concerns on the subject. Printed and visual media in Mexico also devoted considerable attention to issues and consequences of Mexican emigration to the United States.

This renewed awareness was incorporated into commercial movies by film producers and studios. The new wave of representations of immigrants in films coincided with the general cinematic policies of the administrations of presidents José López Portillo (1976–1982) and Miguel de la Madrid (1982–1988) that were characterized by decreasing state film production. This policy shift meant that art films also became more scarce, since the state had been the major single producer of quality artistic cinema. With the demise of state participation in cinema, the private sector once again dominated the production of films in Mexico.[59]

These Mexican private producers had discovered by this time the extensive and growing Mexican and Latin American–origin population in the United States as a potential important market for their films. They hoped that this audience would generate lucrative profits in dollars. It was assumed that films that depicted a familiar experience, immigration (even in an unrealistic manner), would gross well and be a sure investment.[60] Unfortunately their assumptions proved correct. According to film industry statistics of the time, many, if not all, of the immigration films produced did indeed make a sizeable profit at the box office, particularly in the Mexican border states and in the United States.[61]

The private sector producers were interested solely in the profit aspect of film. They had little regard for creativity, interest, or good taste. It is difficult to find much artistic, cultural, or social value in these contemporary genre films.

As with classic genre features, the titles, minor plot details, and characters vary little in this contemporary cycle of Mexican immigration films. They all have much in common and collectively share the following characteristics: (1) This wave of films was produced, almost without exception, purely for commercial, exploitative purposes. (2) Their narrative discourse is filled with excessive violence and sex. (3) The narration and the action (setting) always take place within the United States, adhering to Mexican official immigration policies that stress the violation of human rights of migrant workers and accentuate the benefits of Mexican workers to the United States economy. (4) The main emphasis of the plot is on the violence and subjugation directed at the Mexican workers by Anglo-American individuals and institutions. (5) There is a total disregard in the narrative of the "push" factors in Mexico that are greatly responsible for immigration. (6) Never or seldom shown are the structural problems, political questions, or socioeconomic effects of the contemporary Mexican crisis upon society. (7) The production formula for such features is evident: complete the film in the shortest possible shooting schedule, place one or two major stars in the film, include ample sex and violence (the more the better), and inundate the theater chains, particularly in *provincia* (term used in Mexico to denote all areas outside of Mexico City) and the U.S. border states. (8) Although not directly financed by state film-producing entities, these immigration films, nonetheless, receive governmental support in distribution and exhibition both in Mexico and abroad. (9) The earning power of these films derives in a large measure from the Hispanic market in the United States and provincia. (10) There is a distinct class bias in recent immigration genre films. The immigrants are always represented as peasants and working class individuals; the reality of Mexican immigration seriously contradicts this portrayal since data has shown gender and class diversity in the makeup of recent Mexican immigrants.[62]

In the period from 1976 to 1997, Mexican filmmakers produced approximately sixty commercial genre films based entirely upon the theme of immigration to the Unites States. In the discussion that follows, for the sake of clarity, Mexican immigration genre films are further divided by the following subgenre: the immigrant experience, the avengers of immigrants, comedies, women immigrants, violence and crime on the Río Grande, and the return to Mexico. Since there is a great deal of repetition in the contemporary immigration films of Mexico, as in all genre cycles, a representative number was selected for analysis based on popularity, importance of themes covered, and narrative elements in the plot.

THE IMMIGRANT EXPERIENCE

A popular production is Arturo Martínez's *Deportados*, which traces the hardships suffered by a family when the father, Rafael, desperate for work, joins a group of neighbors and friends to become an undocumented worker in the United States. Tragedy soon strikes on both sides of the border. On the U.S. side Rafael is exploited and abused repeatedly, while back home his wife Carmela is killed fighting off an attempted rape. The son, Rafaelito, left homeless, decides to search for his father in the United States. Rafaelito finds his father's friends and together they search for Rafael. In the meantime, Rafael learns of the fate of his wife and son when he places a call to his village. His only thoughts are to find his lost son and return to Mexico. On the journey back he is detained by the U.S. Border Patrol. In his grief and desperation, he attempts to flee and is killed by the agents. After learning of the death of his father, Rafaelito and the two friends return to Mexico to rebuild their lives and start again, this time in their native land.[63]

Another film with a similar narrative is *Murieron a la mitad del río*. The film, based on a popular novel by Luis Spota, attempts to focus on character development more than on exploitive action or sensationalism. The narrative deals with the misadventures of three indocumentados who illegally cross into Texas to seek employment. Instead of securing decent jobs and monetary rewards, two of the immigrants are killed by ruthless Anglo-Texans, and the one survivor returns to Mexico, a humiliated and broken man. The moral of the story is reminiscent of earlier films: don't go to the United States; only tragedy awaits you.

Murieron a la mitad del río is a film with a better than average script for this genre, a solid cast (headed by Hector Suárez), authentic scenery, and well-intentioned direction. Yet such positive elements do not prevent this film from suffering the same ills as most other Mexican immigration genre films.[64] The main problem is that the focus of the narrative is upon the constant exploitation of the three main characters. Their representation as helpless victims with no control over their circumstances or destiny is excessive. The events are so repetitive that the viewer loses interest after the first part of the film.

La jaula de oro is a more interesting immigration narrative that takes a different approach and addresses a recent concrete immigration issue, the passage of the Simpson-Rodino bill and its impact upon the undocumented immigrant population. As a case study, this narration focuses on one undocumented extended family of two brothers and their wives and offspring. When the bill is made law, the dilemma arises as to whether to apply for legal residency as stipulated by the guidelines of the bill and thus stay in the United States, remain undocumented, or return to Mexico.

One brother, along with most members of the family, decides to stay in the United States and apply for residency. The other brother, disillusioned with U.S. society and displaying strong nationalistic sentiment, leaves his adopted surroundings along with his wife and grandson and returns to Mexico, refusing to give up Mexican citizenship or their mexicanidad.[65]

Although treating complex issues somewhat superficially and presenting a return to Mexico in a romanticized fashion, *La jaula de oro* is a welcome film, devoid of violent and unreal sequences. The narration is developed through character study, dialogue, and realistic human situations.

THE AVENGERS

The single most improbable and far-fetched immigration film to date is *Santo en la frontera del terror* (see fig. 4.6). The legendary wrestling star El Santo stars in this incredible story of indocumentados being systematically entrapped and killed by a ruthless doctor and his gang members for the purpose of selling their organs—particularly the eyes—to the highest bidder in the United States or elsewhere. After numerous fights with the doctor's thugs and accomplices, El Santo predictably defeats the villains. The mad doctor is himself killed in a helicopter while attempting to escape, and the border is safe once again for indocumentados to cross. This film is recommended exclusively for die-hard fans of El Santo that are compelled to see every single one of his movies. Needless to say, indocumentados and the immigration experience are only a minor excuse for one of the final adventures of El Santo.[66]

A contemporary western, or more precisely an offshoot of the classic Lone Ranger or masked avenger theme, is *El chicano justiciero*, directed by Fernando Oses.

177

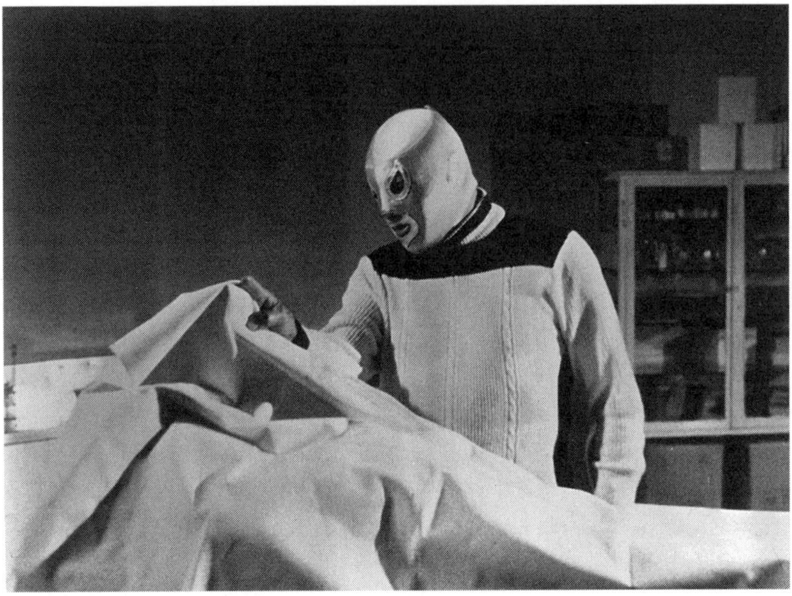

Figure 4.6. El Santo, an action hero and popular culture icon, views the body of an undocumented worker in the film *Santo en la frontera del terror*. Courtesy Filmoteca Nacional/UNAM.

The narrative unfolds with a group of undocumented workers returning to Mexico, but they never arrive at their final destination. The villain of the story, "El Bobo," has planted a deadly bomb in the truck carrying them. The bomb explodes and all the passengers appear to be dead. El Bobo cleans out the truck and abandons the bodies. One of the workers, however, is barely alive. A young Chicano passing by finds him, tends to his wounds, and offers him shelter. The survivor swears vengeance and goes on a campaign against the evil coyotes and criminals along the border. He becomes a government agent, helping both countries fight crime. After numerous adventures, the main contraband gang is captured in a gunfight with the hero. El Bobo is killed. "El Chicano Justiciero" triumphs and rides off in search of further adventures.[67]

From this plot outline one can ascertain that the main goal of the film was sheer entertainment. The director and producers felt that the popularity of the film would be assured by the combination of two themes: immigration and an imitation of the masked ranger. But neither was done particularly well.

COMEDIES

Alfonso Arau, an experienced actor in various comedy roles, produced, directed, and starred in *Mojado Power*. This lighthearted film attempted to merge comedy with a political message. The story centers upon an undocumented worker who, after observing the parallels that immigrants share with Chicanos in their work experiences, devises a plan to unify indocumentados and Chicanos in common causes. His emblem is a decal advocating "Mojado Power"—that is, the alleged unity of all persons of Mexican origin in the United States.

Although the theme and message are valid and important, the narrative and characters are not. Arau reverses the Hollywood formula of films with Chicano or Mexican characters. In the case of Hollywood, the Anglo main character would display his superiority in a paternalistic manner by outwitting the Mexican or Chicano and would always be cast as the protagonist and role model. In *Mojado Power*, Alfonso Arau's Mexican characters assume the traits of Anglo heroes, thus presenting the very same vision as Hollywood. The difference is that in his film, it is a Mexican illegal who shows the "weak" Chicanos the way toward organization and strength. Overall, and in spite of a few good moments, *Mojado Power* is an opportunistic and condescending film.[68]

The single most popular contemporary immigration film is *Ni de aquí, ni de allá*. This well-received production was written and directed by star María Elena Velasco, "La India María," who is the one superstar of comedy in recent Mexican cinema. In this film, La India María is faced with living in extreme poverty and therefore decides her only option is to look for work in the United States. As the story unfolds, after she manages to cross to the United States, La India María begins to be pursued by a Russian spy after she inadvertently witnessess a murder in a bathroom. Throughout the film she is constantly forced to outwit the Russian spy, the INS (Immigration and Naturalization Service), and the FBI.

In her incomparable style, La India María employs the immigration genre to satirize American institutions and attitudes toward immigrants, while at the same time visually addressing the difficult life faced by undocumented Mexicans in the United States. Questions of tradition versus modernity and democratic discourse versus the reality of economic and racial discrimination are themes that resonate well with Mexican society. Finally, after a series of misadventures—where as usual La India María is able to outwit the evil, the corrupt, and the arrogance of power— she is caught and deported to Mexico. Unlike previous genre films that portrayed

179

the immigrants as assimilating or becoming Americanized, La India María never relinquishes her native dress, traditions, or values.[69]

Ni de aquí, ni de allá not only added to the reputation of La India María as the superstar of Mexican cinema today, but also showed a successful effort at combining social parody with the emigration question. The character of La India María has a large following in Mexico. She is the continuation of a rich legacy of talented comedians like Mario Moreno "Cantinflas" and Germán Valdés "Tin Tan" that so successfully employed parody and humor to satirize and expose the social ills of Mexico. In a very astute way, María Elena Velasco placed the setting of this India María narrative on the border and with immigration as the central theme. It is not surprising that *Ni de aquí, ni de allá* is the most viewed immigration genre film of recent Mexico.

WOMEN IMMIGRANTS

Indocumentadas also became central characters in contemporary immigration genre films.[70] A recent production in this trend is *La ilegal* starring the popular actors Pedro Armendariz Jr., Fernando Allende, and the celebrated television star Lucía Méndez (see fig. 4.7). The director of the film is the respected Arturo Ripstein.

In spite of such talent, the film is nothing more than a familiar soap opera. The heroine is courted and seduced by Pedro Armendariz Jr., who later abandons her to her fate after she becomes pregnant. After having her baby, Lucía Méndez's character decides to follow Pedro Armendariz, who lives in Los Angeles. She crosses illegally (hence the movie title) and finally tracks him down, but has serious setbacks in her encounters with both Armendariz and his wife. The protagonist is framed for robbery by the jealous wife and ends up in jail with no money, documents, or friends. When all seems hopeless, she is aided by a sympathetic Chicano lawyer, who emerges as her champion and new love interest. In the end, retribution is accomplished as the film closes with the couple being punished and the protagonist having found a good man who marries her; therefore, she is assured of a comfortable life in the United States.[71]

The sole purpose of the movie was to cash in on the drawing power of the stars. In no way is the plight of undocumented workers ever explored. No social message exists in *La ilegal*. The usual copyright statement at the end of the final credits, which claims that all characters in the film are fictitious and that any resemblance to actual people is purely coincidental, is certainly the case here.

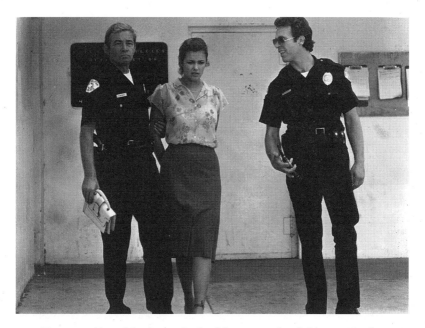

Figure 4.7. Lucía Méndez, as *La ilegal*, being apprehended by two Border Patrol agents. Courtesy Cineteca Nacional.

One of the very worst of recent Mexican immigration genre movies is *Las Braceras*. The story concerns two sisters who emigrate illegally to the United States in an attempt to uncover the details of their father's mysterious death. In actuality, the father, who was working as an indocumentado, was murdered by two corrupt and evil U.S. Border Patrol agents. Through their contacts, the agents learn of the daughters' presence. In order to assure the coverup of their crime, they systematically eliminate the various persons who are aiding the two women. The agents trap one of the daughters, rape, and ultimately kill her. When the agents finally confront the other daughter, she is prepared for them. She pulls out a revolver and shoots them both dead; thus, justice is served even at a very high human cost.

Las braceras is one of the most degrading and violent contemporary Mexican films ever produced. This is an exploitive, brutal, and tasteless movie. The film uses as protagonists the popular exotic striptease dancer Lyn May and the sensual Maritza Olivares for cheap thrills and selling power.

181

VIOLENCE AND CRIME ON THE RÍO BRAVO

In 1977, Alejandro Galindo of *Espaldas mojadas* fame returned to the theme of immigration in the film *Los mojados*. This narrative, unlike his previous effort, was clearly representative of the contemporary genre.[72] The narration concerns a group of Mexican migrant workers who, unable to secure employment in Mexico, decide to cross the border and emigrate into the United States. They plan their crossing at night and are successful in their initial attempt to reach the American side. Feeling secure, the group continues on its march not knowing that the U.S. Border Patrol lies in wait. The officers indiscriminately open fire without any warning or attempt at apprehension. The entire group falls under a hail of bullets. All are left for dead, although the protagonist of the film, Juan García (portrayed by the well-known action star Jorge Rivero), barely escapes after being severely wounded.

The hero of the story manages to get to a nearby town where he is befriended by sympathetic Chicanos. Rumors of this incident and other acts of violence have become common at the border. A Mexican lawyer enters the picture as a dedicated civil servant of the Mexican government attempting to uncover those responsible for the atrocities. He tracks down Juan García and the two form a partnership. As the story unfolds, we learn of a Mafia connection in partnership with certain officers of the U.S. Border Patrol involved in the traffic, control, and placement of undocumented workers throughout the Southwestern United States. Large profits are made by the ring at the expense of the indocumentados.

Juan García devises an ingenious plan that enables him to infiltrate the ring. He gains the ring members' confidence by acting in a ruthless and cunning manner, outfoxing and physically battering immigration officers. He is given a leadership role by the coyotes within the Mafia and, as such, is in a position to learn firsthand of the activities and people involved in the gang. An elaborate scheme is implemented and, after a furious shootout in the final trap, all the major criminals are either killed or captured by the authorities.

After receiving congratulations, the protagonist reveals that he is a special Mexican government agent sent on a mission to clean up the border, and, like a typical western hero, he rides off after defeating the bad guys. In a surprise ending, though, Juan García and his newly assigned partner are ambushed by the remaining Mafia members and brutally killed. The moral of the story is that the struggle for the border, including control of the trafficking of human contraband, will continue.[73]

Malditos polleros narrates the tragic story of the violence and oppression faced by indocumentados on U.S. soil. Full of illusion and in search of a better life, a group of emigrant families travel to the border where all they find is a band of swindlers. For a considerable sum, these swindlers (polleros) promise to take them into the United States illegally and transport them to places of guaranteed employment. But what awaits these poor people is nothing but tragedy, because they have fallen into the hands of killers who make their fortune through cruelty and brutality directed at the defenseless immigrant.[74]

RETURN TO MEXICO

A great number of the Mexican immigrants working in the United States are temporary laborers and return regularly to their sending communities. A story of the impact of these returning immigrants on their communities is applicable to many towns throughout Mexico. This issue forms the basis of *Tiempo de lobos*, written and sensitively directed by Alberto Issac. The plot focuses upon the return of two brothers who work as indocumentados in the United States to their hometown in the state of Colima. This state-produced narrative, unlike the majority of others, is not filled with exploitive sex or graphic violence but with character and story development. Another element that differentiates this movie from others is the excellent acting by a cast that includes Ernesto Gómez Cruz, Gonzalo Vega, Ignacio Retes, and Carmen Salinas.

The construct for the narrative of this film is provided by the socioeconomic conditions of rural agrarian Mexico, the generational conflict, and the distance between those working and residing in the United States and their family members who still reside in the traditional provincia. The consequence of the immigrant experience upon individuals and their sending communities in Mexico is especially well developed in the film. *Tiempo de lobos* is able to capture the transformation of a town that now relies heavily upon the money that the indocumentados send back.[75]

Current Perspectives

The 1990s brought about two distinct trends in Mexican cinema. First, the private sector film industry reached crisis proportion. Given the repetitiveness, dullness, and cheap format of their productions, their audiences disappeared, ending the demand for their films, including immigration genre ones. The other distinct direction is that prominent, established art-film directors for the first time incorporated Mexican immigration as a central theme in their narratives. Maria Novaro and Alberto Isaac, known for innovative and artistic cinema, filmed the sensitive and well-crafted immigration features *El jardín del Edén* and *Mujeres insumisas.*

These two films, because of their structure and individuality, do not fall into the classification of genre films, but rather under the concept of *auteur's.*[76] That is a narrative film in which the director is acknowledged to conceive the idea and theme of the film, write or co-write the script, supervise each and every aspect of the filmmaking process, and participate actively in the post-production of the film —including frequently having a major say in the final cut of the film. Auteur film criticism approaches the director "as an artist and is concerned with the quality of his imagination, and his sensitivity and sensibilities."[77]

In *El jardín del Edén* (1994), María Novaro, one of the most acclaimed directors of the generation of the 1990s, offered a different textual representation of the San Diego–Tijuana border through the lives of those who seek the "promised land." The film opens with a dramatic sequence of images of nameless immigrants waiting for the opportunity to cross to the American side at night. Immigration is the single most critical and unifying theme for the various characters in the narrative.

Director and co-screenwriter María Novaro attempts an unconventional and creative approach to the immigration question. Her discursive narrative is not concerned with the social reality of immigrants crossing the border and their work experiences, but with the individual human complexity of "being" a Mexican immigrant.[78] Unlike most immigration films that represent immigrants solely as members of the working class, *El jardín del Edén* offers a glimpse of various immigrants separated by class, gender, and purpose. From the traditional single male immigrant and a middle-class teenager to families and women, the representations are well developed and complex.

Mujeres insumisas (1995) is the latest Mexican narrative film that encompasses the theme of immigration. Directed and written by the veteran and respected filmmaker Alberto Isaac and based upon a true story, the film recounts the lives of three women, all of them housewives, from a small town in the state of Colima. They reach a breaking point in their daily lives because of alienation and oppression from machismo. In an attempt to opt for the only way out, they decide to abandon their houses and emigrate to Los Angeles, California.

The narrative of the film takes the three women on a liberating odyssey in their quest to reach El Norte. Excellent performances by lead actresses Patricia Reyes Spíndola and Lourdes Elizarrarás, combined with a solid script and an interesting story of changing and evolving gender roles make *Mujeres insumisas* one of the most accomplished Mexican films on this subject matter.

The one serious problem of the film is its representation of Los Angeles and the United States as a panacea. Once they arrive in California, all is effortless and they prosper. The protagonists are even able to quickly secure immigrant visas. Shortly after their arrival in L.A., they manage to open a restaurant that quickly succeeds. These situations are totally unreal and approximate more a fantasy than the actual experiences of the majority of Mexican women immigrants.[79]

The Immigrant Experience in Chicano Cinema

Chicano narrative cinema is a very recent development in the business of moviemaking. Creatively self-determined, full-length narrative features—written, directed and/or produced by Chicanos—first received wide theatrical distribution as late as the 1980s.

As an artistic body of work, Chicano narrative cinema debuted only a few years earlier, in the mid-seventies. Since then, it has continued to evolve and develop aesthetically through increasingly compelling stories, strong characterization, varied genres, and original and innovative narrative styles. Its evolution in focus and style, which covers its less than twenty-year history, reflects the times in which the works were produced and mirrors an implied audience and community posture.[80]

Most Chicano narrative cinema to date has been produced as independent films outside the major Hollywood studios. In a select number of cases such as *El norte*, *The Ballad of Gregorio Cortez*, and *El mariachi*, corporate studios did incorporate Chicano films in their distribution packages. A few cinematic productions were produced from the onset by a leading studio. Chicano films definitively fall under the category of auteur's film.

Thematically, Chicano narrative films have shared certain original trends. Mexican/Latino emigration to the United States is one dominant and recurring theme of Chicano cinema. There exist two distinct explanations for this constant preoccupation and interest by Chicana/o filmmakers. First, they have realized that commercial mainstream cinema will not change its established constructs and purposes in producing films on immigration. Thus, if the Mexican immigrant experience were to have any humanity, soul, or sensitivity in the big screen, it would

185

Figure 4.8. A dramatic labor demonstration by Chicano/Mexican workers is the final scene in Jesús Salvador Treviño's film *Raíces de sangre*. Courtesy Filmoteca Nacional/UNAM.

have to be filmed by an alternative cinema, such as Chicano cinema. And secondly, Chicanas/os are themselves intimately and personally part of the Mexican immigrant experience in this country, since many are descendants of immigrants.[81]

In 1976, Jesús Salvador Treviño received an invitation from the Mexican government film production company CONACINE to cast and direct his script, *Raíces de sangre* (Roots of Blood) (see fig. 4.8). The overly ambitious plot focused upon community and labor organizing against the *maquiladoras* (assembly plants), which divide and exploit the Mexican-origin communities on both sides of the border.[82]

As a related issue, emigration to the United States figures as an important subplot in *Raíces de sangre*. In one sequence of the film, the narration follows a family that decides to emigrate illegally to the United States as a last desperate recourse for survival. They, like so many of their compatriots, just cannot live under the existing conditions in Mexico. Their search for El Dorado, though, ends in tragedy. After giving up all their savings to coyotes for the promise of secure employment, the family is abandoned in a sealed cargo truck by those same smugglers. When they are finally discovered, it is too late; all have suffocated.

Raíces de sangre also highlights the commonalities of the struggles of the Mexican-origin working class on both sides of the border. The exploitive nature of the institutions that dictate their lives are at the heart of the story.

Alambrista (Fence Cutter, 1979), directed by Robert Young, is a landmark film. This sensitive feature narrates the journey of a Mexican undocumented worker named Roberto from his native village in rural Mexico to the agricultural fields in California. During the protagonist's work experiences, he undergoes the constant oppressive conditions faced by undocumented workers in this country. Roberto's existence of living the life of a fugitive, always in fear of being discovered, captured, and deported, is vividly captured in *Alambrista*. The lack of any hope for social justice or advocates for the undocumented is also well addressed in this powerful narrative. Progressively, he is overtaken by feelings of intense alienation and hopelessness that lead him to voluntarily turn himself in to the authorities, so they can deport him back to Mexico.[83]

This movie is one of those rare films in which artistic quality and social commentary are superbly linked. The script and performances achieve their purpose in every detail, capturing both the human emotions as well as the material circumstances that characterize the migratory experience. The film dialogue is in both English and Spanish (with appropriate subtitles), lending great authenticity to the story line. The docudrama format has seldom been better employed in a feature film. *Alambrista* certainly ranks as one of the most outstanding immigration films of all time.

Director and screenwriter Gregory Nava debuted with *El norte* (1983) (see fig. 4.9). This independent film, originally produced and planned for the PBS series "American Playhouse," became one of the most successful independent productions of recent times.

El norte traces the plight of a Guatemalan brother and sister. They are forced to flee their native country and seek refuge in the United States, out of fear of being killed by the military like their parents. The narrative is developed in three segments. The first sets the stage for their exodus from their village, San Pedro, Guatemala. Their father Arturo picks coffee beans, enduring the exploitation of the landowners and their tool of oppression, the military. One evening their father, played by Mexico's leading dramatic actor Ernesto Gómez-Cruz, goes to a secret meeting with other *campesinos* (peasants). They plan an agrarian rebellion against their oppressors. Tragically, they are betrayed by one of their own who informs the landowners of their meeting place. The military ambushes and kills all the campe-

Figure 4.9. Rosa (Zaide Silvia Gutiérrez) meditates beside a lake in her native village in a scene from *El norte*. © 1983 Cinecom International Films.

sinos. During an attempt to save his father, Enrique encounters a wounded soldier and in self-defense kills him. The next day the military arrest Enrique's mother. The only possible salvation for Enrique and Rosa is to escape from Guatemala. With the help of their godparents they start out for "El Norte."

The plot then moves to Mexico. Rosa and Enrique have successfully crossed the Guatemalan-Mexican border and are on their way to Tijuana. After further setbacks with a treacherous coyote, they find a former family friend who helps them over their last hurdle. They attempt to cross the U.S. border through a sewage tunnel. Halfway along the tunnel their journey turns to terror as they are attacked by a pack of rats. Finally escaping, they manage to reach the end of the tunnel and are reunited with their friend. As they reach the top of a cliff that overlooks the lights of San Diego, they behold the sight with awe and in anticipation of their new life.

The third and final part of the narrative opens in Los Angeles. Rosa and Enrique have been able to find housing and employment. However, just when all appears to go well, tragedy strikes once more. Enrique loses his job in an immigration raid. Rosa becomes seriously ill and is rushed to a hospital. She is diagnosed as having advanced typhus acquired from the rats. On her deathbed, Rosa sums up her fateful existence for Enrique: "En México solo hay pobreza. Tampoco hay lugar allí para nosotros. En el norte no somos aceptados pues. ¿Cuándo vamos a encontrar un lugar?" (In Mexico there is only poverty. Neither is there a place for us. In the North we are not accepted. When are we going to find a home?) The movie closes with Enrique, although very aware of the hopelessness of his situation, becoming more assertive in seeking employment.

El norte has been acclaimed for its creative photography, inspiring musical score, careful direction, and overall outstanding acting performances, particularly by the two leading stars, Zaide Silvia Gutiérrez and David Villalpando, who debuted in this feature.[84] The dialogue is maintained in the native languages, Spanish or Maya, adding realism to the story. Among North American critics and audiences, the film received high praise and significant box office success.

A careful reading of El norte, though, reveals certain critical issues that detract somewhat from its overall merit. The film is overly melodramatic at times. In addition, certain characters and events are overly stereotypical. For example, the heavies are all of U.S.–Latino or Latin American origin. In addition, the film plays on the empathy of the viewer through the dramatic outcome of the narration. Withstanding these observations, though, El norte is an important and well-crafted film. It is certainly one of the most accomplished Chicano productions in terms of directing, script, photography, acting, and musical score.

Born in East L.A. (1985) addresses the theme of immigration from a strikingly original perspective (see fig. 4.10). Combining parody with social satire, director, writer, and star Cheech Marín takes direct aim at various U.S. and Mexican institutions, archetypes, and attitudes. As the story unfolds, Rudy Robles, played by Marín, accidently gets caught in an INS raid, and, unable to prove his legal citizenship, is deported to Tijuana, Mexico. Rudy, who cannot speak Spanish, finds himself experiencing tribulations similar to Mexican immigrants in a foreign country. After a series of mishaps while attempting to cross to the United States, he begins to adapt to border circumstances. The film closes with hundreds of undocumented immigrants led by the protagonist overrunning the Border Patrol and crossing into the United States with the popular song "Coming to America" as background music.[85]

Inasmuch as Born in East L.A. was the first narrative comedy of Chicano cinema with an interesting theme and solid acting, it enjoyed critical acclaim and

Figure 4.10. Scenes from *Born in East L.A.*: (Top) Cheech Marín in a Tijuana jail and (bottom) with his love, Dolores, played by Kamala Lopez. © 1987 Universal City Studios, Inc.

respectable box office success.[86] This movie was the recipient of a major award in the prestigious Havana Film Festival of 1988 because of its many artistic and political merits.

However, this film is not without its detractors. The central concern, particularly of feminist critics, is that certain of the female characters are shown with titillating dress and manner.[87] In addition, the few times when women are featured, they have the least developed roles in the film. Nonetheless, *Born in East L.A.* is an important film that addresses critical issues related to Mexican immigration with imagination and soul.

Break of Dawn (1987), written and directed by Isaac Artenstein and produced by Jude Eberhard, is based upon the true life of Pedro J. González, the first Spanish-language radio celebrity in the United States, in the late 1920s (see fig. 4.11). Pedro J. González, like thousands of his compatriots, was swept up by the vortex of the Mexican Revolution. He volunteered and served as a telegraph officer of the army of Pancho Villa for most of the campaigns of the Division of the North. After the defeat of Villa, fearing reprisals against ex-villistas, González along with his family fled to the U.S.–Mexican border. Residing in Ciudad Juárez for a short time, he was forced to cross the border after attacks against the followers of Pancho Villa became intense. Having relatives in Los Angeles, Pedro J. González traveled there and settled permanently.

After working at various odd jobs, he landed employment at a local radio station announcing products in Spanish. Since he was a talented composer as well as a good singer, as an experiment he expanded from commercials to a musical variety show. The acceptance was tremendous. He was given a daily show at the break of dawn called "Los madrugadores." Soon he became a major celebrity not only in Southern California but also throughout the United States, since many other radio stations in the border states picked up his show.

In addition, Pedro J. González became a political and community activist on behalf of the rights of the Mexican-origin population during the decade of the 1930s. When a policy of massive repatriation against Mexicans was implemented and violations against the civil rights of Chicanos and Mexicans occurred on a daily basis, González forcefully and defiantly spoke out. As a consequence of his struggles for his people, he fell victim to injustice. In a devious plot to silence him, he was falsely accused of rape, tried, convicted with total disregard for the facts, and imprisoned in San Quentin. The film masterfully traces all these events and concludes with his release from prison after six years when his case was reopened and his sentence was finally overturned by the California authorities.

A true story
of passion,
power and
betrayal
in 1930s
Los Angeles.

"A bold and impressive piece of work
chipping away at the slanderous
Hollywood stereotype of Hispanics ...
the music is marvelous!
San Diego Tribune

"A passionate
independent film"
San Francisco Chronicle

"Sparkling lead
performance . . . a
touching human story"
Hollywood Reporter

"A compelling drama"
Santa Fe New Mexican

"History rises with
skillful direction"
Columbus Dispatch

Bulk Rate
U.S. Postage
PAID
Permit No. 449
San Diego, CA

PLATFORM
RELEASING
700 Adella Lane
Coronado, CA 92118

BREAK OF DAWN
A TRUE STORY

Figure 4.11. Film poster of *Break of Dawn*. © 1988 Cinewest Productions.

The script of *Break of Dawn* reveals a deep sympathy for and understanding of the story and the events. History and film are seldom combined with such outstanding results. This film is an important and creative production that has been the recipient of well-deserved praise and awards. However, the lack of an adequate production budget as well as the fact that no U.S. major studio distributed it claiming "too much" usage of Spanish, seriously limited its audience and popularity.[88]

Comedian/actor Paul Rodriguez starred in and directed *A Million to Juan* (1994), a comedy-fable that narrates the harsh reality faced by Mexican undocumented workers in the United States. The character portrayed by Rodriguez is a widower and father of a young boy, who struggles for survival against a harsh reality. One day, an angel (played by Edward James Olmos) appears to him, giving him a loan of a check for one million dollars as a catalyst to change his life. After various tribulations, he is able to overcome adversity, find true love, receive his green card, and pursue his aspirations.

The film has certain contributions to the immigration theme. The character of Rodriguez and other indocumentados portrayed in the narrative exemplify the near impossibility of achieving any sort of success for Mexican workers when all is stacked against them. Indocumentados are represented as hardworking, lawful individuals, who just want the chance to compete for the American dream.

Since the production is supposed to be seen as a fantasy, much of it is on that level. Thus, totally improbable situations occur, such as the INS agent being not only sympathetic toward Rodriguez, but also winding up falling in love and staying with him. And, of course, the film has a happy ending for this kind, warm, and decent Mexican immigrant.

The latest Chicano film that squarely addresses the immigration experience is director Gregory Nava's *My Family/Mi familia* (1995), the story of three generations of the Sánchez family (see fig. 4.12). The family's origins are from a small rural village in the mountains of Michoacán. The protagonist, like so many of his compatriots at the turn of the century, emigrates from Mexico to the United States seeking a better life. After months of difficult travel, he finally reaches his destination, Los Angeles. He finds and settles with his uncle "El Californio" in his small home which is called Mexico. There, he meets María, falls in love, and marries her, and thus begins the story of this family in early East Los Angeles.

Moving on to the early 1930s, the family encounters its initial great crisis when wife María, out on a shopping trip to the local market, is rounded up and illegally repatriated from the United States to the interior of Mexico in a deportation campaign. Although she is a U.S. citizen, the fact that she looks Mexican is enough for her to be repatriated without due process of law. At the time of deportation, she is pregnant. During her stay in Mexico her baby is born. After a year, when her newborn son is strong enough to travel, she begins the long trip north.

Figure 4.12. Young María (Jennifer Lopez) carrying her infant son, Chu-cho, risks her life to return to her husband and children in *My Family/Mi familia.* © 1995 New Line Productions, Inc. Photograph by Rico Torres.

She endures a hazardous journey and is finally reunited with her husband and children in Los Angeles.

In the contemporary period, immigration continues as a central issue for the family. An elder son, well played by Jimmy Smits, agrees to marry a Sal-vadorean undocumented worker who would face sure death if deported. As in *Born in East L.A.*, Mexican immigration is well combined with Latin American immigration as a unifying element of the current Chicano/Latino reality in the United States.

A second important element in the film is the issue of change and continuity of the members of the Sánchez family. There are differences in the behavior and the goals of the three generations portrayed. At the same time, Mexican values, traditions, and the legacy of this Chicano family, such as the love for the land, the care and enjoyment of food, the importance of the extended family, and ethnic pride are captured as unifying elements in *My Family/Mi Familia*.

There is no doubt that the theme of Mexican immigration will continue to be paramount in Chicana/o cinema. Given the current political climate on this issue, Chicana/o filmmakers can do nothing else.[89]

Conclusions

It is evident that immigration from Mexico has been a constant and important theme in the narrative films of the United States, Mexico, and the Chicano community. From 1912 to the present, over one hundred features have centered their narrative discourse on the issue of Mexican immigration. In fact, they have established a distinct genre in film. Yet these commercial films for the most part have not served the Mexican immigrant experience well. Generally, these films reflect and follow national concerns and public opinion, and have even established or proposed policies on issues concerning Mexican immigration. Although films are not designed or even expected to be historical or sociological documents, these representations on the silver screen go far beyond artistic liberty. They seriously distort or loosely play with reality solely for commercial purposes.

In the case of American cinema, Mexican immigration only served as a secondary theme for action films in the classic Hollywood formula — the hero against the villains and the predictable ending of good defeating evil. The one variation in the genre of American immigration films is a clear and constant preoccupation with the control of the southern border with Mexico. Hollywood films clearly exemplify a deep-seated public attitude and official policy designed to better control and regulate undocumented Mexican labor in the United States, particularly in times of economic downturn in America.

With the possible exception of *Border Incident*, Hollywood immigration films have not revealed much of the human dimension of Mexican immigrants, nor have they reflected or portrayed the substantial contributions that Mexican immigrants have made to the U.S. economy and to the social and cultural matrix of the nation. In fact, although the immigrants are presumably central to the narratives of the films, in actuality, they are nonexistent as visible characters. Immigrants are only portrayed as defenseless people who are in dire need of a white champion to come to their aid. In such cinematic representations, reference to the white man's burden is clearly transmitted.

Mexican cinema employed its initial immigration films as didactic constructs. From early in its developmental history up to the 1960s, the cinema of Mexico displayed a constant if somewhat static portrayal of its immigrant community in the United States. From the first production in 1922, *El hombre sin patria*, to the decade of the 1960s, two central themes stand out. First and foremost is the representation of the immigrant experience of those unfortunates that crossed the Río Bravo to the land of dollars in search for an illusive and false El Dorado. Whether the film reflected a dramatic plot or introduced a comic element, the ideological premise and didactic message was similar: No good awaits you in the United States. Not a single Mexican immigrant feature follows the typical immigrant success story of Hollywood. Mexican immigrant genre films opted for movies that either reinforced official policy of attempting to dissuade further immigration by its portrayals of the tragic lot of immigrants, or responded to Mexican internal concerns and popular cultural representation of immigrants in journals, corridos, and folklore more than reality. Such films never brought to the screen thoughtful, well-researched and well-written scripts that would enlighten and examine the experiences of immigrants in the United States. The viewer learns much more about Mexico's attitudes and policies toward its emigrants, or the historical condition of the country at the time of the making of the production, than about the immigrants themselves. The one exception to this rule is the excellent *Espaldas mojadas*.

A second theme in Mexican immigration cinema in this early period is the characterization of Mexicans in the United States as pochos. Mexican films from these four decades consistently display immigrants who have spent a period of time in the United States as assimilated, anti-Mexican, and pro-American way of life individuals who have lost their identity, attempting to become participants of American society at the expense of their mexicanidad. In opposition to this process, certain Mexican characters in films like *Soy Mexicano de acá de este lado* accentuate their nationalism and are portrayed as true Mexicans, not second class citizens (both figuratively and politically) like the pochos.

On the whole, these productions followed and hardened Mexican stereotypes and broad generalizations about the Mexican-origin community in the

United States more than contributing to a more sensitive and complex understanding of the "other Mexico." It was indeed unfortunate that filmmakers in the pioneer and Golden Age periods of Mexican cinema who produced such classic films and reflected such a wealth of creativity and talent did not do so in the case of the immigrant experience.

In the contemporary period, immigrants did not fare any better in Mexican cinema. Producers originated a distinct cycle of close to sixty immigration films, responding in an opportunistic manner to the political climate of the times and the potential untapped market in the United States. Almost all follow a basic discursive formula: set the plots on the U.S. border, include lots of sex and violence in the narrative, and exhibit the films in the Mexican border states and the U.S. Southwest in theaters or through video. This unfortunate genre cycle ran from the late 1970s to the early 1990s.

The recent films of art directors María Novaro and Alberto Issac might signal a positive new direction in immigration films. However, to make such an assessment from only two films is premature.

As the analysis has shown, the viewing audience will learn from immigration genre films much more of the two countries' attitudes, public opinion, and the political climate toward the issues surrounding Mexican immigrants than about the actual immigrant experience. What is not covered or represented in immigration films is equally revealing and just as critical in the study of the immigration genre films. In American cinema, the contributions and institutionalization of immigrants in the economy and social life of the United States are fully dismissed. Mexican films, on the other hand, go to great lengths to ignore the "push" factors—high unemployment and underemployment, recurring economic crisis, repeated devaluation of the peso, meager wages, exploitation, and few alternatives—that compel Mexicans to emigrate to the United States as a last resort. Mexican cinema also evades the select success stories of immigrants (with the exception of *Mujeres insumisas*) who have bettered their lives in their new surroundings.

It is only Chicana/o cinema that has consistently represented the immigrant experience from a realistic perspective. For Chicana/o filmmakers, Mexican immigration is an essential part of the making and the growth of their community. Since many Chicano/a filmmakers are themselves sons and daughters of Mexican immigrants, this preoccupation toward the subject matter is a highly personal one. More than a political question, immigration involves issues of identity, self-discovery and ethnic consciousness. Moreover, as committed artists striving toward the creation of cultural manifestations that combine artistic worth

197

with a social/political message, their purpose in filmmaking is diametrically different from the commercialization of the two discussed national cinemas. For Chicana/o filmmakers, success of a film is not derived exclusively from box office returns.

In essence, then, the celluloid immigrant has appeared on the silver screen in hundreds of features. For the most part, though, the representation on film of Mexican immigration, with the exception of a few select features, does not do justice to the complexity, humanity, triumphs, and tragedies of the journey "North from Mexico."

Notes

1. "Inside Proposition 187," *Los Angeles Times*, 10 November 1994, p. A-28.

2. Juan Gómez-Quiñones, "Una interpretación de las relaciones entre la comunidad chicana y México," in David R. Maciel, ed., *El México olvidado: la historia del pueblo chicano* (El Paso and Ciudad Juárez: University of Texas El Paso/Universidad Autónoma de Ciudad Juárez, 1996).

3. Richard M. Blumenberg, *Critical Focus: An Introduction to Film* (Belmont, Calif.: Wadsworth Pub. Co., 1975), pp. 3–4.

4. Garth Josett and James M. Linton, *Movies as Mass Communication* (Beverly Hills, Calif.: Sage Publications, 1980).

5. See various articles in B. Rosemberg and D. M. White, eds., *Mass Culture: The Popular Arts in America* (Glencoe, Ill.: Free Press, 1957).

6. Daniel Talbot, ed., *Film: An Anthology* (New York: Simon and Schuster, 1959), pp. 16–17.

7. Cited in Robert C. Allen and Douglas Gomery, *Film History* (New York: Knopf, 1985), p. 160.

8. Ibid., p. 161.

9. Norma Iglesias, *Entre yerba, polvo y plomo: lo fronterizo visto por el cine mexicano*, 2 vol. (Tijuana: El Colegio de la Frontera, 1991).

10. Alejandro Galindo, *Una radiografía histórica del cine mexicano* (Mexico, 1968), addresses this theme in detail.

11. The two longest lasting Spanish-language newspapers in the Southwest, *La Opinión* from Los Angeles and *La Prensa* from San Antonio, trace the growth and popularity of the Mexican cinema in the United States.

12. Gerald Mast's *A Short History of the Movies* (Indianapolis: Bobbs Merrill, 1976) discusses the influence of Hollywood on world cinema in an excellent manner.

13. Stuart M. Kaminsky, *American Film Genres: Approaches to a Critical Theory of Popular Film* (Dayton, Ohio: Pflaum Pub., 1974).

14. Harry M. Geduld and Ronald Gottesman, *An illustrated Glossary of Film Terms* (New York: Holt, Rinehant, and Winston, 1973), p. 73.

15. The anthology edited by Barry K. Grant, *Film Genre: Theory and Criticism* (Metuchen: Scarecrow Press, 1977), discusses this and other key points of genre films.

16. Barry Keith Grant, *Film Genre Reader* (Austin: University of Texas Press, 1986).

17. Ibid., p. 52.

18. Joseph M. Boggs, *The Art of Watching Films* (Palo Alto, Calif.: Mayfield Pub. Co., 1985), p. 351.

19. Ibid., p. 351.

20. Judith Hess Wright's "Genre Films and the Status Quo," in *Jump Cut* I (May-June 1974), is a suggestive essay on this point.

21. The following two articles offer important elements in genre films: Thomas Sobchack, "Genre Films: A Classical Experience," *Literature/Film Quarterly* III, 3 (Summer 1975), pp. 196–204; and Thomas Schatz, "The Structural Influence: New Directions in Film Genre Study," *Quarterly Review of Film Studies* II, 3 (August 1977), pp. 302–312.

22. Allen in *Film History* addresses this theme in an exceptional manner.

23. *El Dorado* was a mythical city of gold sought by the Spanish conquistadors in their travels in what is now the U.S. Southwest.

24. David R. Maciel, "Aztlán and Mexico: A History of Chicano/Mexicano Relations, 1836–1990," unpublished manuscript.

25. Juan Gómez-Quiñones, "Piedras contra la luna. Mexico in Aztlán and Aztlán in Mexico: Chicano-Mexicano Relations and the Mexican Consulates," in *Contemporary Mexico: Papers on the IV International Congress of Mexican History*, ed. James Wilkie (Los Angeles: University of California Press, 1975), pp. 10–18.

26. David R. Maciel's "The Unwritten Alliance: Mexican Policies on Immigration to the United States," *The World and I: A Chronicle of our Changing Times* 7 (1985), pp. 678–679, examines this theme in detail.

27. Ibid., p. 680.

28. Federico Dávalos Orozco y Esperanza Vázquez Bernal, *Filmografía general del cine mexicano* (Puebla: Universidad Autónoma de Puebla, 1985), pp. 91–92.

29. Aurelio de los Reyes, *Medio siglo de cine mexicano* (Mexico: Editorial Trillas, 1987), pp. 89–94.

30. Interview with the widow of Miguel Contreras Torres, Medea de Novaro, Mexico City, 12 July 1987, provides extensive analysis of the career and films of Miguel Contreras Torres.

31. Francisco E. Balderrama, *In Defense of la Raza* (Tucson: University of Arizona Press, 1982), pp. 4–6.

32. Mark Reisler, *By the Sweat of Their Brow* (Westport, Conn.: Greenwood Press, 1976), p. ix.

33. F. Rand Morton's *Novelistas de la Revolución Mexicana* (Mexico: Editorial Cultura, 1947) includes an excellent chapter on the writings of José Rubén Romero.

34. Specifically, the label *pocho* was placed on Chicanos whom Mexicans believed consciously attempted to assimilate into U.S. society at the expense of their Mexican roots. This term signifies a negative view of *lo mexicano*. Many Mexicans alleged that Chicanos have also a condescending attitude toward their homeland. Later, class biases were incorporated into the stereotypes; most Chicanos were thought to be descendants of lower classes, because it was widely believed in Mexico that only the poor, the unskilled, and the illiterate emigrated to the United States.

35. Iglesias, *Entre Yerba*, p. 24.

36. David Maciel, *El bandolero, el pocho y la raza: imágenes cinematográficas del chicano* (Mexico: UNAM, 1994), pp. 57–58.

37. David Maciel's "The Unwritten Alliance" examines this theme in detail.

38. Alejandro Galindo, *Espaldas mojadas* (Mexico 1953), original screenplay provided by author.

39. Ibid.

40. Ibid.

41. García Riera, *Historia documental* VII, pp. 133–134.

42. Interview with Tomás Pérez Turrent, Mexico City, 14 June 1984.

43. Eulalio González, *El bracero del año* (Mexico City, 1962), original screenplay provided by the author.

44. Eulalio González, *El pocho* (Mexico, 1963), original screenplay provided by the author.

45. Alfred Charles Richard, *The Hispanic Images of the Silver Screen* (New York: Greenwood Press, 1992), pp. 67–68.

46. Ibid., p. 124.

47. Blaine P. Lamb, "The Convenient Villain: The Early Cinema Views of the Mexican American" *Journal of the West* XIV, 4 (October 1975), pp. 75–81.

48. Arthur Pettit, *Images of the Mexican-American in Fiction and Film* (College Station, Texas: Texas A&M University Press, 1980), pp. 111–131.

49. See the recent study by David G. Gutiérrez, *Walls and Mirrors* (Berkeley: University of California Press, 1995), pp. 39–69.

50. Ricardo Romo and Raymond Paredes, eds., *New Directions in Chicano Scholarship* (Santa Barbara: Center for Chicano Studies, 1977), pp. 183–201.

51. William K. Everson, *The Hollywood Western* (New York, 1969), pp. 166–167.

52. David R. Maciel, "Hollywood Views on Mexican Immigration," in *Voices of Mexico* (Spring 1995), pp. 25–35.

53. Ibid.

54. Ibid.

55. *The San Diego Union*, 22 October 1980, p. B-7.

56. *Motion Pictures*, 13 February 1982, p. A-18.

57. Interview with Fernando Macotela, Mexico City, 17 June 1987.

58. Moisés Viñas, *Historia del cine mexicano* (Mexico: UNAM, 1987), pp. 275–281; Interview with Gustavo García, Mexico City, 12 July 1988.

59. Interview with Andrés de Luna, Mexico City, 19 July 1988.

60. Interview with Carlos Monsiváis, Mexico City, 12 January 1989.

61. The monthly publication *Cámara*, of the Cámara Nacional de la Industria Cinematográfica, publishes all relevant information on the film industry in Mexico.

62. The book by Marilyn P. Davis, *Mexican Voices/American Dreams* (New York, 1990), conveys this point well.

63. *Deportados*, original screenplay (Mexico City, 1987).

64. Interview with José Nieto Ramírez, Mexico City, 7 May 1987.

65. *La jaula de oro*, original screenplay (Mexico City, 1987).

66. *Santo en la frontera del terror*, original screenplay (Mexico City, 1978).

67. *El chicano justiciero*, original screenplay (Mexico City, 1978).

68. Allen Woll, *The Latin Image in American Film* (Los Angeles: UCLA Latin American Center Publications, 1985), pp. 6–16, discusses Anglo heroes and Mexican characters in Hollywood films.

69. Interview with María Elena Velasco, Mexico City, 22 July 1986.

70. The best general analysis of women in contemporary Mexican cinema is Jorge Ayala Blanco, *La condición del cine mexicano* (Mexico: Editorial Posada, 1986), pp. 115–139.

71. Interview with Arturo Ripstein, Mexico City, 19 November 1986.

72. Interview with Alejandro Galindo, Mexico City, 4 June 1985.

73. Interview with Alejandro Galindo, Mexico City, 29 May 1987.

74. *Malditos polleros*, original screenplay (Mexico City, 1985).

75. Interview with Alberto Isaac, Mexico City, 23 June 1987.

76. Gerald Mast and Marshall Cohen, *Film Theory and Criticism* (New York, 1985), pp. 527–541, is an excellent discussion of auteur film theory.

77. Ibid.

78. Interview with María Novaro, Mexico City, 18 July 1994.

79. Pierrette Hondagneu-Sotelo, *Gendered Transitions: Mexican Experiences of Immigration* (Berkeley, 1994), provides a documented update panorama of women immigrants from Mexico.

80. Chon A. Noriega, ed., *Chicanos and Film: Essays on Chicano Representation and Resistance* (New York: Garland Pub., 1992), pp. 156–167.

81. David R. Maciel, *El Norte* (San Diego, 1990), p. 71.

82. Jim Miller, "Chicano Cinema: An Interview with Jesús Salvador Treviño," *Cineaste*, VIII (1978), pp. 38–41; and Jesús Salvador Treviño, "Raíces de sangre: First Feature Film

Directed by a Chicano," *Somos*, June-July 1978, p. 17, are two informative published interviews with Jesús Treviño.

83. *Variety*, 14 July 1978.

84. Vincent Canby, "El Norte: A Fine Movie Fueled by Injustice," *New York Times*, 22 January 1984, p. H-17; Jane Maslin, "Film: 'El Norte' Promised Land for Guatemalans," *New York Times*, 11 January 1984, p. C-15.

85. Juan Rodríguez Flores, "Cheech Marín, humor con preocupación social," *Proceso*, 19 September 1987, pp. 20–21.

86. Chon Noriega, "Cafe Orale: Narrative Structure in Born in East L.A." *Tonantzin* (San Antonio, Texas) 8 February 1991, pp. 17–18.

87. Rosa Linda Fregoso's "Born in East L.A. and the Politics of Representation," *Cultural Studies* IV, 3 (October 1990), addresses critical issues of sexism and gender representation.

88. Interview with Isaac Artenstein, Coronado, California, 11 June 1990.

89. David Maciel, *El bandolero, el pocho y la raza: imágenes cinematográficas del chicano* (Mexico: UNAM, 1994), pp. 106–107.

5

JOKELORE,

CULTURAL DIFFERENCES,

AND LINGUISTIC DEXTERITY

The Construction of the Mexican Immigrant in Chicano Humor

o o o o
o o o o

José R. Reyna and María Herrera-Sobek

Although there are only two comprehensive scholarly collections of Chicano/ Mexican jokes, one from Texas[1] and the other from Texas and Mexico,[2] both reflect the extent and array of themes found in joke tradition among Chicanos in general. In fact, those two collections have generated several other studies of more specific joke themes such as *curanderismo* (folk medicine) jokes,[3] Pancho Villa jokes,[4] "Contemporary Myths in Chicano Jokelore,"[5] and "Linguistics and Humor."[6] In addition, José Limón wrote an insightful article on the *agringado* (anglocized) phenomenon among Chicanos,[7] and Rafaela Castro studied "Mexican Women's Sexual Jokes."[8] All of these studies indicate firstly that by the mid-twentieth century, jokes not only had supplanted the traditional folktale as the most popular prose narrative genre among Chicanos, but also may have become the most popular genre altogether.[9] Secondly, and more importantly, we propose that jokes reflect the gamut of issues that are of interest and concern to Chicanos. Among the favorite topics in the Chicano joke tradition is that of immigration.

Our study is divided in two parts. "The American Dream" analyzes immigration jokes from a thematic, ideological, and cultural perspective. The jokes cited in this section include those from José Reyna's personal collection, i.e., recollections from his childhood years in South Texas and later jokes heard during his adult years while living in New Mexico and California. Some of the salient themes examined are: (1) The American Dream, (2) The Crossing, (3) Initial Contacts, (4) Culture Clash, and (5) The Land of Equal Opportunity.

"Verbal Play and Mexican Immigrant Jokes" focuses on María Herrera-Sobek's collection. Here the corpus of jokes is analyzed with respect to the linguistic manipulations used to produce humor in the immigrant jokes and toward constructing a theoretical model that aids in the interpretation of these jokes with respect to their function in Chicano/Mexican society.

Historically, Mexican emigration to the United States has been such a problematic issue that immigration and humor are two subjects that would seem to be mutually exclusive. Yet it is precisely that kind of incongruity that is the basis of humor itself. Moreover, it is likely that neither immigration nor the humor of immigration are new. Certainly in folklore there is a long tradition of jokes not necessarily about immigrants exclusively, but about racial groups, ethnic groups, regional groups, and other "outsiders."[10] In the United States, a nation that is often characterized as "a nation of immigrants" or as a "melting pot" of immigrant groups from around the world, there have been plenty of groups—Irish, Italians, Poles, Czechs, Finns, and Norwegians, to name but a few—that have been the object of derision in American humor.[11] To be sure, by now most Americans of European descent have assimilated to such an extent that the traditional immigrant joke seems to have become passé in this age of "political correctness." But because Mexican immigration continues to be a vital part of American society and culture, and because people continue to be people, jokes about the Mexican immigrant continue to be a popular theme. Nevertheless, it should be pointed out that there is a difference between what we call "in-group joking" and "out-group joking." In-group jokes are those that are told amongst people of the ethnic or national group itself, while out-group jokes are those that make fun of other ethnic groups or nationalities. Jokes told about Polish Americans are generally told by out-group people (i.e., people who are not Polish Americans), whereas Mexican immigrant jokes are told by the in-group members themselves (i.e., Chicanos or Mexican immigrants). Needless to say, Euroamericans also engage in jokes about Mexicans and Chicanos.

Although we shall address other related themes later, what may be called the Mexican "pilgrim's progress" takes us from the initial decision to come to the United States, through the border crossing, and to the myriad experiences that immigrants encounter once they are in this country.

The American Dream

Although in ancient times such longed-for places as the Hispanic Tierra de Jauja, where rivers flowed with honey, or the Irish Avalon, where the dead were healed, were entirely imaginary,[12] the Mexican's dream is much closer to home. That is, it is not a greener pasture or the hereafter that Mexicans dream of, but rather orchards where money "grows on trees" on the other side of the border:

> A man who has been to the United States returns to Mexico and tries to convince his compadre to join him there by telling him all kinds of stories about the opportunities that await them north of the border. "In fact," he says, "in the United States you can walk down the streets and just pick the money right off the trees." Convinced by the exaggerations, the friend agrees to come with him.
>
> As soon as they cross the border they see a dollar bill on the ground. When the more experienced man reaches down to pick it up, the newcomer grabs his arm and says, "Hey, don't bother picking that one. Let's just go to the other end of the orchard and work our way back to the border!"[13]

The irony of this joke is that although the Mexican is portrayed as falling for the dream, it also suggests that, in reality, Mexicans only wish to stay in the United States long enough to earn a little money and leave at the earliest opportunity. This is certainly more in keeping with the theme of immensely popular songs such as "Canción mixteca" and "México lindo y querido," in which the Mexican's ultimate wish is to return to his homeland, even if only to be buried there. The joke, then, is further evidence of the fact that Mexicans are not always eager to come to the United States; as in this case, they sometimes have to be cajoled, perhaps with a dream. Even the prospect of becoming American has never been attractive, especially since they have to renounce their Mexican citizenship. For generations Mexicans have taken this to mean that they must literally trample their beloved flag (los hacen pisotear la bandera) before they can become citizens. In one joke, a prospective citizen, when asked if he swears to "support the Constitution," replies that he already has ten kids to support![14] In another, we learn that Mexicans hate Abraham Lincoln because he introduced "L'Incoln Tax."[15] Of course, Mexican men are especially apprehensive about becoming assimilated, which means that they will surely be henpecked. (*Allá manda la mujer.* [Over there (in the U.S.) women are the bosses.] *En los Estados Unidos la mujer lleva los pantalones.* [In the United States women wear the pants.][16]

THE CROSSING

Other jokes reflect the fact that even if Mexicans were eager to leave Mexico, and if money were there for the asking, they still could not just go to their nearest consulate, obtain a visa or passport, pack their bags, catch a convenient flight to the Los Angeles airport, report to the employment office, and secure a lucrative job. In reality, given restrictions on legal immigration, the majority of those who come in search of work must resort to other, less glamorous (and downright illegal) means of entry. Indeed, over the years Mexicans have used so many ingenious ploys just to cross the border that the theme has found its way into joke tradition:

> Two friends had tried to come to the United States legally but had been turned back. Undaunted and determined to become less conspicuous, they decided to pass themselves off as, of all things, Arabs, since Arabs were then enjoying favored status.
>
> When they got to the border all wrapped in sheets and wearing towels around their heads, the guards became suspicious and asked them what they knew about Arab culture. Necessity being the mother of invention, they quickly improvised a border version of "El corrido del caballo blanco" that started out, "Este es el corrido / del camello blanco . . ." ("This is the ballad of the white camel . . ." instead of the correct "This is the ballad of the white horse.")[17]

Among the themes in this joke would be: (1) crossover from joke to corrido; (2) the incorporation of a contemporary theme (i.e., the recent rise to power of OPEC and oil-producing Arab nations) in a joke with a traditional theme (Mexican illegal immigration); (3) Mexican ethnocentricity (i.e., even Arabs should know José Alfredo Jiménez's corrido); and (4) stereotyping by Mexicans (all Arabs wear certain attire and ride camels).

As can be seen from the preceding joke, in many instances Mexican immigrant jokes merge with other motifs. The following joke, for instance, combines the immigrant theme and another equally ubiquitous Mexican joke cycle, *perico* (parrot) jokes.[18] In this case, the parrot-as-immigrant theme would seem to be a natural development inasmuch as parrots, too, must sneak into the United States illegally, and usually under very similar conditions:

> *A woman who owned a parrot wanted to punish him for some misdeeds, so she told him, "I'm going to 'bring you inside.'" The parrot, thinking that she meant she was going to stick him under her dress, panicked and protested, "I was smuggled into this country under a woman's dress. If you're going to do the same thing to me now, I'd rather die!"* [19]

The joke below shows that there is no end to the indignities that the illegal must suffer in order to escape detection, including attacks on his very manhood:

> *A perico mojao (wetback parrot) was so poor that he decided to escape at night, so la imigración would not catch him. On the way back to Mexico he came to a farm and sneaked into the henhouse, figuring he could at least eat some chicken feed. As he was eating, he noticed the rooster was going around "stepping on" all the chickens. When there were no more chickens left, the parrot became suspicious of the rooster's intentions. He looked up from where he was eating and told him, "Look here, Mr. Rooster, let's be friends. I'm starved and I'm a wetback. Please don't screw me. Just let me eat in peace."* [20]

Even though smuggling and smugglers—from *bulegas* (bootleggers) during Prohibition to *narcotraficantes* (drug smugglers) in our day—have been popular themes in corridos and songs, we have found no jokes about those themes in the Chicano jest tradition. The only contraband item, other than parrots, that we have come across in joke tradition is the cow's udder mentioned in the following joke:

> *A man returning from Matamoros on the bus was smuggling a cow's udder in his pants. One of the teats slipped out and was noticed by a lady. She mistook it for something else and complained to the driver. In the meantime, the man took his knife and was about to cut it off when the lady said, "Never mind, it's no big deal."* [21]

There are various interpretations for this joke. One may read in this text the lady's false modesty ("The lady doth protest too much") as humorous. A second interpretation may rely on men's insecurity regarding the size of their penises.

INITIAL CONTACTS

Assuming that a Mexican seeking illegal entry into the United States succeeds in outsmarting border officials at the crossing itself, that is still only a pyrrhic
victory, as Mexicans who succeed in gaining surreptitious entry still face a multitude of difficulties, not the least of which is getting caught by *la migra*, the hated
Border Patrol agents. The joke below is about a meeting that would have taken
place in the days when the government hired only Anglos, most of whom thought
they could speak Spanish:

> *Two Mexicans sneaked across the border. One of them, Nacho, had to relieve*
> *himself, so he went behind a tree. In the meantime, a Border Patrol agent*
> *came upon the other Mexican and asked him (in broken Spanish, of course),*
> *"¿Dónde nacho?" (Where were you born?) The man thought he had said,*
> *"¿Dónde está Nacho?" (Where is Nacho?), so he answered, "¡Nacho está*
> *detrás de aquel árbol!" (He's behind that tree.) Then the agent asked him,*
> *"¿Tiene papeles?" (Do you have papers?) And the Mexican replied, "No,*
> *él se limpia con hojas." (No, he'll just use leaves.)* [22]

CULTURE CLASH

Mexicans who succeed in eluding officials at the border and la migra once
they are on this side, still find it difficult to escape detection. Cultural differences
are evident not only between Mexicans and *americanos* but also between Mexicans
and Chicanos. Cultural misunderstandings are common as can be seen in the
following:

> *A Mexican makes it across the border and wants to catch a train, but has*
> *never seen one. A Chicano tells him, "When you see a big black thing coming*
> *down these tracks smoking, that's a train." A short time later a big black guy*
> *comes walking down the railroad smoking a pipe, so the Mexican jumps on*
> *his back and yells, "¡Vámonos pa' Chicago!" (Let's go to Chicago!)* [23]

Another joke relates to cultural objects in American bathrooms:

> *A Mexican who came to the United States had to use the bathroom in the*
> *bus station. The men's bathroom was out of order, so he had to use the*
> *women's bathroom. The janitor told him to push the first two buttons on a*
> *contraption that he would see there, but not to mess with the third one. When*

he was done he pushed the first two buttons, then out of curiosity pushed the third one. Unfortunately, that button was a tampon remover and it yanked and yanked at him.[24]

Although the newcomer may often be portrayed as being less sophisticated in some ways, sometimes these jokes provide an avenue through which commentaries on problems created by modern technology can be aired. Criticism regarding American wastefulness can be detected in this anecdote:

Two compadres were walking home one night, and they got to criticizing American culture, especially about how wasteful Americans are. Just then, they came up to a garbage can that had been put out to be picked up the next day.

The night before, a drunk American woman had fallen in the garbage can head first, with her tail sticking up.

One of the men said, "¿Ya ve, compadre? Tiraron estas nalgas, y ¡todavía están buenas"! (You see, compadre? They discarded this butt and it's still in good shape!) [25]

Perhaps the most important aspect of U.S. culture with which Mexican immigrants come in contact is racism. Although discrimination has assumed more subtle forms in recent decades, the following two jokes illustrate the overt nature of Anglo/Mexicano conflict in the days before the civil rights movement:

A Mexican went into a restaurant and sat down to eat. As they did not serve Mexicans, the waiter went up to him and said, "I'm sorry, sir, you'll have to leave. We don't serve Mexicans here."

The Mexican, who did not understand either the language or the custom, just sat there. The waiter then took the Mexican's coat and hat, handed them to him and said, "¿Comprendy?"

The Mexican said, "Ah, sí, comprendo." As he was leaving, he said, "You got a mother?" The puzzled waiter said, "Yes." And the Mexican said, "¿Comprende?" (He could only hope that the americano was familiar with the old Mexican expression "¡Chinga tu madre!" [Go fuck your mother!]) [26]

It seems there was a big dance in heaven, but only the best people, namely Anglos, were admitted. A Mexican went to the door, and St. Peter promptly informed him, "I don't want any Mexicans in here!"

Offended, the Mexican thought, "We'll see." He went home, took a bath

*and combed his hair, then came back. St. Peter said, "What are you?" The
Mexican said, "I'm an American!" (¡Soy puro gringo!) So they let him in.
Later, there was a fracas, a big fight, a knifing, someone had been killed. So
St. Peter ordered the doors closed so they could find the perpetrator. Knowing
all about Mexicans, he said, "I know, play the Mexican national anthem
and we'll find out if there is a Mexican in here." No sooner had the band
started playing than they heard a loud* grito *(shout) from the patriotic Mexican. "You see," St. Peter said, "there's a Mexican in here," so they took him
by the tail and threw him right out.*[27]

This joke surely adds a touch of irony to the old Mexican expression, *¡Pobre
México, tan lejos de Dios, y tan cerca de los Estados Unidos!* (Poor Mexico, so far from
God, so near the United States!)

In fairness to Anglos, we should say that they are not always portrayed as
being racists. Everyone has heard the joke about José, who goes to his first baseball
game, decides to watch it from the flagpole, then thinks everyone is welcoming him
by singing "José, can you see?"[28] This is probably a joke borrowed by Chicanos
from Anglo tradition. Moreover, Anglos are not the only ones who demean Mexicans. As indicated in the joke about St. Peter and heaven, there are also Mexican/
Chicano conflicts, which may be based on economic as well as cultural conflicts,
differences, or rivalries. These have evidently given rise to jokes in which Chicanos
and Mexicans are portrayed as antagonists, although the rivalry is not as bitter as
is the Anglo/Chicano and Anglo/Mexican rivalries. Most often Chicano immigrant
jokes derive their humor from making fun of the undocumented worker.

*Don Cacahuate made it across the border at Calexico and was wandering
around lost in the desert not far from his destination—Indio, California.
Finally, he came upon a man and asked him how far he was from Indio
("¿Cuánto me falta pa' Indio?"). The man, seeing how dirty and unkempt
he was, chose to interpret the question as: "How close am I to looking like
an Indian?" So he said, "¡Nomás las plumas, desgraciao!" (Hell, all you
need is some feathers!)*[29]

It goes without saying that in the above instance both Indians and undocumented immigrants are slurred. In a Mexican version of the joke, the man is looking
for Lión (i.e., the city of León in Guanajuato) and is told all he needs is to roar. But
in our case, the Chicano is portrayed as being in the best position to help the Mexican
immigrant adjust to a whole new way of thinking. Interestingly, the Mexican's lack

of awareness about things American is made even more poignant when it comes to long-standing Anglo/Chicano conflicts. As in the following joke, that point may be lost altogether on the Mexican:

> A Chicano militant goes to the bus station in Laredo to get his grandfather, who is visiting from Mexico, and drive him to Houston. As soon as they get on the freeway he begins to tell his grandfather all about those americanos. "You see all that, abuelo? It was all México. And the Gringos stole it!" Driving through San Antonio on the beautiful freeways, the Chicano again says, "You see that, abuelo? All of it was México. And the Gringos stole it from us!" When they got to Houston he again reminded his grandfather, "This was all ours. And the damned Gringos stole it from us!" By that time the grandfather had gotten into the spirit of things, so he said, "Those damned Gringos. They kept the best freeways!"[30]

As helpful as Chicanos might try to be, it cannot be denied that on occasion they have been known to take advantage of their unwitting kin:

> A Mexican crossed into the United States, robbed a bank, and was chased and finally apprehended by an FBI agent. Unfortunately, the agent couldn't speak Spanish and the Mexican couldn't speak English. So, a Chicano passerby agreed to perform his civic duty and serve as interpreter.
>
> The agent told the Chicano, "Tell him to tell me where he hid the money."
>
> The Chicano said, "Dice que le diga donde escondió el dinero." (He says to tell him where you hid the money.)
>
> The Mexican said, "Dígale que no le voy a decir." (Tell him I am not going to tell him.)
>
> The Chicano said, "He says he won't tell you."
>
> The agent said, "Well, you tell him that if he won't tell me where he hid the money, I'm going to shoot him on the spot."
>
> The Chicano said, "Dice que si no le dice dónde está el dinero, lo va a matar aquí mismo." (He says that if you don't tell him where the money is, he is going to kill you right here.)
>
> The Mexican said, "Ah, en ese caso dígale que se vaya por esta calle hasta la esquina y que doble a la izquierda y se vaya cinco cuadras. Cuando llegue a una casa de ladrillo, allí detrás verá un árbol muy grande. Cerca del árbol hay una piedra, y allí debajo de la piedra encuentra el dinero." (Oh, in that case, tell him to go down that street until

211

he comes to the street corner, and there to turn left and walk five blocks.
When he comes to a brick house, there in the back he will see a tree that is
very large. Near the tree is a stone, and there underneath the stone, he will
find the money.)
The Chicano turned to the agent and said, "He says he'd rather die!" [31]

Besides the Chicano, there is another well-known type of "helper," and that
is the immigrant who has been in this country only a short time but sees himself
as an old-timer conversant with the culture and language of the *americano.* Like all
the other helpers, though, he usually makes matters worse:

A Mexican was hired by an American to herd some pigs. One of the pigs
wandered away and was run over by a train. When the American patron
found out, he threw a fit and cursed, "You son of a bitch!" The Mexican
asked the "interpreter" what the American had said. The translation: "He
wants to know why you left the pig in the ditch!" [32]

A Mexican who witnessed a killing didn't know English, so another immi-
grant offered to interpret for the police. The witness told the interpreter, "Pues,
dígale que Casimiro le dió un tiro en la sien, y nunca volvió en sí."
(Casimiro shot him in the temple, and he never came to.) The interpreter's
translation: "He said Almost See (casi miró) gave him a bullet (le dió un
tiro) in the one hundred (en la 'sien') and he never came back to yes (volvió
en sí)." [33]

A Mexican worker got fed up with his low wages and told his friend, "Dí-
gale al patrón que si no me paga más, voy a parar mi trabajo y me voy
a regresar a mi tierra." (Tell the boss that if he doesn't give me a raise I'm
going to quit and return to my land.) The friend's translation: "He say if
you don't pay him more, he's going to stand up his work and go back to
his dirt." [34]

As can be seen from many of the examples cited thus far, the language problems that immigrants face cut across many themes. In the joke below, both characters have done their best to prepare themselves for that inevitable first encounter
with an Anglo who does not know Spanish. By now probably totally disoriented,
they end up wasting their best English on another Mexican:

Two Mexicans run into each other in the woods and pretend that they are speaking English.. "Buaynus tardies, sinior, coumou estar ustay?" "Oh, yo estar beayne. Yo trabajar muchou toros las deeaz," and so forth. Finally, they both run out of English and one of them asks the other, "Ouh, sinior, ustay ser Meksicanou?" "Sí, yo ser Meksicanou." Relieved, the first one says, "Ah, entonces ¿qué estamos haciendo hablando inglés?" (Then what the hell are we doing speaking English?) [35]

It should be noted that much of the humor of this joke is based on the performance of the narrator. That is, the narrator must pronounce Spanish with a heavy English accent until the characters find out that they are both Mexican. Only when he finds out that the other character is also Mexican can he switch to normal pronunciation. Nonetheless, the basic theme is that both characters are trying so hard to impress the americano that they cannot see that they are actually both Mexicans.

THE LAND OF EQUAL OPPORTUNITY

In spite of all their travails—and ever more stringent immigrant labor laws—most Mexican immigrants eventually manage to find employment. Although they are often portrayed in jokes as being farmworkers, they can be found in a wide range of occupations, such as musicians, bakers, and teachers, as shown in the following:

A group of musicians came to the U.S. and formed a mariachi group. Taking the bus to their first gig, they neglected to pay their fares. The bus driver tried to explain that they had to pay, but since they didn't understand, he said, "Token, por favor." They thought he had said "Toquen" (Play), so they promptly went into a chorus of "El Rancho Grande." [36]

A Mexican baker was explaining to a customer how he goes about making fancy biscuits, the ones with a little tip on them. He says, "I just take the little ball of dough and press it against my navel. Then he said, "Do you know how doughnuts are made?" [37]

A Mexican teacher was teaching Spanish in the United States. A student omitted the [orthographic] accent in the name María. The teacher corrected her [in a heavy Spanish accent], "Remember, María do not have a deep-thong, María have two strong bowels." [38]

213

If military service can be considered an occupation, then we could also in-clude the plethora of jokes about Mexicans who have fought on the U.S. side in wars. For example:

> *As Mexican paratroopers were bailing out of an airplane they would each yell, "¡Ayúdame, Virgen de Guadalupe!" (Help me, Virgin of Guada-lupe!) There was one Anglo among them. Although he did not understand what they were saying, when his turn came he followed suit and yelled, "Me, too, Miss Lupey!"* [39]

TURNABOUT IS FAIR PLAY

The jokes we have seen thus far illustrate the nature of the Mexican's initial contact with American laws, customs, and language; typically, it is the immigrant who is portrayed as the butt of these jokes. That is, after all, universally part and parcel of the immigrant condition. However, if we examine Chicano/Mexicano joke tradition more closely, we also find a cycle in which americanos take their turn as outsiders, their turn in the barrel, as it were. [40] These are especially poignant when the americano is on the Mexican's turf, i.e., Mexico. [41]

> *An American tourist crosses the border, goes to a marketplace, and sees a small bust of Pancho Villa. He asks how much it costs, and the clerk says it costs $50.00. The American asks why it is so expensive, and the Mexican says it is because it is the "real head of Pancho Villa." He convinces the American that it is authentic and sells it to him. The tourist then goes deeper into Mexico, goes to another marketplace, and sees a similar Pancho Villa bust, only smaller—and it costs $100.00! When he asks why it is so expen-sive, he it told that it is because it is the "real head of Pancho Villa." The tourist then shows the man the larger bust and says, "But this is supposed to be the real head of Pancho Villa!" The Mexican explains, "Sí, señor, but this one is of when he was a little boy!"* [42]

In another twist on the same theme, there are many jokes in which it is the Chicano who is portrayed, or who portrays himself, as the outsider, that is, the Chicano is the one who commits cultural *faux pas*, sometimes in Mexico, some-times in the United States, due to the fact that he is unfamiliar with Mexican customs and language. [43]

A couple from Texas visited some compadres in Mexico City. They were out on the terrace enjoying the sun. When the sun started setting, the hostess said, "Vámonos pa' adentro porque ya está cayendo el crepúsculo." (Let's go in, it's getting dark.) Later, when the couple from Mexico visited them in Texas, the hosts took them out to the terrace too. And when the sun started to set, the Texas compadre tried to impress the Mexicans with her flowery language. Instead, she mangled it and it came out as, "Vámonos pa' adentro, compadre, porque ya se me está poniendo crespo el culo'." [44] (Let's go in, my butt's getting antsy.)

Two Chicanos, a tall one and short one, used to cross over into Matamoros, always together. One time the tall one (el alto) couldn't go, so the short one went alone. Driving around town he ran a stop sign [ALTO], so a police-man stopped him and, in typical fashion, asked him, "Oiga, ¿qué pasó con el ALTO?" (Say, what about the stop sign?) The short guy misunderstood him and said, "He couldn't make it today!" The policeman then said (per custom), "Hey, don't get smart with me, or I'll take your placas (license plates)." The Chicano again misunderstood and said, "No, please, you don't have to beat me, I'll give you my placas (dental plates)!" [45]

It is evident that there is in Chicano tradition a cycle of jokes that deals with the theme of Mexican immigration to the United States, and that, in fact, the theme is so popular that within the cycle there are sub-themes related to various aspects of the immigrant experience. The next section, "Verbal Play and Mexican Immigrant Jokes" will discuss such sub-themes. It is also obvious from the extant collections that the perspective seen in the cycle is, nonetheless, a U.S. (i.e., Chicano or experienced immigrant) perspective. But it would be interesting to see if there has been a Mexican equivalent. That is, has there been in joke tradition a strictly Mexican perspective on the subject of Mexican immigration to the United States, and not only what was found on this side of the border. It would seem to us that, for example, the theme of the Mexican returning home and lording it over other Mexicans, perhaps the Mexican version of the *agringado* phenomenon, would be replete with humorous possibilities. Many years ago, Reyna had the experience of telling a joke about Mexican immigrants to a neighbor who happened to be a home-sick Mexican immigrant himself. He promptly responded in kind, telling Reyna about a *pocho* (assimilated Chicano) who went to a bakery in Mexico and asked for *pan mexicano.* Although such assimilated Chicanas/os have been satirized in songs as well as in literary works and films, in the authors' experience, we have found that Mexicans who have not been to the United States do not really appreciate the bilingual/cross-cultural type of humor that is so popular among Chicanos and Mexican immigrants in this country. Neither have we had success in eliciting such jokes from Mexicans in visits to that country; perhaps they are merely being polite and do not want to hurt a pocha/o's feelings. Clearly, a collection of Mexican jokes would shed light on the subject. Unfortunately, to our knowledge there are no scholarly joke collections from Mexico at all (or from any other Spanish-speaking country for that matter). Consequently, for the time being we must settle for the insights that we can gain from an interpretation of jokes generated by Chicanos and Mexican immigrants themselves. In spite of the fact that these jokes make light of the immigrant condition, they do give us the human dimension, not to mention the "lighter side," of an otherwise very complex and controversial issue.

Verbal Play and Mexican Immigrant Jokes

Another area of folklore humor that has blossomed from the Mexican immigrant experience is the joke based on verbal play between English and Spanish. Analysis of this category will encompass three specific aims: (1) present an explanation of the various techniques and linguistic manipulations employed in order to achieve humor in the anecdote, (2) propose a tentative model that outlines the framework upon which this type of jest rests, and (3) offer a preliminary hypothesis that attempts, in part, to explain the function these jokes play in the Mexican immigrant community.

Eighteen Mexican immigrant jokes were collected between 1977 and 1978, mostly from Mexican immigrant informants living in the surrounding communities of Orange County, California. Five of the jokes cited here were collected by an undergraduate student, Mario Meza, for a class project.[46] All the jokes were narrated in Spanish and the cited texts are Herrera-Sobek's translations. A large number of informants were young male Mexican nationals who were working or studying here. Some crossed the border with proper documentation; others were here without any legal documents. These men seemed to enjoy telling the jokes recorded here.

Careful examination of the texts yielded four main categories:

1. Verbal play between English and Spanish (10)
2. Verbal play using Spanish only (4)

3. Verbal play between French and Spanish (1)
4. Miscellaneous (3)

As is readily evident, category 1, exhibiting the largest number of jokes, depends on the confusion between English and Spanish for its humor. In this particular category two groups of jokes are evident: (1) jokes that rely on phonetic or sound (be it syllable, word or sentence) confusion and (2) those that rely on confusion of both sound and writing. Following is an example of a joke utilizing phonetic or sound confusion alone:

California, Land of All Saints
Two compadres go to work in the United States. After working for some time in the States they return to Mexico to their hometown. All their friends and relatives want to hear about the United States; they want to know how the people are, what language they speak, about the freeways and buildings, etc. One compadre eggs on the other, "You tell them!" The other says, "No, you tell them!" Finally one of the men says, "O.K. I'll tell you. To begin with, let me tell you, California is a very saintly land. All the towns in California bear saints' names: San Isidro, San Diego, San Clemente, Santa Ana, Los Ange-les, San Francisco—all saints' names. Well it was such a saintly land, such a Christian land that they called my compadre 'Son of a Bitch' and they called me 'Son of a Gun!'[47]

The phonetic resemblance between the English word "son" and the Spanish word for saint (*san*) is deftly employed to produce humor.

A variation of this joke with the kernels "son of a bitch" and "son of a gun" used as the main ingredients reads as follows:

One day two Mexicans crossed the border to the United States as is tradi-tionally done—illegally. They were at the outskirts of San Diego trying to come to Los Angeles and were getting tired and desperate. They decided to stand right in the middle of the road so that an oncoming car had to brake in order not to run over them. The mad American driver yelled at them, "Son of a bitch!" One of the fellows asked the other, "What did he say?" and the second one answered, "¡Dice que subas el veliz!" (He says to get your suitcase in the car!) The American driver got even angrier and said, "Son of a gun!" The fellow translating said, "¡Qué te apures que ya se va!" (He says to hurry because he is leaving!)[48]

The resemblance between the phonetic sounds and rhythm of the English words "Son of a bitch" with *Subas el veliz* and "Son of a gun" with *Ya se va* incites the listener to laughter. The added plus that the immigrants supposedly get their ride only increases the pleasure.

Another example of the type of joke that utilizes linguistic confusion as the principal source of humor is found in the following:

> *The Little Old Lady and the Immigration Officer*
> *A little old lady decides to come to the United States. She crosses the border illegally and soon an immigration officer spots her and begins to question her. The little old lady does not answer and finally the immigration officer asks, "Do you speak English?" Whereupon the little old lady answers indignantly, "¡Ayyy, cómo que me quieres picar las ingles desgraciado!" (Ohhh, how dare you want to poke my thighs, you disgraceful one!)* [49]

The use of similar sounding phonemes in English and Spanish and juxtaposing the innocence of the English sentence "Do you speak English?" with the sexual slightly obscene, slightly bawdy meaning of *"picar las ingles"* combine to produce the jest. Here again the fact that the little old Mexican lady scolds the American immigration officer increases the response to laughter. It is obvious that the aggression factor plays a role in this anecdote; however, it is secondary to the verbal play and the sexual connotation inscribed in it.

The second group of jokes displaying verbal play between English and Spanish as the principal element in producing the comical effect depends on the protagonist misreading words or phrases and not on orally misunderstanding them. One joke of this type collected has the immigrant reading a sign on a door with the English words "For Sale, Not For Lease" as reading *"Fórzale no le hace"* (force it open, it does not matter), whereupon a Chicano policeman explains to the immigrant the actual meaning of the words. Reyna has collected the following variant of this joke.

> *A group of Mexicans was arrested for breaking into a vacant house. When they went to court, they told the judge that they were merely obeying a sign that read "For Sale" which they read as "Fórzale" (force it open).* [50]

Another joke collected belonging to this group has the *dramatis personae* misreading a sign in a Coke machine:

> *A recently arrived Mexican immigrant who cannot read English wants to buy a Coke. He sees a Coke machine and takes the smallest coin he has,*

which is a dime, and inserts it in the slot. A red light flashes out reading
"Dime." The man reads it in Spanish with its equivalent meaning of "Tell
me." So the fellow looks around and whispers, "¡Dame una coca!" (Give
me a Coke!) [51]

The jokes found in category 2 consist of verbal play utilizing the Spanish language only. Included in this category is the popular and widely known joke about Ignacio. This joke was a favorite in South Texas in the Río Grande Valley in the 1950s when the Bracero Program (1942–1964) was in full force. The Ignacio joke quoted in its entirety by José Reyna (see page 208) has Ignacio and an unnamed friend crossing the border together without proper documentation. Ignacio needs to relieve himself and hides in the bushes. Meanwhile, immigration officers spot Ignacio's friend and begin to question him: "¿Dónde nació?" (Where were you born?)

The friend confuses the anglocized, mispronounced short sentence (*nacio* for *nació*) as asking for Ignacio and proceeds to tell the officers that Ignacio is behind the bushes. When the officers ask for his papers (i.e., legal documents), the friend thinks they are asking him if Ignacio has toilet paper! Ignacio's friend responds that Ignacio uses leaves to clean himself.

The humor here lies in several cultural areas. First, the Anglo's inability to speak Spanish correctly is a source of humor. That the government officials representing the law sound stupid is comical. The Border Patrol officers' inability to speak Spanish fluently detracts from the government agency's power and status, so the officers are demystified and the audience (mostly Chicanos and Mexican immigrants) can laugh and feel superior to them.

Second, when the phrase "y los papeles" (and the papers) is enunciated, the joke rebounds back at the immigrants and the "culture of poverty" that Mexicans and Chicanos know so well. Poor people do not have the luxury of toilet paper for their daily needs and use instead newspapers, magazine pages, etc., to clean themselves. This cultural fact of life is both an embarrassment and a source of humor. Chicanos/Mexicans have learned to laugh at our own poverty—to transform life's daily inequities and the pain they cause into sources of humor. This process is similar to the "aesthetics of rasquachismo" that Tomás Ybarra Frausto first delineated as the transformation of discarded objects from a consumer and highly urbanized society into decorative objects such as discarded automobile tires or coffee cans used as flower planters (see Introduction). In fact, this would be an early example of recycling.

The Russian theoretician Mikail Bahktin no doubt would categorize the Ignacio joke cycle as extremely subversive, given the ridicule of powerful figures such as Border Patrol officers and the fact that the subject matter is eschatalogical.

One of the jokes collected that can be classified under category 3 involves confusion between French and Spanish.

> *"Ce la vie!"*
> *A Mexican immigrant goes to France or Canada and sees a girl fall, her dress flying out and exposing her private parts. A Frenchman philosophically tells her, "Ce la vie!" (Such is life!), whereupon our picaresque Mexican joins in with "¡Yo también se la vi!" (I, too, saw her private parts!)*

The French phrase is obviously interpreted as a Spanish one. Although most jokes relied on verbal play for their comical effect, a few informants related Mexican immigrant experience jokes based on other aspects of immigrant lore. One of these jokes depends on the commonly held myth that money is abundant in the United Sates and one can "sweep it off the streets." The narrative has Don Cacahuate and his wife, Doña Cebolla, riding a bus from Tijuana to the United States (Don Cacahuate and Doña Cebolla are popular stock characters in Mexican folktales). While on the bus, around the San Ysidro area, Doña Cebolla spots a billfold full of money and very excitedly tells her husband. Don Cacahuate calmly answers, "Don't worry, we will start picking dollars as soon as we reach San Diego!"[52]

As can be seen, many of the jokes are structured by the use of pejorative and insulting phrases. Since in previous research[53] it was found that the Mexican immigrant possessed a very positive self-image and a definite feeling about his personal worth in American society, it was puzzling to find these jests where the fool appeared to be the immigrant himself.

SOCIAL FUNCTION OF MEXICAN IMMIGRANT JOKES

Making a structural model of the Mexican immigrant joke yielded important insights as to the function these jokes play in the Mexican immigrant community. The structural model for this type of jest exhibits four basic components interplaying within a closed system: (1) *Dramatis Personae*—immigrant, (2) The United States as the geographic location, (3) The Experience: English *interpreted* Spanish, (4) Humor.

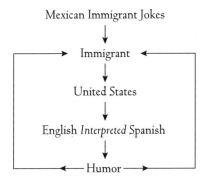

As the structural model demonstrates, the joke is on the protagonist himself. Since the Mexican immigrant is at the receiving end of the jest, it stands to reason that this is not a case of humor as a technique in race conflict (although, of course, given the nature of some of the jokes and the protagonists involved, i.e., Border Patrol and immigrant, there is race conflict expressed). John H. Burma in his article "Humor as a Technique in Race Conflict" calls humor in this category an open system, where hostility flows from the in-group to the out-group. "In conflict, the involved parties make use of a variety of techniques to gain ascendancy or temporary advantage. Since subtle barbs often strike more telling blows than gratuitous insult or rational argument, not infrequently these techniques include humor, satire, irony and wit." [54] He further states that: "In any conflict it is most gratifying to cause one's adversary to appear ludicrous in his own eyes. Where this is not possible, very considerable satisfaction can be secured by making your opponent appear ludicrous in your eyes." [55]

In Mexican immigrant jokes this, of course, is the opposite, for in these jokes it is the immigrant himself who generally appears as the fool. This particular theory of race conflict and aggression, therefore, does not satisfactorily explain the role of these jokes.

A superficial analysis might lead the investigator to conclude that this group of jokes belongs to the category posited by Américo Paredes in his article "The Anglo-American in Mexican Folklore" in which he found a body of folklore "principally the jest" where an "attitude of self-satire" and "masochistic as well as self-degrading" tendencies were evident.[56] There *is* a corpus of jokes that falls into this area. Paredes describes these jokes:

The self-critical jest is told in all Mexican folklore areas, but more than the *corridos* or the jest of veiled hostility it can be identified with the direct influence of United States culture. Some jests of this type are popular with Anglo-Americans, among whom they form part of a corpus of "ethnic" jokes along with stories about Negroes, Jews, or Irishmen. Many undoubtedly were evolved by Mexican-Americans, who as individuals caught between two cultures were more apt to look with a critical and ridiculing eye now at the American, now at the Mexican. Many others no doubt have originated in Mexico, in the more cosmopolitan circles, most likely during recent decades. It is my own experience some 35 years ago this kind of jest was restricted almost entirely to Mexican-Americans, who might have imperiled life or limb by telling them on the Mexican side of the border.[57]

Since the jokes collected here are bilingual and bicultural, their performance requires a specific performer and a specific audience. Otherwise the joke loses its humor in the translation — be it Spanish or English. Furthermore, since Chicanas/os have become politically and socially sensitive to the issue of undocumented workers — as Chicanas/os prefer to call the Mexican immigrant — very few Chicanas/os tell this type of joke. It is generally the immigrants themselves (particularly those who have resided in the United States for several years) who take pleasure in telling these anecdotes.

Our analysis indicates, therefore, that these jokes, rather than being masochistic or self-degrading, can best be understood in terms of their social context and performance.

Basic to the understanding of the deeper function of these jokes is the reconceptualization of folklore in terms of communicative process formulated by Professor Dan Ben Amos in his seminal article "Toward a Definition of Folklore in Context": "To define folklore, it is necessary to examine the phenomena as they exist. In its cultural context, folklore is not an aggregate of things, but a process — a communicative process, to be exact."[58] He elaborates further:

> The ever increasing emphasis on the situational background of tales, songs, and proverbs that developed from Malinowski's functionalism into Hymes's "ethnography of speaking," enables us not only to study but to define folklore in its context. And in this framework, which is the real habitat of all folklore forms, there is no dichotomy between processes and products. The telling is the tale; therefore the narrator,

his story, and his audience are all related to each other as components of a single continuum, which is the communicative event.[59]

Viewed in this light, i.e., folklore performance being a communicative event, two important functions can be discerned for the types of jokes analyzed here: (1) a prescriptive function and (2) a cathartic function. In the first instance the particular message depicted in the joke is a type of humorous advice to the newcomer. The underlying prescriptive message in these jokes seems to be: In order to avoid ridicule and compromising situations, learn how to speak English.

With respect to the cathartic function, we find it to be a corollary to the first function cited above. In formulating or creating a joke there has to be a process of objectifying and reordering of phenomena in order to achieve a desired result—in this case humor. The process of objectifying particular experiences and sharing them in the stylized structure of the joke provides a feeling of solidarity and serves as a public forum for the release of feelings of anxiety, which are great in the transplanted person. The catharsis produced during this particular folkloristic group performance accounts for the popularity of these jests.

Mexican immigrants have found in the dynamics of folklore a socially acceptable and psychologically beneficial escape valve for their feelings of anxiety produced in the new surroundings. As Roger D. Abrahams states in his article "Personal Power and Social Restraint in the Definition of Folklore":

> Folklore . . . gives form to energies set into motion by some shared or social anxiety. This is why we can say that folklore attacks social problems, because it takes the unfocused energies arising out of problems and channels them into forms that have been useful in meeting the same challenges in the past. Furthermore, these forms commonly conform to what is regarded as proper practice. Thus we may say that expressive folklore is the approved and tested rhetoric of a community, it is a set of inherited organized techniques of control and persuasion.[60]

The jokes analyzed here show that the Mexican immigrant has found through the medium of folklore an effective way to deal with an anxiety-ridden situation. The jokes reveal a certain maturity and sophistication in the manner the immigrant has chosen to confront the ego-threatening side effects of being an immigrant in a strange country in which a foreign tongue is spoken. Immigrants could have chosen to express hostility toward their new environment through their jokes. They chose, however, to laugh at themselves and their foibles. This is no small feat. We can indeed admire the immigrants' courage and self-confidence, for to paraphrase an old saying: He who can laugh at himself truly laughs best.

Notes

1. José Reyna, *Raza Humor: Chicano Joke Tradition in Texas* (San Antonio: Penca Books, 1980).

2. Américo Paredes, *Uncle Remus con Chile* (Houston: Arte Público Press, 1993).

3. Américo Paredes, "The Anglo American in Mexican Folklore," in Ray B. Browne, Donald M. Winkelman, and Allen Hayman, eds., *New Voices in American Studies*, ed. Ray B. Browne et al. (West Lafayette, Ind.: Purdue University Press, 1966), pp. 113–128.

4. José Reyna, "Pancho Villa: The Lighter Side," *New Mexico Humanities Review* 7, 1 (1984), pp. 57–62.

5. José Reyna, "Contemporary Myths in Chicano Jokelore," in *Renato Rosaldo Lecture Series* Monograph 3, Series 1985-86 (1987), pp. 24–32.

6. José Reyna, "The Humor of Language: Linguistics and Humor among Chicanos." Paper presented before Encuentro México/Chicano: Homenaje a César Chávez. Universidad Nacional Autónoma de México, Mexico City, 1993.

7. José Limón, "Agringado Joking in Texas Mexican Society: Folklore and Differential Identity," *New Scholar* 6 (1977), pp. 33–50.

8. Rafaela Castro, "Mexican Women's Sexual Jokes," *Aztlán* 13 (1982), pp. 275–293.

9. Reyna, *Raza Humor: Chicano Joke Tradition*, p. 9.

10. Antti Aarne and Stith Thompson, *The Types of the Folktale* (Helsinki: Folklore Fellows Communication, 1961); and Stith Thompson, *Motif-index of Folk Literature*, 6 vols. (Bloomington: University of Indiana Press, 1958).

11. Jan Brunvand, "As the Saints Go Marching By: Modern Jokelore Concerning Mormons, *Journal of American Folklore* LXXXIII (1970), pp. 53–60; Richard M. Dorson, "Dialect Stories from the Upper Peninsula: A New Form of American Folklore," *Journal of American Folklore* LXI (1949), pp. 113–150; Alan Dundes, "A Study of Ethnic Slurs: The Jew and the Polack in the United States," *Journal of American Folklore* LXXXIV (1971), pp. 183–203; and Heda Jason, "The Jewish Joke: The Problem of Definition," *Southern Folklore Quarterly* XX (1967), pp. 48–54.

12. Thompson, *Motif-index of Folk Literature*, p. 238.

13. José Reyna's personal collection.

14. Paredes, *Uncle Remus con Chile*, p. 181.

15. Reyna's personal collection.

16. Paredes, "The Anglo American in Mexican Folklore."

17. Reyna's personal collection.

18. Reyna, *Raza Humor: Chicano Joke Tradition in Texas*, pp. 95–99.

19. Ibid., p. 99.

20. Ibid., p. 97.

21. Ibid., p. 118.

22. Reyna's personal collection; cf. Paredes, *Uncle Remus con Chile*, p. 136.

23. Reyna, *Raza Humor: Chicano Joke Tradition in Texas*, p. 92.

24. Ibid., p. 91.

25. Reyna's personal collection.

26. Reyna, *Raza Humor: Chicano Joke Tradition in Texas*, p. 92.

27. Ibid., p. 90.

28. Paredes, *Uncle Remus con Chile*, p. 141.

29. Reyna's personal collection.

30. Reyna, "Contemporary Myths in Chicano Jokelore," p. 30.

31. Reyna's personal collection.

32. Reyna, *Raza Humor: Chicano Joke Tradition in Texas*, p. 41.

33. Reyna's personal collection; cf. Paredes, *Uncle Remus con Chile*, p. 51.

34. Reyna's personal collection.

35. Reyna's personal collection; cf. Paredes, *Uncle Remus con Chile*, pp. 173, 175.

36. Reyna's personal collection.

37. Alicia María González, "'Guess How Doughnuts Are Made': Verbal and Nonverbal Aspects of the 'Panadero' and His Stereotype," in Richard Bauman and Roger D. Abrahams, eds., " . . . *And Other Neighborly Names: Social Process and Cultural Image in Texas Folklore* (Austin: University of Texas Press, 1981), p. 121.

38. Reyna's personal collection.

39. Reyna, *Raza Humor: Chicano Joke Tradition in Texas*, p. 43.

40. Paredes, "The Anglo American In Mexican folklore," pp. 113–128.

41. Reyna, *Raza Humor: Chicano Joke Tradition in Texas*, pp. 25–27.

42. José Reyna, "Pancho Villa: The Lighter Side," *New Mexico Humanities Review* 7, 1, p. 61.

43. Reyna, *Raza Humor: Chicano Joke Tradition in Texas*, pp. 29–30.

44. Ibid., p. 47.

45. Ibid., pp. 44–45.

46. My sincere thanks to Mr. Mario Meza who collected five jokes analyzed here for a class project. This study was later published in *Southwest Folklore Journal* 4 (1980), pp. 14–22. The topic of Mexican immigration to the United States has been widely researched. For an older study see Ernesto Galarza, *Merchants of Labor: the Mexican Bracero Story* (Charlotte / Santa Barbara; McNally and Loftin, 1964) for an excellent analysis of Mexican migration to the United States. For an extended bibliography on Mexican migration and the *corrido*, see María Herrera-Sobek, *Northward Bound: The Mexican Immigrant Experience in Ballad and Song* (Bloomington: Indiana University Press, 1993).

47. Joke collected by Mario Meza. This joke is similar to "The Fool," a reversal of AT-Type 1322, Words in a Foreign Language Thought to Be Insults; Aarne, Antti, and Stith Thompson, *The Types of the Folktale*, 2d rev. FFC, no. 184 (Helsinki, 1961). See Richard M. Dorson's *Buying the Wind* (Chicago and London: The University of Chicago Press, 1964), pp. 450–451.

48. Joke collected by Mario Meza.

49. Joke collected by Mario Meza. See also Dorson, p. 450.

50. Reyna's personal collection.

51. Joke collected by Mario Meza. See also Dorson, p. 451.

52. Joke popular during the 1950s and heard repeatedly during my childhood. See variant collected by José Reyna and Dorson, p. 451.

53. María Herrera-Sobek, *The Bracero Experience: Elitelore versus Folklore* (Los Angeles: Latin American Studies Publication Series, 1979).

54. See also John H. Burma, "Humor as a Technique in Race Conflict," *American Sociological Review* II (1946), p. 710.

55. Burma, p. 711.

56. Paredes, "The Anglo-American in Mexican Folklore," p. 115. Three other interesting studies done on the image of the Anglo North American in another genre of folklore, the corrido, are the following: Merle E. Simmons's chapter "Mexican Relations with the United States" in his book *The Mexican Corrido as a Source for an Interpretative Study of Modern Mexico (1870–1950)* (Bloomington: Indiana University Press, Indiana University Publication Series, 1957); Simmons's article, "Attitudes Toward the United States Revealed in Mexican Corridos," *Hispania* 36:1 (1953), pp. 34–42; and an article by Julio Rodríguez-Puértolas, "La problemática socio-política chicana en corridos y canciones," *Aztlán* 6:1 (1975), pp. 97–116. Another source related to the above issue is John T. Reid's *Spanish American Images of the United States 1790–1960* (Gainesville: University of Florida, 1977).

57. Paredes, "The Anglo-American in Mexican Folklore," p. 126.

58. Dan Ben Amos, "Toward a Definition of Folklore in Context," in *Toward New Perspectives in Folklore*, ed. Américo Paredes and Richard Bauman (Austin and London: University of Texas Press, 1972), p. 9. See also Jan Harold Brunvand's article, "The Study of Contemporary Folklore: Jokes," *Fabula* 13 (1972), pp. 1–19.

59. Ibid., p. 10.

60. Roger D. Abrahams, "Personal Power and Social Restraint in the Definition of Folklore," in *Toward New Perspectives in Folklore*, p. 19.

6

THE CORRIDO AS HYPERTEXT

Undocumented Mexican Immigrant Films and the Mexican/Chicano Ballad

o o o o
o o o o

María Herrera-Sobek

It may appear strange to associate an ultramodern technological word such as "hypertext," a word linked to the cyberspace world of the information high-way, with a traditional literary genre such as the *corrido* (Mexican ballad). The corrido traces its roots in the Americas to the early sixteenth century with the coming of the Spanish *romance*, or ballad.[2] Nevertheless, its persistence in Mexican/ Chicano culture should not surprise us since this folk genre possesses such a flexible poetic structure that it has managed to survive throughout the twentieth century in spite of the dire predictions about its impending demise by some corrido scholars.[3] Indeed, the corrido has made its recent debut on the internet via elec-tronic mail (e-mail) — on April 12, 1995, I received, through one of my listserves, a corrido freshly penned mourning the death of Selena, the popular Texas-Mexican singer who had recently been murdered.

With respect to the relationship between corridos and films, this ballad genre has made itself a staple of Mexican movies since the 1920s and has, in fact, been the source and inspiration for developing narrative films from original corrido plots or corrido heroes. Examples abound, including the famous "Juan Charras-queado" and "Rosita Alvírez" corridos. Both ballads have been made into feature-length films. Some corridos have spawned serial movies such as "El corrido de

Camelia La Texana," which gave birth to a movie bearing the title *Contrabando y traición* [La Camelia o Camelia La Texana] (Contraband and Treachery [La Camelia or Camelia La Texana], 1976) plus such sequels as *Mataron a Camelia La Texana* (They Have Killed Camelia the Texan, 1976); *La hija de Camelia* (Camelia's Daughter, 1977); *Emilio Varela vs. Camelia La Texana* (1979); *Ya encontraron a Camelia* (They Have Found Camelia); *El hijo de Camelia La Texana* (Camelia the Texan's Son, 1989); and *La muerte de Camelia* (The Death of Camelia). Several corridos related to these films and bearing similar titles accompanied them.

Before expounding on the function of the corrido as hypertext, I want to define the computer-linked term. In computer science manuals the word "hypertext" is defined as

> a metaphor for presenting information in which text, images, sounds, and actions become linked together in a complex, nonsequential web of associations that permit the user to browse through related topics, regardless of the presented order of the topics. These links are often established both by the author of a hypertext document and by the user, depending on the intent of the hypertext document. For example, traveling among the links to the word *iron* in an article might lead the user to the periodic table of the elements, to a map of the migration of metallurgy in Iron Age Europe. The term *hypertext* was coined in 1965 by Ted Nelson to describe documents, as presented by a *computer*, that express the nonlinear structure of ideas, as opposed to the linear format of books, film, and speech.[4]

More simply put, a hypertext is a text containing embedded sources of information. The hypertext allows the computer user to highlight a word and be referred to additional information on the subject.

In this chapter, I am using the word "hypertext" as a metaphor for how the corrido or other popular songs are inserted into film narratives and serve to introduce and provide the themes for various film segments. My study will specifically analyze a special genre of film — those films focusing on the undocumented Mexican immigrant experience — and examine the important functions corridos and popular songs have in the development of plots and story lines.

I posit in this study that corridos and popular songs function as hypertexts within narrative films since they provide the story line with additional information, thus expanding the parameters of the scene and the message it is conveying. In this manner, corridos and popular songs aid the plot action in moving forward and backward, and simultaneously expand a particular scene by musically and verbally adding to the visual effects and the dramatic import.

In addition, corridos, folk songs, and other popular songs inserted in the film's plot structure represent ideological configurations directly connected either to nationalist projects or to the structuring of social protest articulations. The interpolations of songs in films, therefore, are not fortuitous or mere sources of musical entertainment but serve specific ideological purposes in the production of the films.

Although I have collected approximately thirty films for this study, I have selected five representative ones about undocumented Mexican immigrants for my analysis. These include *Espaldas mojadas* (Wetbacks, 1954), *Maldita miseria* (Damned Misery, 1981), *Pasaporte a la muerte* (Passport to Death, 1988), *El jardín del Edén* (The Garden of Eden, 1994), and *Arizona* (1985).[5] I collected the videos by doing fieldwork: i.e., canvassing video stores in the Santa Ana, California, area and in Puerto Vallarta. In addition, David Maciel made available to me two important films: *Espaldas mojadas* and *El jardín del Edén*.

The five films selected represent distinct categories of corrido intertextuality and specific points in the history of the undocumented Mexican immigrant film genre. Their dependency on corridos and songs for plot development and ideological constructs make them particularly interesting for my project. My analysis is based on the video versions of the films and not on the original celluloid texts themselves. This is due to the relatively easy availability of the videos and the feasibility of repeatedly playing them in my home for this study. I am aware, nevertheless, that there is a significant difference between the original film and the video version of it.

Authors David Bordwell and Kristin Thompson, in their lucid textbook on film analysis, *Film Art: An Introduction* (1993), point out the importance of sound in films: "in the process of film production the sound track is built up separately from the images, and it can be manipulated independently. This makes sound as flexible and wide-ranging as other film techniques."[6] They further elucidate:

> Yet sound is perhaps the hardest of all techniques to study. We are accustomed to living in a largely invisible sound environment. Our primary information about the layout of our surroundings comes from sight, and so in ordinary life sound is often simply a background for visual attention. Similarly, we speak of "watching" a film and of being movie "viewers" or "spectators"—all terms which suggest that the

sound track is a secondary factor. We are strongly inclined to think of sound as simply an accompaniment to the real basis of cinema, the moving images.

Three types of sound are typical in films: speech, music, and noise. With respect to music Bordwell and Thompson note:

> The rhythm, melody, harmony, and instrumentation of the music can strongly affect the viewer's emotional reactions. In addition a melody or musical phrase can be associated with a particular character, set-ting, situation, or idea. By manipulating such motifs, the filmmaker can subtly compare scenes, trace out patterns of development, and suggest implicit meanings. It is obvious that sound, and particularly music, affords the filmmaker an infinite array of creative possibilities.

Structural analysis of the thirty films in video form collected for this project yielded five distinct categories of how corridos function within the structure of the film.

1. Corridos used to frame the film. Here the corrido introduces the film and sets the theme that the film will be developing.
2. The corrido used as a coda. Ballads used in this manner provide closure to the film.
3. Corridos interspersed throughout the film. These songs, inter-textual corridos, are used to underscore or develop a particular theme in the film.
4. Corridos used as foreshadowing agents. These corridos prime the audience for events to come.
5. Informational corridos. These corridos are used to provide addi-tional information on the film's plot. This information may be political, economic, psychological, etc.

Framing-the-Film Corridos

On July 3, 1987, the *Los Angeles Times* reported the death of eighteen undoc-umented workers who were trapped in a railroad boxcar and died of heat and asphyxiation in the town of Sierra Blanca, Texas.[7] The event was duly recorded in a corrido titled "El vagón de la muerte" (The Boxcar of Death), and a film was made using the same title.[8] Two other movies with similar themes surfaced: *Pasa-*

porte a la muerte (Passport to Death; film 1988, video 1989) and *El carro de la muerte* (Death Car).[9] Although *El vagón de la muerte* incorporates three songs within its plot—including the corrido "El vagón de la muerte," which gives closure to the film—I will focus my analysis on *Pasaporte a la muerte* since it has a corrido at the inception of the action and closes with the "Canción mixteca"—a popular Mexican immigrant song about nostalgia for the homeland.

The back of the video box of *Pasaporte a la muerte* summarizes the film's plot: "El drama real de dieciocho ilusos que soñaron triunfar en los Estados Unidos y lo único que encontraron fue un pasaporte a la muerte" (The real life drama of eighteen "dreamers" [i.e., workers] who dreamt of success in the United States and all they found was a passport to death). The film opens with a scene depicting a husband and wife arguing about the husband's proposed trip to the United States in search of the man who has raped his wife. The wife is begging her husband not to leave, to forget the unfortunate incident, but he is full of rage and intent on seeking revenge. As the husband walks out of their bedroom, where the scene has been taking place, and slowly walks down the stairs, the corrido "Pasaporte a la muerte" is sung:

Con la ilusión de llegar	With the illusion
a estar en el otro lado	Of going to the other side [USA]
se platicaba la gente	The people told each other
que aquí vivía sin trabajo	Those who were without work
ya conocemos a un hombre	We know a man
que puede darnos la mano.	Who can give us a hand.
Es el famoso pollero	It is the famous smuggler
que le apodaban "Ojitos"	Nicknamed "Little Eyes"
y su patrón don Octavio	And his boss Mr. Octavio
un hombre cruel y asesino	A cruel murderer
el amo del contrabando	The king of smuggling
y aterrado de los vicios.	And supplier of drugs.
Dicen que tiene mi pueblo	They say my people
la culpa de tantas cosas	Are to blame for many things
por engañar a los pobres,	Because they deceive the poor
con mil mentiras piadosas	With a thousand white lies
que les ayuda en el campo	That they will get help for their land
y allí no llega su ayuda.	And they never get help.

231

Aquí se acaba el corrido	Here the corrido ends
del tren que tanto soñaban	The ballad of that train you dreamt so much about
ya no escucharán silbidos	You will no longer hear its whistle blow
pues muy atrás se quedaron	You have been left behind
la muerte sin pasaporte	Death without a passport
sólo los cuerpos quedaron.	Only the bodies remained.

The corrido cues the spectator in on the action to come and foreshadows the death of those who will journey in the doomed boxcar. The film narrates the story of a greedy smuggler and his partner in crime who smuggle undocumented workers to the United States. Unbeknownst to the head smuggler, Don Octavio, his son is among the group that is to journey in the killer boxcar. The unfortunate group will be transported through the Texas desert inside an airtight refrigeration railroad boxcar locked from the outside. Eventually a railroad worker discovers the locked boxcar and opens it. All the people inside the car except one (the enraged husband seeking revenge) are found dead from heat exhaustion and lack of air. The film ends when the bodies are discovered and taken out for burial.

The above corrido summarizes what is later going to transpire. It sets the stage, so to speak, by recounting the dreams and aspirations of a people who are doomed to find only death. The first stanza in the corrido succinctly captures the reasons for people risking their lives to journey to the United States in search of a better life. Basically the ballad puts forth the "push/pull" theory of immigration, i.e., unemployment in Mexico and the belief there is work in the United States.

The ballad "Pasaporte a la muerte" is permeated with an atmosphere of tragedy. Almost from the inception of the song, with the third word *ilusión* (illusion), the audience is psychologically tuned in to a tragic denouement. The word connotes a hope and an optimism that oftentimes are not realized. Given the literary, folk song, and film traditions of depicting the Mexican immigrant experience to the United States as tragic, the film viewer has a historical and mass media context from which to draw the conclusion that the film will not have a happy ending. The ballad aids in structuring a sense of foreboding.

The corrido further frames the movie by summarizing the plot. The protagonists are the group of people seeking to cross the border into the United States without proper documentation. The "bad guys" are the coyotes, or smugglers, who are depicted as evil and greedy in the second stanza. The coyotes are "cruel assassins" who love to engage in contraband, be it humans or drugs.

The third stanza engages in spreading blame to the general population. Mexico's upper and middle classes are to blame for deceiving the poor working class.

The fourth stanza provides closure to the song and more explicitly informs the viewer the film will have a tragic ending. Those seeking the train of salvation are only given a ride to their doom.

The film is thus placed within the context of the structure of many heroic-type corridos where the death of the hero is announced at the beginning of the song. Suspense is then created in the narrative about how the doomed hero comes to meet his death. The film's narrative thus begins where the corrido ends, and the ballad provides a preview of events to come; it serves almost as a teaser because golden nuggets of information are dropped. These nuggets will create great suspense and empathy for the characters in the story. The audience immediately connects with the various protagonists since they know beforehand the fate of these people. To a certain extent, the viewer becomes a god, albeit a helpless one, in knowing the future of the people. The viewer feels powerful in knowing but powerless in not being able to do anything about it. The tension between these two states oscillates between feelings of enjoyment (power) and sadness (powerlessness).

Identification with the characters is produced during the psychological feelings of powerlessness since we, the viewers, are like them, not knowing the tragedies that await us in the future. We happily go about our business making plans, without realizing that death is just around the corner.

The corrido is an important element in configuring both the film's narrative plot and the psychological feelings elicited by the celluloid images. The corrido's plaintive wail frames the film, which is appropriately titled *Passport to Death*.

The Corrido as Coda

The film *Arizona* (1985) is based on a true incident that happened in the Arizona desert. A small group of people from El Salvador—some political exiles, others seeking to find employment in California, while others were simply wishing to join family members in Los Angeles—were lost in the hot Arizona desert. The movie narrates their tragic story. The story line begins at the Guatemalan-Mexican border, where a small group of people are dodging bullets from unseen soldiers and a smuggler greets them on the Mexican side among bushes and reeds. One of the members of the group informs the smuggler that three of the original group of exiles are dead and only twelve have survived the Guatemalan border crossing.

233

The journey of these would-be immigrants across the Mexican nation is re-counted at a fast pace and the story picks up again at a border town called Las Juntas. Here three coyotes are to guide them across the Organ Pipe section of desert. However, their U.S. contact does not show up. The guides assure the group that they are fairly close to the freeway (Interstate 10) where a second group of smugglers is supposedly waiting to pick them up and transport them to Los Angeles.

Unfortunately, the guides lose their bearings and get lost. The group desperately keeps walking across rough mountain terrain. The lack of food and water, plus the unforgiving burning sun, soon begin to take their terrible toll. The guides keep insisting they are not far from Interstate 10 but as time passes people begin to die from the blazing heat and their unquenchable thirst—a diabetic, a baby, two little girls, a man—until eventually only three survivors are left: two men and a woman who are rescued by the Border Patrol and taken away in the patrol car.

There are two songs sung in the movie: "Qué lejos ando" and "Arizona." The song "Qué lejos ando" underscores the feelings of displacement and deterritorialization felt by the men and women in the film. The song is played while they await the arrival of the guides who are to take them across the border and they are lodged in a large house run by the coyotes. As the group settles in for a night's rest, a guitar strums the tune and a voice begins to sing:

Qué lejos ando	How far I am wandering
y yo sin poder volver.	Without being able to return
Qué lejos ando	How far I am wandering
de mi pueblo,	From my town
ay tan querido.	Oh so beloved.
Cuanta nostalgia	Oh what nostalgia
me recorre el pensamiento.	Runs through my mind
El no poder regresar	Not being able to return
es lo que siento.	Is what I feel most.

The song underscores the psychological feelings of the exiles. As the movie progresses, we hear their tales of woe: the oppression in their country and the death squads killing their beloved family members. Each person has a tragic tale to tell. Thus through their stories, the viewer understands the rationale for undertaking such a dangerous journey.

No other song is played until the film ends. The song "Arizona" serves as a coda and provides closure to the narrative.

The song begins with a scene from the film in which several men are lined against a wall and unidentified government soldiers begin to take aim with rifles to execute them. Both the government soldiers and the men being shot are anonymous because they represent any and all repressive governments in Latin America. A plaintive wail intones, "Arizona desierto de lago." Then a strong voice interrupts:

"Allí donde se han roto las garantías individuales." (There where all guarantees [of freedom] to the individual have been broken.)

A second voice screams, "¡Muera la represión!" (Death to repression!)

"La posibilidad de huir es al menos una forma de retrasar la muerte." (The possibility of escaping is at least a form of delaying death.)

The song "Arizona" is then sung in earnest.

Arizona desierto de lago	Arizona, desert lake
testigo obligado	Forced witness
de tanta traición	Of so many treacheries
Cuantas vidas	How many lives
en ti se han quedado	Have been left here
que se han sepultado	Have been buried here
debajo del sol.	Underneath the sun.
Arizona desierto de arena	Arizona, sand desert
la gloria o la pena	Glory or pain
lo mismo te da.	Is the same to you.

The song, while not a classic corrido, shares the narrative style of the genre. It personalizes a state, Arizona, as the song's addressee. The narrator directly speaks to Arizona and her desert, and the killer desert is transformed into the enemy of the people. It becomes the main protagonist and is blamed for the sufferings of humanity. The desert is viewed as analogous to killer Latin American governments who are implacable and always get their "man." The song provides closure to the film by mourning the deaths of those whose lives have been taken by the burning sands under Arizona's hot summer sun.

Intertextual Corridos

The film *Espaldas mojadas* (1954), directed by Alejandro Galindo, is permeated with a strong nationalist ideology in which the folk songs interpolated within

Figure 6.1. Mexican undocumented workers waiting to cross the Río Grande in a scene from *Espaldas mojadas*. Courtesy Filmoteca Nacional/ UNAM.

the plot function as ideological supports for the construction of the film's message (see fig. 6.1). The message is explicitly stated in the beginning of the film after the opening credits are given.

> Nuestro propósito es advertir a nuestros con nacionales de la inconveniencia de tratar de abandonar el país en forma ilegal, con el riesgo de sufrir situaciones molestas y dolorosas que podrían hasta crear dificultades en las buenas relaciones que venturosamente existen entre ambos pueblos.

> Our purpose is to warn our countrymen of the hardships encountered when abandoning our country illegally. There is a risk in encountering unpleasant and painful experiences that could conceivably result in creating difficulties between the two countries, which up to now have had a good working relationship.

The film then proceeds to depict the misadventures of an *espalda mojada* (wetback or undocumented worker) who is recruited to work in the United States and crosses to the "other side" without legal documents at the Juárez/El Paso border. The musical compositions interpolated within the movie are all undergirded by nationalistic themes, love of country, homesickness, and desire to return to the motherland. The songs include such Mexican immigrant favorites as "Nací de este lado" (I Was Born on This Side), "Canción mixteca," "El desterrado" (The Exiled One), "Dos arbolitos" (Two Trees), and "La pajarera" (The Bird Woman). These are all folk songs with strong emotional content, because the lyrics of most of them depict an idealized view of Mexico and its people. The film is constructed with a firm didactic message, and the songs interspersed at key places throughout the narrative reinforce the message — return to Mexico — to the protagonist who is in the United States, and by extension, to all Mexicans residing in the United States. Indeed, the protagonist at the close of the narrative does return to Mexico and brings back with him a *pocha* (Mexican-American woman) and an expatriate. Throughout the movie, nationalistic sentiments are expressed and the evils of emigrating to the United States are underscored. The songs can be viewed as underpinning a nationalistic theme running throughout the film. We can analyze these songs within the parameters of contemporary post-colonial theories such as those posited by Homi Bhabha and Benedict Anderson. In particular their ideas are pertinent to the analysis of Mexico's literary production and the role this plays in "imagining a nation." Bhabha states:

> Nations, like narratives, lose their origins in the myths of time and only fully realize their horizons in the mind's eye. Such an image of the nation — or narration — might seem impossibly romantic and excessively metaphorical, but it is from those traditions of political thought and literary language that the nation emerges as a powerful historical idea in the west. An idea whose cultural compulsion lies in the impossible unity of the nation as a symbolic force.[10]

Timothy Brennan likewise posits that "Nations, then, are imaginary constructs that depend for their existence on an apparatus of cultural fictions in which imaginative literature plays a decisive role."[11]

The concept of nation in the Mexican corrido is an old one and begins to appear as early as the 1810s when the inhabitants from what was then New Spain declared their independence from the mother country, Spain, and initiated the Wars of Independence. These wars lasted eleven years, and it is from these years that a few corridos have survived with the theme of nation as defined by contemporary political theory. In *Espaldas mojadas* I center my analysis on the corridos in it and assert they function as discursive acts that, in Benedict Anderson's terms, aid the Mexican people in the "imagining" of Mexico as a nation, as a site for nationality, and as a strategic element in the construction of a nationalistic spirit being forged against foreign aggressors.

Webster's Collegiate Dictionary defines "nation" as deriving from *natio*, "race, originally a being born, or to be born." It further defines it as "a people connected by supposed ties of blood generally manifested by community of language, religion, customs," and adds that "nation" implies "any aggregation of people having like institutions and customs, a sense of social homogeneity and mutual interests," and a "body of inhabitants of a country united under a single independent government; a state." Theoretical political scientists, on the other hand, have a more restrictive definition of the term. In a now famous lecture delivered at the Sorbonne on March 11, 1882, titled "What Is a Nation?" the French historian Ernest Renan questions the specificity of the term, stating at the inception of his talk that "What I propose to do today is to analyze with you an idea which, though seemingly clear, lends itself to the most dangerous misunderstandings." [12] He then proceeds to enumerate what he calls "vast conglomerates" of men found in "China, Egypt or ancient Babylonia, Hebrews and Arabs, [city states such as] Athens or Sparta . . . the various territories in the Carolingian Empire . . . nations such as France, England . . . confederations such as Switzerland or America," and after enumerating all these "nations" surmises that race is not a significant factor for any of them as they all have numerous races within their territories. And, in fact, in many countries, it is what Renan calls "the fusion of their component populations," which is in the final analysis their "defining feature." He therefore views those that would seek race as the defining characteristic of nation to be in "very great error, which if it were to become dominant, would destroy European civilization." The French thinker proved prophetic if we recall Germany's attempt at race purification during Hitler's regime. Renan proceeds to dismiss other prevailing concepts such as "dynasty" and "language" associated by many with the notion of nation. With respect to the latter, he underscores the pernicious danger to the intellect if one is a language chauvinist. In splendidly eloquent terms he admonishes, "Let us not abandon the fundamental principle that man is a reasonable and moral being, before he is cooped up in such and such a language, before he is a member of such and such a race, before he belongs to such and such a culture. Before French, German, or

Italian culture there is human culture." Religion is likewise disdained by Renan as a defining characteristic. Finally he rejects natural geographic boundaries as an integral ingredient in the construction of a nation. Neither rivers nor mountains in the final analysis are the primary limiting factors in a nation's borders.

Renan defines nation in more reified terms. He asserts:

> A nation is a soul, a spiritual principal. One lies in the past, one in the present. One is the possession in common of a rich legacy of memories; the other is present-day consent, the desire to live together, the will to perpetuate the value of the heritage that one has received in an undivided form. . . . The nation . . . is a culmination of a long past of endeavors, sacrifices, and devotion.

Cultural studies critics point to the importance of literature as a primary ingredient in the construction of nations—an indisputable force in "imagining" communities. Yet the studies underscore either a Eurocentric view or lack of folkloristic knowledge in pinpointing the importance of what literary texts were the most instrumental in imagining the nation state. While in Europe the novel may have been the form par excellence evidencing a new thought formation in the construction of nation, for Third World countries, the novel was not only an expensive commodity but implied having the leisure time to read it. For peasants in Latin America and Mexico, this was unattainable. Thus, while agreeing with Brennan that in Europe "literature participated in the formation of nations through the creation of 'national print media'—the newspaper and the novel—in Latin America conditions for the widespread dissemination and reading of novels were quite different and inappropriate. Flourishing alongside what Francesco de Sanctis has called 'the cult of nationality in the European nineteenth century,' it was especially the novel as a composite but clearly bordered work of art that was crucial in defining the nation as an 'imagined community'" and that in Europe "nationalism coincides especially with one form of literature—the novel."

The novel in Europe was indeed an appropriate instrument that helped impose a single language on a heterogeneous population (i.e., English, French, Spanish) and to have them accept subconsciously the concept of "nation." Brennan thoughtfully integrates Mikhael Bakhtin's and Eric Hobsbawm's ideas of epic narrative and their theories regarding how epic was displaced by the novel as a tool in the formidable task of nation formation.[13]

Likewise, Benedict Anderson is correct in underscoring the importance of

239

print-capitalism in the dissemination of ideology and the creation of a mind state that was receptive to the notion of nation.[14] Equally important for European nation-building was the novel's role in coalescing the upper and the lower classes within its narrative structure by commingling subjects in novels of realism. The novel's bringing together disparate groups was in fact very attuned to the ideological goal of nation building.

Bakhtin correctly pinpointed the prototype of the novel in the folk tales and folk songs of the people. His statement "The novel's roots must ultimately be sought in folklore" evidenced great insight and knowledge.[15]

Nevertheless, if for Europe the novel served as a primary energizing and stabilizing force in the construction of nations, for Mexico it was the Mexican ballad, or corrido, that enveloped a newly born nation at the dawn of the nineteenth century in a discourse that sought to unify a heterogeneous population. While few corridos have been collected from this period, the few that are known mark the beginning of the corrido's history as an instrument used in the constructing of a national consciousness. The corrido, as an aid in nationalistic propaganda, will reach stratospheric heights during the Mexican revolution, the socialist-leaning years of the 1930s and the beginning of the 1940s modern Mexican era. After the early 1940s, the corrido's nationalistic bent in Mexico will decline, although it will not disappear altogether.

Although political theorists negate the categories of race, language, geography, and religion as being of primary importance in defining a nation, the corrido does indeed underscore these areas and seeks to unify a nation by invoking these concepts. The film *Espaldas mojadas* closely demonstrates how corridos and other types of folk songs can be used to structure a nationalistic message.

Foreshadowing Corridos

The most artistically conceived film of those considered here, and one that incorporates both traditional folk songs as well as more contemporary ones is *El jardín del Edén*, which appeared in 1994 (see fig. 6.2). This film is an excellent example of corridos and songs functioning as foreshadowing agents. The songs frequently serve as cues to the scenes that follow. Thus the songs expand our knowledge about the characters in the story or the events encompassed within the plot's structure. There are a total of fifteen songs; each is related and tied to a specific scene. The beginning chords of the songs generally cue in the scene that is

Figure 6.2. Scenes from María Novarro's film *El jardín del Edén*. Courtesy IMCINE, Instituto Mexicano de Cinematografía.

taking place or cue in the scene that immediately follows. Thus the song "Baby, baby, corazón regresa" with the lyrics is played as background music to the reunion of two close friends—the Chicana Liz and the Anglo Jane—as Liz utters, "It took you long enough to come!"

> Yo no puedo comprender
> porque tardas en volver
> baby, baby
> corazón regresa.
>
> [Sung in English]
> So you promised to come home
> . . . [music fades]
>
> I do not understand
> Why you delay in returning
> Baby, baby
> My heart, come back.

The film's narrative traces various events experienced by the two young protagonists, Liz and Jane; both are trying desperately to find themselves in Tijuana, Mexico (of all places!). The two young women will be introduced to a series of individuals as they try to make sense of their lives, including Felipe Reyes, a young man who is attempting to emigrate to the United States but lacks the proper documents.

Liz is a non-Spanish-speaking Chicana in search of her Mexican roots. When she acknowledges her inability to be fluent in Spanish and speaks in a mixture of Spanish and English the song "Hey Baby que pasó" is played. The song, rendered in a mixture of Spanish and English, reiterates the Spanglish theme introduced by Liz. The song's lyrics include:

Hey baby que pasó (what happened?)
Are you with another vato (dude)
Hey baby que pasó
Won't you give mi un beso (a kiss)
come on baby yo te pido (I beg of you).

While the song is playing, highly decorated low rider automobiles parade, emphasizing other aspects of Chicano culture. Each song played serves as a prelude to the introduction of the characters in the plot. Such songs as "Juanita," "Margarita," and "Mujer paseada" (A Woman Who Has Been Around) serve as introductory notes to the women who bear the name of the title of the song or in some way depict the characteristics of the women.

The use of music falls within the cinematic stylistic technique of parallelism. The film's story line follows a series of parallels that reinforce the juxtaposition of the two worlds presented: the United States and Mexico. We can discern the parallel structures through the pairing of persons and events such as the juxtaposition of the would-be migrants on one side of the corrugated steel fence and the *migra* on the other. The migra and undocumented migrants will continually be paired throughout the film's plot. Other parallel figures include the whales as migratory animals juxtaposed to the human migrants. Again the whale motif, like the migra motif, runs throughout the film. The characters and their actions also form a series of pairs such as Felipe and Frank, Liz and Jane, and Father dying in the hospital and Felipe lying in bed badly hurt. Other pairs include Frida Kahlo and Liz, and the Virgin of Guadalupe and the little girl, Lupita. The songs are an integral part of these parallel structures.

El jardín del Edén is one of the most artistic films belonging to the undocumented Mexican immigrant film genre. Nevertheless, the genre has not achieved its full potential.

Information-Type Corridos

Information-type corridos are used to provide additional information, be it political, economic, or psychological in the film's plot. An example of a film using this type of corrido is *Maldita miseria* (1988 video). The film was directed by Julio Aldama, produced by Orlando R. Mendoza, and featured in starring roles Rafael Inclán, Gerardo Reyes, Lupita Castro, Mercedes Castro, Juan Valentín, and Jorge Rivero. This film depicts the travails of a Mexican peasant family. Suffering under the weight of extreme poverty the main protagonist, José Manuel Ramos, decides to risk his luck and seek his fortune in the United States. He departs with a friend, Lorenzo (Lencho) Rojas, who previously had worked in the United States and is knowledgeable about the coyote system and how to cross the border without documentation.

This movie is typical of many undocumented worker-type genre films with respect to the songs played. *Maldita miseria* contains ten songs that are showcased and are an integral part of the plot. These songs include "Ojos provincianos," "Rumbo al sur," "Novillo despuntado," "Por tu culpa," "Segundo lugar," "Inmortal," "Me caí de la nube," "Vuelve gaviota," "Bésame, quiéreme," and "Pero ¿qué te parece?" The tune of "Maldita miseria" serves as an introductory musical composition. The lyrics are not sung but the musical score is played as background music. The opening scene presents an agricultural field with a one-room mud hut (*jacal*) where a family of four lives. The camera focuses on a man working the fields with a plow driven by a pair of oxen. The song, played in mournful dirgelike tones accompanied by a harmonica and a guitar, emotionally colors the scene with pathos. The spectator is visually and aurally struck by the dire circumstances of this impoverished family.

The director, in planning the introductory musical score, knew that the song's lyrics narrated the events transpiring in the movie. He therefore prudently withheld the lyrics so as not to give the plot away and have the audience lose interest. Instead, the music foreshadows future events without explicitly surrendering the main ingredients of the plot and eliminating suspense.

The song's lyrics (which can be heard at the conclusion of the film) are as follows:

243

Maldita miseria	Damned Misery
(1)	(1)
Mi prieto del alma	My dark darling
te juiste pa'l norte	You left for Northern lands
dejaste la siembra	You left the crops
por una ilusión.	For a dream.
(2)	(2)
Vendiste los bueyes	You sold the oxen
para el pasaporte	For the passport
maldita miseria	Damn the poverty
la de 'sta región.	Of this region.
(3)	(3)
Con un burro viejo	With an old donkey
hicimos labranza	We plowed the land
hicimos la escarda	We weeded and planted
con un hazadón.	With a hoe.
(4)	(4)
Miramos al cielo	We looked at the sky
con una esperanza	With some hope
pero las nubes se fueron	But the clouds left
como maldición.	As if by a curse.
(5)	(5)
Mis hijos lloraban	My children cried
dejándome sorda	A deafening sound
me fui pa' la hacienda	I went to the hacienda
y quise robar.	And tried to steal.
(6)	(6)
Les traje nopales,	I brought them cactus
quelites y gordas	Weeds and tortillas
pero ya sin fuerzas	But lacking strength
me puse a llorar.	I started to weep.
[Hablado:]	[Spoken:]
¡Ay maldita miseria la	Oh damned be the poverty
de esta región!	found in this region!

(7)

Los güeros mandaron
la plata a montones
por unos papeles
que había que firmar.

(7)

The Anglos sent
Plenty of money
And sent some papers
That I had to sign.

(8)

Mi prieto había muerto
piscando limones
no quise la plata
y me puse a llorar.

(8)

My dark love had died
Picking lemons
I didn't want the money
And started to cry.

Several thematic issues displayed in the song are faithfully represented in the movie. The first stanza correctly states the male leaves his home to journey north (i.e., to the United States), but incorrectly insinuates it was for a mere illusion. In truth, it was hunger, the failure of the crops to yield adequate sustenance, that drove José Manuel to seek a change of fortune. Conditions in the region were not conducive to staying home. According to the movie, it was either leave or die of hunger together with his wife and children.

The second stanza again correctly portrays the events that transpired in the film's plot but has a part that deviates from it. The song faithfully renders the selling of the oxen in order to acquire money for traveling to the United States but does not coincide with the movie's plot of crossing the border without proper documentation. The lyrics narrate how money from the sale of the oxen was used for purchasing a passport, while in the film the money was used to defray the coyotes' fee. Of course, José Manuel was unaware they were going to cross the border as *mojados* (wetbacks). He genuinely thought the money he had was for acquiring a passport.

The third stanza depicts an old burro working in the fields. The movie has the protagonist riding his tiny burro to town. The riding of the burro (instead of riding a horse or a bicycle or driving a car) further underscores the peasant status of the rider. During the colonial period, Indians were forbidden to ride horses; these animals were reserved for the sole use of the Spaniards. The horse was an important strategic element in the conquest of the Aztec empire and the Spaniards promoted the horse as one of their symbols of a superior status. In the present case, the burro serves to connote both the poverty and the status of the peasant. The song, nevertheless, focuses on the utility of the burro for agricultural purposes, although calling the animal an "old burro" also conveys the dire situation of the protagonists.

The fourth stanza again serves to describe the rationale for leaving Mexico: crop failure due to drought. Since Mexico still does not have fully irrigated agricultural systems throughout the country, some nonirrigated areas depend on rainfall. When rainfall does not come, the campesino suffers crop failure. This seems to be the situation described both in the movie and the song. Of further interest in this stanza is the concept of the biblical "curse." The stanza portrays the lack of rain as a punishment from God. Thus the biblical connotations of drought and curse are linked together. This interjects the concept of the sacred, of a mythic conceptualization of the weather. No such conceptualization is evident in the film.

The lyrics of the song are sung by a woman—José Manuel's wife, Mercedes, nicknamed "Mencha." The fifth stanza focuses on the effects poverty and Mencha's husband's departure have on her family. Both film and song depict the hunger the children and mother experience. They both narrate how the mother is forced to steal from the hacienda where she had worked and had been fired when she refused the sexual advances of the *hacendado* (landowner).

The sixth stanza continues describing the harsh reality of the woman and two children left behind to fend for themselves. They are forced to eat wild vegetation—cactus and weeds. A note of pathos is introduced with the description of how the narrator cries upon witnessing her children's hunger.

While stanzas one through six recount the story in fairly chronological order, stanzas seven and eight are reversed. Stanza seven narrates how money was sent back home while stanza eight explains why: the death of José Manuel.

Immigrant films fall into two basic subgenres: tragedy and comedy. *Maldita miseria* belongs in the tragedy subgenre since a series of unpleasant experiences are narrated throughout with the culmination of the main protagonist dying of a blow to the head after falling from the ladder he was using for picking lemons.

The musical score from the song "Maldita miseria" introduces the movie and is played as background music while the film's credits are projected on the screen. The song, complete with lyrics, brings closure to the movie and is played in its entirety while the final credits are flashed on the screen. Thus the song "Maldita miseria" frames the movie from its beginning to its end. The final playing of the song serves to reiterate the principal events in the film's plot. It reminds the audience of the terrible price immigrants pay for emigrating to the United States.

The film, however, makes excellent use of the other songs throughout. The songs are carefully chosen for their lyrics, which either foreshadow events, underscore a specific theme, or add information, thus expanding our knowledge of the characters, their motives, or personality traits. They are all integrated into the plot and function to release and lighten up the extremely depressing nature of the theme of Mexican immigration as viewed from a Mexican perspective.

The first song introduced (after the musical score of "Maldita miseria") is "Ojos provincianos" (Eyes from the Province). The song is very peppy and has a happy, uplifting tune. It underscores the love between husband and wife (Mercedes and José Manuel) and also the optimism felt upon making the decision to emigrate to the United States. It is assumed that all their problems will be over once José Manuel finds employment in the United States and earns plenty of dollars.

Ojos provincianos

¡Qué bonita está la tarde	How beautiful is the afternoon
no hace frío ni hace calor	It is not hot or cold.
bonito es ir a pasearme	How wonderful to take a stroll
con la dueña de mi amor!	With the love of my life!

The next song appearing in the film is sung while the transaction is being made between the would-be undocumented workers and the coyotes. The song is of the *canción ranchera* (country or rural song popular among farmworkers and working-class people) type. The words are not easy to hear and serve as background music; however, one part can be deciphered as:

Si tú no vuelves	If you do not return
me vuelvo a casa	I shall return home.
me vuelvo loco	I shall go crazy
si tú no estás.	If you are not here.
Yo soy tu esclavo	I am your slave
tú eres mi reina	You are my queen
vuelve conmigo	Come back to me
llorando estoy.	I am crying for you.

Although the song serves as background music, the lyrics are still pertinent to the narrative story. As can be seen, both stanzas decry the departure of a loved one and begs for their return. The song foreshadows the fact that José Manuel will not return and his *reina* (queen) will be left inconsolably weeping.

The next song is the first one heard while José Manuel and Lencho are working in the United States, "Bésame y quiéreme" (Kiss Me and Love Me). It is sung by one of the characters in the movie, Lupita Stalling, the daughter of the U.S. farmer. Lupita is a Chicana, and she and her father are portrayed in a very positive light. Indeed, it is Lupita who, upon meeting the newly arrived immigrants Lencho and José Manuel, begs her father to hire them at their ranch. Lupita is attractive and José Manuel immediately falls in love with her. Thus the song, although sung by Lupita, is really expressing the sentiments José Manuel has toward her.

Bésame, quiéreme
Mira cariñito tus labios me tienen prendida
cada que me besas me dejas más confundida
Tú me das de todo besos, caricias ardientes
pero lo que quiero ya siempre se queda pendiente.
pero lo que quiero ya siempre se queda pendiente.

Quiéreme, quiéreme, quiéreme como yo te quiero
bésame, bésame, bésame porque estoy sufriendo
desde ante todo necesito besos y caricias ardientes
pero lo que quiero ya siempre se queda pendiente
pero lo que quiero ya siempre se queda pendiente.

Kiss Me, Love Me
Look, darling, your lips have me on fire
Each time you kiss me you leave me more confused
You give me everything: kisses and hot caresses
But what I really want is always left hanging
But what I really want is always left hanging.

Love me, love me, love me as I love you
Kiss me, kiss me, kiss me because I am suffering for you
Above all else I need kisses and hot caresses
But what I really want is always left hanging
But what I really want is always left hanging.

The song introduces the audience to Lupita's interest in music. This interest will lead to a future linkage between José Manuel and Lupita, which will prove disastrous for the former since he will fall even more in love with the young, pretty woman.

After working hard all week, the men head for town for a relaxing evening. It is at a bar-restaurant that we hear a canción ranchera performed by the well-known and popular singer, Gerardo Reyes. This is an example of a featured singer performing a particular song. The song's lyrics, nevertheless, are completely woven into the general plot of the story, for they underscore the love for the girl left behind—whether in the South or in the North.

The song's title is "Rumbo al sur" (Southbound) and is similar in theme to another immigrant love song "Rumbo al norte" (Northbound). Both songs describe tender feelings for the sweetheart left at home. The men are sitting at a table in the bar-restaurant with prostitutes at their sides. Gerardo Reyes is announced as the performer who will be singing. With a mariachi band behind him, he descends from the top of a stairway in the restaurant down to where the customers are seated eating and drinking. All narrative action stops and the song "Rumbo al sur" is sung.

Rumbo al sur
(written by Francisco Vidal)
Me voy en ese tren
que va con rumbo al sur
y quiero que esta noche
tú me des mi despedida.

Southbound
I am leaving on that train
Heading for the South
And tonight I want you
To bid me good-bye.

The song is meant to evoke a longing for José Manuel's wife and by extension the wives and sweethearts of all who are working far away from home. As stated above, the setting where the song is performed is in a bar-restaurant and the hardworking laborers are taking a respite from the arduous farm work done during the week. They are happy, drinking, listening to music, and enjoying the company of working bar women. José Manuel is despondent and worried about his wife, whereupon Lencho offers him one of the bar girls. It is interesting to see the double standard Mexican men have. Here is a married man enjoying the company of prostitutes and no one appears to disapprove. In fact, they seem to approve of such behavior. José Manuel's wife is having the opposite experience. Although she is a faithful woman who rejects the advances of a wealthy man who could save her and her children from hunger, the gossip in the town leads the townswomen to believe she is having an affair with the hacienda owner and they begin to ostracize her and verbally abuse her.

The next scene transports us back to the farm where the men are resting after a day's work and José Manuel is singing "Segundo lugar."

Segundo lugar
No te olvides que no pude darte
el lugar que ya estaba ocupado
yo no se porque quieres dejarme
si yo ya toda mi vida te he dado.

Second Place
Don't forget I couldn't give you
The place already taken
I don't know why you want to leave me
When I've given you all my life.

Lupita overhears the singing and enthusiastically asks José Manuel to teach her to play the guitar. This, of course, will encourage José Manuel to fully develop his crush on Lupita, which will end in tragedy.

The lyrics of the song are again indicative of the double standard. Here the male, a married man, is asking his mistress to accept second place, his wife occupying first place. This seems to be in the *casa chica* (small house) tradition, where the husband has a wife and, in addition, a second household. Again the narrator of the song does not seem to have any guilt feelings about being unfaithful to his wife and, in fact, is pressuring the mistress to accept her situation. It is not clear whether José Manuel is actually telling Lupita via the song that although he is in love with her his wife comes first. Lupita is oblivious of José Manuel's love for her.

Music is also associated with the women left behind. In *Maldita miseria* the camera returns to Mexico, to the wife left behind, and captures her mournfully working while the song "Vuelve gaviota" (Return, Seagull) is sung in the background by a female singer.

Vuelve gaviota
(written by Hermanos Zaízar)
Tiende tu vuelo, triste gaviota
que así mis penas volando van
aunque en el vuelo dejes tus plumas
en las espumas, del ancho mar.

Return, Seagull
Begin your flight sad seagull
For my grief is flying thus
Though flying you lose your feathers
In the foam of the wide sea.

The singing stops here, although the song contains one more stanza pertinent to the woman's condition in Mexico.

The song conveys the psychological state of mind Mercedes is laboring under.
She longs for José Manuel's return. It is ironic that the faithful wife at home yearns
for her husband's presence and fends off unwanted and unwelcome suitors (the evil
hacendado), but meanwhile José Manuel is falling in love with the North American
farmer's daughter, Lupita, and is keeping company with prostitutes. The double standard is very evident here and the movie does comment on it in an implicit manner,
i.e., through the lyrics of the next song, "Novillo despuntado" (Wild Young Bull).

While the farmworkers are picking tomatoes, two women—Las Jilguerillas,
a famous singing duet that has been well known in Mexico for several decades—
pose as farmworkers and begin to sing "Novillo despuntado":

Novillo Despuntado
¡Ando buscando un novillo
que del corral se salió
Pero ay!
tiene la cara morena
como la tiene mi amor.
Pero ay,
¡qué risa me da!

Wild Young Bull
I am looking for a young bull
Who got out of the corral
But oh, ho, ho
His face is dark brown
Like my love's face.
But oh, ho, ho,
How this makes me laugh!

251

The above song is interesting for various reasons: it criticizes in a picaresque, tongue-in-cheek manner José Manuel's infidelities and simultaneously show-

cases the famous female duet Las Jilguerillas. Furthermore, the singing takes place in the tomato fields while workers, including Las Jilguerillas, pick tomatoes.

The tragedy pivots around the jealousy José Manuel experiences toward Lupita's boyfriend. The moment that initiates a series of events leading to the ultimate tragedy begins with a song. Lupita's boyfriend is in an office meeting with friends that include a group of singers, Los Grillos. They begin singing "Me caí de la nube" (I Fell from a Cloud).

> Me caí de la nube
> Me caí de la nube que andaba
> como viento mil metros de altura
> por poquito yo pierdo la vida
> esa fue mi mejor aventura
> por mi suerte caí entre los brazos
> de una linda y hermosa criatura.
> Me tapó con su lindo vestido
> y corriendo a esconder me llevó
> me colmó todo el cuerpo de besos
> y abrazada conmigo lloro.

> I Fell from a Cloud
> I fell from the cloud I was flying in
> As the wind one thousand feet high
> I almost lost my life
> That was my best adventure
> By sheer luck I fell in the arms
> Of a beautiful, lovely girl.
> She covered me with her beautiful dress
> And quickly ran to hide me
> She covered my whole body with kisses
> And hugging me cried with me.

The group of men listening to the song, including Lupita's boyfriend, join in the singing at this point.

The song serves as an example of male bonding. The lyrics depict the alleged suffering of males at the hands of "ingrate" and "treacherous" females.[16] The lusty singing of the song by all the males in the room brings forth a warm camaraderie among them. In addition, the song foreshadows the actual fall José Manuel will experience picking fruit.

After the song is sung, Lupita's boyfriend requests that the Grillos perform a serenade for Lupita, who is celebrating her birthday. The Grillos agree whole-heartedly.

That night Los Grillos sing the love song "Inmortal" to Lupita.

Inmortal
A que linda se mira la vida
cuando estoy en tus brazos mi amor
como que algo me incita y me dice
que te quiera con loca pasión
hasta siento que el alma me brinca
y me lleno de mucho valor.

Immortal
Oh how beautiful life looks
When I am in your arms, my love!
Something inside incites me and tells me
To love you with great love
I feel my soul jump for joy
And I am filled with great valor.

The song of course is a declaration of love Lupita's boyfriend is making to her. However, since José Manuel had been asked by the foreman to come and sing for Lupita, he witnesses this display of love between the young woman and the man he perceives as his rival. He becomes extremely jealous and begins to behave in a pouting, unbecoming manner. Los Grillos begin to sing a second song fairly pertinent to the situation.

Pero ¿qué te parece?
Pero ¿qué te parece?
enamorarte de mi
después que tantas veces
indiferentemente
pasaste por mi.

But How Do You Feel Now?
How do you feel now?

> Being in love with me
> After so many times
> You so indifferently
> Passed by my side.

The song refers to José Manuel's impossible love for Lupita; it reminds him he has his true love already back home. Nevertheless, José Manuel persists in desiring Lupita's love.

Events begin to take an ominous turn during Lupita's birthday festivities. José Manuel at first had refused to participate in the merrymaking because, having fallen in love with Lupita, he had become extremely jealous of her fiancé. His friends convince him to attend the party, and while inebriated he sings a *canción de despecho*, or a jilted lover's offensive song. Lupita's friends are shocked by the rude behavior and insolent lyrics of José Manuel's song.

> Por tu culpa
> Que tristeza yo traigo por dentro
> que no calma ni el vino ni nada
> voy sufriendo y no encuentro el remedio
> *pa'* curar lo que traigo en el alma.

> Because of You
> What sadness I have inside of me
> A sadness nothing, not even wine quenches
> I'm suffering and I can't find a remedy
> To cure what I have in my soul.

José Manuel's downfall is imminent. We know his abominable behavior will not go unpunished. This is equivalent to a hero's hubris—a weak flaw that will lead to a tragic ending. Indeed, the next day, José Manuel wakes up with a horrendous hangover. The foreman kindly advises him to stay home and sleep off the hangover. José Manuel stubbornly refuses and joins the lemon picking crew. As he climbs a high ladder he experiences dizziness and falls, hitting his head on a stone. José Manuel dies on the spot. The camera next focuses on a funeral service at the cemetery—José Manuel's. Soon thereafter Lencho travels to his hometown to inform Mercedes of the tragic ending José Manuel had in the United States. He offers the money paid by the farm company where José Manuel worked, but Mercedes refuses to take it. The movie closes with a painful irony. Mercedes runs weeping toward the now verdant and fertile fields she has worked hard to revive, with the help of the nourishing rainfall that came after José Manuel had left for the United States. Implicit in this scene is a critique of José Manuel not being patient enough. The song "Maldita miseria" is sung as Mercedes, kneeling among the rows and rows of new green sprouts of corn, looks upward at the sky in supplication, wanting an answer. The credits at this point are projected on the screen, and obviously, no answer is given.

The plot, as cited earlier, dwells on the hardships an immigrant encounters on both sides of the border. Nevertheless, the film is liberally sprinkled with songs. At least a third of the movie (eight songs at three minutes per song equals twenty-four minutes) is spent performing songs. If the topic were not so tragic, this movie, and others like it, could very well be classified as a musical because of the various musical groups and musical compositions showcased in or made an important aspect of the film. In this type of movie, groups or famous singers are frequently showcased and the audience is presented with musical performances.

As pointed out in the analysis, the songs are an integral part of the narrative sequence of events in *Maldita miseria*. They are integrated to support thematic structures in the story line. They either highlight or expand on the film's themes.

Nevertheless, in spite of the director's attempts at integrating the stories and making them part of the plot, the songs stop the narrative action of the story line. They tend to distract the viewer from the main story line, particularly when the movie is attempting to showcase a featured famous singer or musical group. The songs generally function better at the beginning of a movie or at the end. When inserted throughout the movie, if done in a showcase-type manner, they tend to interrupt the narrative flow. This is one of the reasons Mexican immigrant movies tend to fall into the *B* movie category. The plot is loosely structured and the songs are at times inserted for entertainment purposes. Stoppage of the action misdirects the attention of the viewer and undermines the seriousness of the topic presented, i.e., the travails of being a Mexican immigrant.

The corridos in Mexican movies in general and in Mexican immigrant movies in particular serve as founts of information, or "hypertexts," in which are inscribed a series of codes; these discursive codes are made evident as the movie plot progresses. When the corrido frames a plot at the inception of the film narrative, several events are foreshadowed. When corridos appear strategically sprinkled throughout the film narrative, they serve to encode specific messages or to underscore certain points structured in the main plot. When the corrido is sung at the close of the film narrative, the ballad reiterates the main message and recalls for the audience the moral encoded in the film. It often recapitulates the story line as in

Maldita miseria and in *Arizona*. Corridos are an integral part of filmmaking in Mexican film productions. They are a mainstay in both plot production, such as the "Corrido de Camelia La Texana," and in plot development.

Many of the films analyzed that related to the undocumented Mexican immigrant theme follow the tradition of Mexican musical films established in the 1940s and 1950s in which major movie figures such as Pedro Infante, Jorge Negrete, and Antonio Aguilar starred. Thus at times the Mexican immigrant films resemble, in part, variety shows where different songs are performed. Nevertheless, films about undocumented Mexican immigrants, while not artistically superior, are important sources of information sociologically and historically speaking. They are material documents that encode in great detail and from various perspectives a historical event not related to the "Great Man as Historical Agent" motif, but from the "little people's" historical experience.

Notes

1. My sincere thanks and appreciation to the following University of California units for their financial support in researching this article: Chicanos in a Global Society SCR-43 Funding, director Leo Chávez; Humanities' Research and Travel Committee; dean of humanities, Spencer Olin; and Steven Topik, director of the Latin American Studies Program.

2. See Américo Paredes, *"With a Pistol in His Hand": A Border Ballad and Its Hero* (Austin: University of Texas Press, 1958); and "The Mexican Corrido: Its Rise and Fall," in *Madstones and Twisters*, ed. Mody C. Boatright (Austin: Texas Folklore Society Publications, 1958), pp. 91–105. See also Merle E. Simmons, "The Ancestry of Mexico's Corridos," *Journal of American Folklore* (1963) 76:1–15; Vicente T. Mendoza, *El romance español y el corrido mexicano* (México: Ediciones de la Universidad Nacional Autónoma de México, 1939); and Margarita Prieto Posada, "Del rabel a la guitarra: El corrido mexicano como un derivado del romance español" (master's thesis, Facultad de Filosofía y Letras, Universidad de México, 1944). For an opposing view, see Celedonio Serrano Martínez, *El corrido mexicano no deriva del romance español* (México: Centro Cultural Guerrerense, 1973).

3. See Vicente T. Mendoza's views on the uprise and "decline" of the Mexican *corrido* in the introduction to his book *Lírica narrativa de México: El corrido* (México: Instituto de Investigaciones Estéticas, Universidad Nacional Autónoma de México, 1964).

4. *Microsoft™ Encarta*, 1993, n.p.

5. *Espaldas mojadas* (Ata Films, 1953); *Maldita miseria* (Million Dollar Video Corp., 1988); *Pasaporte a la muerte* (Mexicinema Video Corp., 1989); *El jardín del Edén* (Incine, 1994); and *Arizona* (Producciones Latinoamericanas, S.A., 1985). Other movies with related themes include *Contrabando humano* (Mexicinema Corp., 1987); *Memorias de un*

mojado (Million Dollar Video Corp., 1988); *De sangre chicana* (Mexicinema Video Corp., 1987); *Mojado power: El mojado remojado* (Million Dollar Video Corp., 1986); *El Pocho* (Million Dollar Video Corp., 1986); *Jaula de oro* (Million Dollar Video Corp., 1988); *Tres veces mojado* (Mexicinema Video Corp., 1989); *El puente* (Million Dollar Video Corp., 1986); *Ni de aquí ni de allá* (Million Dollar Video Corp., 1987); *El Milusos llegó de mojado* (Million Dollar Video Corp., n.d.); *La ilegal* (Million Dollar Video Corp., 1980); *Frontera* (Televicine, 1979; Million Dollar Video Corp., N.D.); *Mauro el mojado* (Million Dollar Video Corp.); *Las braceras, El vagón de la muerte, El norte, Alambrados,* and *Rompe el alba* (Million Dollar Video Corp., 1990); *Los dos amigos* (Video Visa, 1985); *El remojado* (Arte y Diseño Videovisa, Inc., 1988 and Televicine, 1984); *Tiempo de lobos* (Million Dollar Video Corp., 1988); *Como fui a enamorarme de ti* (Million Dollar Video Corp., 1990); *Los chacales de la frontera* (Mexicinema Video de México, S. A. de C. V., 1990); and *Discriminación maldita* (Million Dollar Video Corp., 1988). For an expanded list and summary of films with Mexican immigrant content see Norma Iglesias, *Entre yerba, polvo y plomo: Lo fronterizo visto por el cine mexicano,* vols. I and II (Tijuana, Baja California: El Colegio de la Frontera Norte, 1991).

6. David Bordwell and Kristin Thompson, *Film Art: An Introduction* (New York: McGraw-Hill, 1993).

7. *Los Angeles Times,* 3 July 1987.

8. *El vagón de la muerte.*

9. *El carro de la muerte.*

10. Homi K. Bhabha, *Nation and Narration* (New York: Routledge, 1990), p. 1. See also Benedict Anderson, *Imagined Communities* (London: Verso and New Left Books, 1983).

11. Timothy Brennan, "The National Longing for Form," in *Nation and Narration,* ed. Homi K. Bhabha (New York: Routledge, 1990), pp. 44–70.

12. Ernest Renan, "What Is a Nation?" in *Nation and Narration,* ed. Homi K. Bhabha (New York: Routledge, 1990), pp. 8–22.

13. Brennan, p. 52.

14. Ibid.

15. Michael Holquist and Katerina Clark, *Mikhail Bakhtin* (Cambridge: Harvard University Press, 1984). See also Brennan, p. 53.

16. For a discussion of this theme, see my articles "Mothers, Lovers, and Soldiers: Images of Women in the Mexican Corrido," *Keystone Folklore Journal* 23(1-2) (1979): 53–77; and "The Treacherous Woman Archetype: A Structuring Agent in the Corrido," *Aztlán* (1982) 13:136–146; and my book *The Mexican Corrido: A Feminist Analysis* (Bloomington: Indiana University Press, 1990), pp. 54–76.

Source Acknowledgments

CONTRIBUTORS

MARÍA ROSA GARCÍA-ACEVEDO, whose fields of specialization are comparative politics, Latino politics in the United States, and public policy, has held academic appointments at the Centro de Investigación y Docencia Económicas, Universidad Iberoamericana, the Universidad Autónoma de Ciudad Juárez, and the University of New Mexico. She has been a policy analyst for the Ministry of Foreign Relations of Mexico. Publications include articles and book chapters on U.S.–Latin American diplomatic relations, Mexican emigration to the United States, and Chicana/o politics. She is completing a major study on the political links between the Chicano community and the Mexican state from the early 1970s to the present.

JUAN GÓMEZ-QUIÑONES is a professor of history at UCLA. His areas of teaching and research specialty include the fields of political, labor, intellectual, and cultural history. He was director of the Chicano Studies Research Center at UCLA for fourteen years. In addition, he was a founding co-editor of *Aztlán: International Journal of Chicano Studies Research*. In 1990 Professor Gómez-Quiñones received the Scholar of the Year Award from the National Association of Chicano Studies. He has more than thirty publications including *Mexican American Labor, 1790–1990; The Roots of Chicano Politics, 1600–1940; Chicano Politics 1940–1990; Sembradores, Ricardo Flores Magón, and the Partido Liberal Mexicano: 5th and Grande Vista;* and *Mexican Nationalist Formation: Political Discourse, Policy and Dissidence.*

ALBERTO LEDESMA, an assistant professor in the Institute for Human Communication at California State University at Monterey Bay, completed doctoral studies in the Department of Ethnic Studies at the University of California, Berkeley. His doctoral dissertation addressed the representations of undocumented immigrants in Chicana and Chicano narratives. He has taught Chicano literature and Chicano cultural history at California State University, Northridge, and Berkeley. In addition he has published numerous short stories and poems dealing with the Mexican immigrant experience.

JOSÉ R. REYNA received a B.A. in Spanish from Michigan State University and an M.A. and Ph.D. from UCLA, with a specialization in folklore. He has held academic appointments in Texas and New Mexico. Currently he is a professor of Chicano folklore, literature, and dialectology at California State University, Bakersfield. Among his extensive publications are *Raza Humor: Chicano Joke Traditions in Texas; Folklore Chicano del Valle de San Luis Colorado; Modismos de Texas;* and *Mexican-American Prose Narrative in Texas.*

VICTOR ALEJANDRO SORELL is Professor of Art History, Associate Dean of the College of Arts and Sciences, and Director of the Center for Global Studies at Chicago State University (CSU). He is also Institutional Director of the CSU–University of Minnesota MacArthur Foundation Undergraduate Honors Program in International Studies. He has held a number of visiting professorships at the University of Chicago, UCLA, the School of the Art Institute of Chicago, and at Michigan State University. Between 1980 and 1983, he served as a Senior Program Officer at the National Endowment for the Humanities (NEH). He has published and lectured widely in the United States and internationally on Chicana/o, Latina/o, Afro-American, and Latin American art theory and criticism. He is also very active as an exhibition curator and consultant in the production of documentary films. He is the recipient of NEH and Rockefeller fellowships. Current monographs in progress include co-editorship of *Identidades Nuevomexicana/os: The Culture of Empowerment and the Empowerment of Culture* and co-authorship of *Illuminated Handkerchiefs and Prison Scribes: The Rudy Padilla Paño Collection.*

ABOUT THE EDITORS

DAVID R. MACIEL is a professor of history and chairperson of the Department of Chicana/o Studies at California State University, Dominguez Hills. His teaching interests and research fields include Chicana/o history, Mexico, modern Latin America, and the U.S. Southwest. He has held academic appointments at the University of New Mexico, the University of Arizona, Arizona State University, and the University of Houston. In addition, he has been a visiting professor at the National Autonomous University of Mexico (UNAM); the University of California, San Diego; the University of Arizona; and the University of Guadalajara. He has been the recipient of two Fulbright teaching and research postdoctoral fellowships to Mexico and research fellowships by the Ford Foundation and the National Endowment for the Humanities. He has served as a media consultant on the film *Break of Dawn* and on numerous documentaries in the United States and Mexico. His published research has focused upon the Chicano community, Mexican cultural history, and film. Selected books include *Ignacio Ramírez: Ideólogo del liberalismo social en México; Al norte del Río Bravo: Pasado inmediato 1930–1982; El México olvidado; El Norte: The U.S.–Mexican Border in Contemporary Cinema; El bandolero, el pocho, y la raza: Imágenes cinematográficas del chicano*; and (co-edited with Isidro D. Ortiz) *Chicanas/Chicanos at the Crossroads: Social, Economic, and Political Change* (University of Arizona Press). He has also published numerous articles, book chapters, and reviews in scholarly journals of the United States and Mexico. Currently, he is completing a monographic study of the cinema of Mexico.

MARÍA HERRERA-SOBEK holds the Luis Leal Endowed Chair in Chicano Studies and is a professor of Chicano Studies at the University of California at Santa Barbara. Among her extensive publications are *The Bracero Experience: Elitelore versus Folklore* (1979); *The Mexican Corrido: A Feminist Analysis* (1990); and *Northward Bound: The Mexican Immigrant Experience in Ballad and Song* (1993). In addition, she has edited three books: *Beyond Stereotypes: The Critical Analysis of Chicana Literature* (1985); *Gender and Print Culture: New Perspectives on International Ballad Studies* (1991); and *Reconstructing a Chicano/a Literary Heritage: Hispanic Colonial Literature of the Southwest* (University of Arizona Press, 1993). She co-edited *Chicana Creativity and Criticism: Charting New Frontiers in American Literature* (1988, new edition 1995) and *Chicana Writes: On Word and Film* (1995) with Helena María Viramontes, and the textbook *Saga de México* (1991) with Seymour Menton. In addition, she has published more than eighty articles in various journals and as book chapters.

Herrera-Sobek is a recognized poet. Her collection of poems, "Naked Moon/Luna Desnuda," appeared in the anthology *Three Times a Woman*, which featured also the work of Demetria Martínez and Alicia Gaspar de Alba. Her poems have been published in numerous journals and poetry collections.

INDEX